McLAREN!

McLAREN!
The Man, the Cars & the Team

EOIN S. YOUNG

BOND, PARKHURST PUBLICATIONS   NEWPORT BEACH, CALIFORNIA

For Bruce, to whom I owe so much

English edition published by Eyre and Spottiswoode (Publishers) Limited, London

ISBN 0-87880-007-7

Library of Congress Card No. 72-155023

Bond, Parkhurst Publications, Newport Beach, California

Printed in the United States of America

CONTENTS

Preface   7

Introduction   10

1 New Zealand's Driver to Europe   20

2 Grand Prix Racing with Cooper   38

3 The Zerex Special & the First McLarens   56

4 Can-Am Domination   80

5 Designing the McLarens   104

6 Racing Engine Development   126

7 Team Manager Teddy Mayer   148

8 Denis Hulme, Can-Am Champion   164

9 Tyler Alexander & the Mechanics   182

10 McLaren Racing as a Business   200

11 At the Track   210

12 The Commercial Importance of American Racing   218

13 Production Cars & Special Projects   228

Looking Ahead   238

McLaren Cars by Type Number   240

Index   269

PHOTO CREDITS
By page number:

Tyler Alexander   19, 100, 104, 108, 112, 128, 130, 214
Lionel Birnbom   61, 74, 75, 89, 90, 91, 172, 187, 192-193, 217, 218 top, 227, 266 top
Pete Biro   123
Alice Bixler   93, 178, 260 top
Don Bok   264 bottom
Jim Chini   182, 198, 210
Gordon Chittenden   80, 181, 260 bottom
Dennis Cipnic   79
Pete Coltrin   72, 132, 135
Michael Cooper   10, 13, 15, 17, 260 lower middle, 268
Richard Corson   164
Peter Deacon   40
Charles Gellis   205 left
Geoffrey Goddard   48, 59, 62, 63, 67, 68, 73, 77, 78, 85, 86, 88, 102, 106, 110, 114, 115 both, 118 bottom, 134, 136, 138, 139, 153, 170, 173, 174, 180 top, 200 bottom, 231, 233, 236, 240 middle, 242 bottom, 244 bottom, 246 top, 248 top, 250 bottom, 252 top, bottom, 254 middle, bottom, 256 both, 258 top, 262 middle, bottom, 264 top, middle, 266 middle two, 268 bottom
Michael R. Hewett   43, 46-47, 101
Jack Inwood   50, 66
Ron Laymon   248 middle, bottom
Henry N. Manney   49, 131, 161, 199, 213, 260 upper middle
Barry McKay   41, 167
Gunther Molter   20, 71, 244 top, 252 middle, 254 top
Bill Motta   242 top
Bill Neale   179, 195
Bill Norcross   44
Mati Palk   142-143 (drawing)
David Phipps   95, 98, 118 top, 250 middle
Evan Selwyn-Smith   56
Ray Simpson   54
Nigel Snowdon   177, 232
Bob Tronolone   64, 70, 76, 83, 84, 87, 94, 109, 145, 146, 159, 175, 176, 180, 218 bottom, 235, 240 top, 242 upper middle, 258 bottom
Bill Warner   148
Cameron A. Warren   69, 82, 92, 144, 157, 163, 171, 189, 212, 250 top, 258 middle
George Wilkes   65
Kurt Worner   38, 133, 244 middle
Others are from the collections of Bruce McLaren Motor Racing Ltd., Eoin S. Young and the McLaren family.

EDITOR   Jonathan Thompson
DESIGNER   Hal Crippen

All text, type and captions for this book are set in Baskerville, designed by the great English printer; this face has become the parent of the so-called "modern" faces.

The book was printed in Phoenix, Arizona by Datagraphics, Inc., a division of Bond, Parkhurst & Bond.

PREFACE

Bruce McLaren always felt that credit should go to his racing team—"I would like to think they couldn't do it without me, but I know I certainly couldn't have done it without them"— and for that reason I have written this portrait of the McLaren team, setting the scene with Bruce's career to help the reader understand why the other members of the team who are introduced later could be carried along by the infectious McLaren enthusiasm for work and success.

I am indebted to Denny Hulme, Teddy Mayer, Phil Kerr, Tyler Alexander, Robin Herd, Gordon Coppuck, Colin Beanland, George Bolthoff and Ron Smith for taking the time to talk with me about their special departments in the team and remembering what it was like working with Bruce. Thanks also to Ken Tyrrell, Peter Agg, Roy Lunn, Jim Kaser and all the others who helped me compile the various sections of the book with anecdotes and details that I had either forgotten or never knew.

I started working with Bruce as his secretary in 1962 and I was one of the first directors of Bruce McLaren Motor Racing Limited when the company was formed late in 1963. In those early days we made up company procedure as we went along. Bruce used to say that we were a two-man act—he was the nice guy and I was the baddie. If deliveries were late or other problems had arisen it was my job to telephone the offender and deliver a verbal caning. That was when Bruce stepped in as the nice guy, to smooth things over and apologize for his secretary's wrath; we inevitably succeeded in getting instant delivery, or satisfaction, and the person on the other end of the phone would hang up wondering how an extraordinarily nice chap like Bruce could employ a swine like me.

We worked together on his regular magazine articles for *Autosport* in England and we syndicated these features to other magazines and to newspapers in New Zealand. It reached the stage eventually where Bruce became so polished on the tape recorder that he virtually dictated the story just as it appeared in the magazine without the need for any tidying-up by me. If the tape was done while he was in the bath there were splashes, muffled exclamations, and giggles interspersed with his report. On occasions he would tape the story as he drove to work in his Mercedes and he would add a running commentary on the dozy habits of some of the other commuters. I never ceased to be amazed at the way Bruce could find words and descriptions for his experiences that were always so much better than I could have managed, and I was supposed to be the writer! I left McLaren Racing in 1966 to start my own business as a freelance journalist and racing consultant but I still worked closely with Bruce and the team in both these areas.

Bruce never seemed unduly worried about time, particularly if he was engrossed in working on a new car at the factory and it wasn't until the staff started to expand that he came to realize that not everyone lived and breathed racing, that some people had a life of their own to lead outside the sport. It always seemed to be easier to work long hours when the boss was there beside you—and this often made it more difficult to leave before he did. As a driver, however, Bruce was often ordered to bed the night before the race. On one famous occasion in 1967 when the new M6A Can-Am car had won three races in a row, Bruce made the mistake of mentioning in front of Tyler that their success hadn't really seemed all that hard to achieve. "Hard?" Tyler gave him an incredulous look. "I didn't see *you* in the garage at four o'clock this morning!"

The fact that Bruce was the same age, or younger, than many of the people in his team helped to start the tremendous sense of family loyalty that made the McLaren team easily the most cheerful on any track in Europe or America. Bruce and Denny were like brothers.

When I walked into the offices of *Autocar* just after lunch on June 2 this year and Martin Lewis told me he had heard on the radio that Bruce had been killed at Goodwood, I simply didn't believe him. It took hours for the terrible reality to sink in, and then I realized that for years I had regarded him as a brother too. He had introduced me to the European racing world and I was very much aware that whatever success I had achieved since I left the team I owed solely to Bruce. But he was such a larger-than-life person that now it wouldn't surprise me at all if he walked round the corner and said "Hi." That helps to make this book easier to write.

I want to thank *Autosport* and Frederick Muller Ltd, publishers of Bruce's original book *From the Cockpit,* for allowing me to quote passages here, and the authors of *Autocourse* and *Grand Prix Racing Facts and Figures* for their reams of historical facts. Any errors that occur are my fault, not theirs.

This book would not have been possible without the support of Patty McLaren, help from Bruce's mother and father in New Zealand, and the ceaseless cups of coffee from my wife Sandra as I typed the manuscript.

Bruce was a great friend to so many people all over the world that I would like to think this book is a tribute from them to him, and perhaps it will help Bruce's international friends to know what made him the way he was, and what made his racing team so successful. If I have done that, I have succeeded.

Eoin S. Young
East Horsley, December 23, 1970.

10

INTRODUCTION

WESTHAMPNETT AERODROME was one of a string of fighter bases along the south coast of England during the Battle of Britain.

Before the war it had been a quiet Sussex farm a couple of miles from Chichester and half a mile from the Goodwood horse racing course. When war threatened, the flat fields were taken over and landing strips were laid out, connected around the perimeter by taxying and access roads. One of the Hurricane pilots who flew from Westhampnett was Squadron Leader Tony Gaze, an Australian flying with the Royal Air Force.

In 1946 when the fighting was over and there was time to think about motor sport again, Brooklands and Donington Park were gone, swallowed up by war factories. New tracks had to be found if racing was to be revived and it was then that Tony Gaze remembered the narrow strip of asphalt perimeter roads around Westhampnett. Gaze suggested the old fighter field, already becoming overgrown, to the Duke of Richmond and Gordon, who owned the nearby Goodwood estate.

The Duke had raced at Brooklands before the war as Freddie Richmond, the Earl of March, winning the 1930 BRDC 500-mile race in a little Ulster Austin Seven with Sammy Davis, and a year later he won the JCC Double Twelve—a 24-hour race run in daylight over two days—sharing an MG Midget with Chris Staniland. Bruce McLaren learned about motor racing with an Ulster Austin in New Zealand when he was fourteen, and years later, when he saw a large oil painting of an Ulster in action, he bought it and hung it in pride of place in his home. It was the Duke winning at Brooklands in 1930.

The Duke asked Wing Commander Tommy Wisdom, well known as a racing driver and a journalist, for his opinion of Westhampnett as a possible motor racing venue and when Tommy endorsed Gaze's opinion, Goodwood was born.

Stirling Moss started his racing career with his first major drive in a Cooper 500 in 1948 at Goodwood and 14 years later that sparkling career finished in the bank at St. Marys. He had been out to beat the lap record which John Surtees had set and Stirling had equalled earlier in the race at 1 minute 22 seconds (105.37 mph). Stirling had stopped to check sticking throttles on the apple-green UDT-Laystall Lotus-Climax V-8 and he was making up time when the car inexplicably lunged off the road into the bank and Stirling was lucky to escape with his life. He never raced again.

The first race on the Goodwood circuit was in 1947 and the last was in 1966. The threat of high lap speeds from the new 3-liter Grand Prix cars would have meant costly modifications to the safety measures and the Duke decided to close the track. Racing stopped, but the lap speeds rose fantastically during private testing. The grandstands, the pits, the covered paddock area, the control buildings and the concrete-protected marshal's posts were left where they were.

When the track finally closed the lap record stood to the two Flying Scots—Jim Clark and Jackie Stewart—in their 1.5-liter Lotus and BRM Formula 1 cars at 1 minute 20.4 seconds (107.46 mph), but already in unofficial testing Bruce McLaren had lapped at 1 minute 17.2 seconds in one of his McLaren-Oldsmobile sports cars. Bruce loved Goodwood. He knew every inch of the 2.4-mile track. It was only an hour from his factory at Colnbrook, and the team always used Goodwood to try new cars and new developments.

In 1967 Dan Gurney and Jack Brabham were lapping at 1 minute 15.4 seconds in their Formula 1 cars and that season Denny Hulme got down to 1 minute 13.4 seconds in the new McLaren M6A Can-Am sports car. Three years later, in the early summer of 1970, Hulme had lowered the test record to 1 minute 7.8 seconds with the newest sports car, the M8D, which had been christened the "Batmobile" because of the high side fins

sloping back to the tail with a wing slung between them.

Lap speeds in figures mean little more to the average reader than an earthquake toll in Tibet, but to lap a track like Goodwood as a passenger in a Can-Am sports car is to appreciate the difference between good racing drivers and mere mortals.

With the 630 horsepower of the Chevrolet V-8 engine bellowing in the back, the car accelerates down the pit lane. The aluminum engine is bolted to a plate directly behind the cockpit, acting as part of the chassis. Two hip-hugging seats are scooped into the riveted aluminum monocoque box that forms the frame of the car and accommodates 64 gallons of fuel stowed in bag tanks. Every ounce of the 1420-pound car is built for pace. Sixty-five hundred revolutions per minute on the dial directly in front of the driver is 110 miles per hour in low gear. Up to 140 mph in second and you're into the never-ending right-hander at Madgwick. The scenery starts to blur. Third gear and 175 mph through the flat-out kink to the right at Ford- **13** water. In top gear on a flying lap the car goes through this kink as fast as it does on the main straight. Back into third for St. Marys and flashing by on your left is the bank where Moss crashed. Foot hard on the floor through the tricky left-hander at 115 mph and you're charging at the sharp Lavant right-hander.

Lavant calls for delicate horsepower ballet as you grab second momentarily right on top of the corner. You're already hard on the brakes, but the lower gear snatches the rear tires into an oversteering slide. The instant the car is aimed for the straight you whack it into third and surge away from the corner. A hundred yards away and you're into top at 130 and still accelerating judderingly hard with the engine transmitting all its power through the pair of rear Goodyears, each a flat-treaded rubber roller 14 inches across. You use a lot of road through the slight left-hand kink leading to the main straight because it's a kink that gets tighter the faster you go.

Woodcote, the right-hander at the end of the straight, looks as though it's been loaded into a cannon and fired at you point blank as the needle on the rev counter jumps up to sixty-six hundred—180 mph. Suddenly, like a giant hand, the brakes arrest the car in full flight, snatching you from certain destruction against the far bank. In the passenger's seat the g force of retardation is so powerful that your knees feel like they're slicing through the riveted dash panel. Woodcote is lined up and gone, the maneuver planned 100 feet before the turn and executed automatically. At that speed your mind works at computer speed. Instantly there is a wall across the road. There is no hope of stopping but an arrow indicates salvation to the right and as you plunge toward the wall a gap opens on the far side and you slither through with the exhaust bark bouncing off the walls. The relaxing of tension as the car swerves into the pits is beautiful.

A lap like that from a standing start, with two aboard, would have equalled the old Grand Prix lap record, shared by two of the fastest drivers in the world!

After his tests with the prototype M8D which was to be driven in the series by Denny Hulme, Bruce flew to Indianapolis to oversee the running of the first McLaren entries in the 500. He was enthusiastic about the performance of the latest in the line of McLaren title-winning Can-Am cars. Bruce had won the Can-Am championship in 1967 and 1969 and Denny had filled the gap in 1968. The Can-Am McLarens were unbeatable; they had won all eleven races in the championship the season before,

and Bruce was anxious to get back from Indianapolis to test the second car, which he would drive on the 1970 series.

The car was ready to run on the Tuesday after the 500, but the fiberglass body had not been completed so it was decided to fit Bruce's car with the body from Denny's for the tests.

Bruce arrived back from America on Monday, June 1, and the following morning he drove down to Goodwood in his 250SE Mercedes with Ron Smith, a friend who managed Patsy Burt's McLaren M3 sprint car and her garage at Bookham in Surrey. Ron had worked for Moss in the early days and he often helped the McLaren team by looking after management duties during test sessions. It was a test day like any other.

On the hour trip down Bruce told Ron about the various problems they had come up against at Indianapolis where Carl Williams' McLaren had finished 9th and Peter Revson's had quit after 87 laps. Bruce confessed that it was a new world totally unlike Grand Prix racing, but he was bubbling over with new ideas for a 1971 Indianapolis McLaren.

It was a sunny June morning with a slight breeze across the airfield, rippling the windsock. The Hurricanes and Spitfires which had scrambled from Westhampnett thirty years earlier had been replaced by leisurely light aircraft doing touch-and-go landings.

A Formula 1 McLaren had been brought along as well as the new Can-Am car, because Peter Gethin was to take Denny Hulme's place for the Belgian Grand Prix at Spa the next week-end and he had to get the cockpit tailored to fit. Denny was still recovering from burns received during practice at Indianapolis three weeks earlier.

Peter hadn't arrived and the Can-Am car was being trundled around by New Zealand mechanic Cary Taylor who had raced a 1.5-liter Brabham at home before he came to England to work for the Brabham team and later joined the McLaren Can-Am crew. He was breaking the new car in, and had been chuntering around since 9 o'clock, making sure there were no leaks or other problems before Bruce got down to sorting it out at speed. Out of curiosity, Ron clocked Cary on one lap at 1 minute 28.4 seconds.

The Formula 1 car was sitting fueled and ready to run, so Bruce decided to do a few laps in it. He came in after a best lap of 1 minute 12.2 seconds and waited for the Can-Am car to have the brake balance adjusted and five gallons of fuel added. At 3½ miles to the gallon it was easier to keep adding fuel than to park out on the circuit with dry tanks. For testing the car ran with tanks only about a third full.

At quarter to eleven Bruce drove out of the pits for the first time in his new car and after a standing-start lap and a flyer he headed back for the pits. There was more high-speed oversteer than he liked and he mentioned to Ron that the special steering wheel with a flattened bottom they had made for the Indianapolis cars would be better than the normal wheel with its fat leather-bound round rim. The flattened rim was more comfortable on the tops of the thighs in the wriggle-fit cockpit.

The mechanics raised the wing just a fraction to increase the downthrust and try to curb the oversteer. Bruce went out again and after four laps, two of which equalled his earlier time with the 3-liter Formula 1 car, he came back to the pits to have the wing angle raised another notch. He said the sports car felt a lot softer everywhere compared with the precision of the open-wheeled Grand Prix car at the same speed, so the crew checked the fat Goodyears, making the pressure 22 psi all around. They

put tape under the front duct in the nose to check the possibility of grounding, and as an efficient test driver Bruce rattled off the instrument readings he had checked coming down to Woodcote on the last lap: oil temperature 90 degrees C, water temperature 70 degrees C, fuel pressure 140, oil pressure 60.

After another four laps and a best of 1 minute 11.2 seconds he was back for a further notch on the wing. Taking advantage of the stop they filled the tanks just to the top of the first layer of safety foam. That made it about 20 gallons on board. Six more laps and a best of 1 minute 10.8 seconds (122.03 mph) and he reported that the high-speed oversteer had been cured. Instead he now had a trace of understeer. He was pulling only just over 6400 rpm on the straight and he wondered what had happened to the other 200 rpm. Perhaps he was losing time coming out of Lavant onto the straight, so he asked for adjustments to the rollbars front and rear. Another five laps to equal his previous time and he came back to say that the handling was better and he was back up to six-six again on the straight.

The oil temperature was up five degrees but the other instruments were normal. They checked tires and shock absorbers to see why it might be oversteering at Madgwick just past the pits.

At 12:19 by Ron's pit watch the big orange finned McLaren rumbled away down the pit lane. Another few laps and they would stop for lunch. All was well as Bruce twitched the tail coming out of the chicane and set off on the flying lap.

He never completed it. At 12:22 p.m. he was dead, killed instantly when the car left the road just after the left-hand kink on the main straight and slammed into a marshal's protective embankment on the right-hand side of the track. An investigation of the scattered wreckage showed that a section of the tail must have lifted at around 170 mph, causing immediate instability and a situation that was beyond human control.

In the dark days that followed it was realized that Bruce, the complete man, had virtually penned his own epitaph in the closing paragraph of his book *From the Cockpit*, written in 1964. He had put down on paper the grief he felt at the death of his teammate Timmy Mayer, killed in a practice crash in Tasmania, but he had also recorded his justification for going racing and those last few sentences in his book are a fitting beginning for this one:

"The news that he had died instantly was a terrible shock to all of us, but who is to say that he had not seen more, done more and learned more in his few years than many people do in a lifetime? To do something well is so worthwhile that to die trying to do it better cannot be foolhardy. It would be a waste of life to do nothing with one's ability, for I feel that life is measured in achievement, not in years alone."

1

NEW ZEALAND'S DRIVER TO EUROPE

BRUCE LESLIE McLAREN was born in Auckland, New Zealand, on August 30th, 1937, under the sign of Virgo, the craftsman. It was prophetic.

Leslie and Ruth McLaren were proud of their first son and second child, a brother for their seven-year-old daughter Patricia. Les McLaren had recently bought a service station and garage in the wealthy suburb of Remuera and their home was just around the corner in Upland Road. With his three younger brothers Les had helped to maintain something of a McLaren domination in local motorcycle sport and he was thinking of switching his enthusiasm to cars. "Pop," as he was known to everyone later in the racing world, may have known that in Europe during that August, Mercedes-Benz W125s had won the Grands Prix of Monaco and Germany, but he certainly would never have imagined that 21 years hence his infant son would make his name in international racing on the Nurburgring and in 25 years time he too would win the Grand Prix round the streets of Monaco.

After the war, Les sold his Singer Le Mans sports car and bought a 1935 SS1—the forerunner of the Jaguar—ostensibly because the larger car would help to accommodate the fifth member of the McLaren family, Janice, who was born in 1947.

The sporty SS also served as a competition mount and Les competed in sprint events and beach races. To have a racing driver as a father must have been good value at school where Bruce was captain of the junior's rugby football team, and like every husky young New Zealander he dreamed of being a top-rated "All Black" and playing for his country.

He was nine and a half when the pains started in his left hip. A polio epidemic was sweeping the country and anxious mothers watched their children for any sign of an ache or pain. In fact Bruce had probably been so determined *not* to get the dreaded polio that he never told his parents about the pain that was starting in his hip and causing him to favor his left leg at school. Eventually the pain became too much even for the captain of the rugby team to ignore and his confession brought panic to the household at Upland Road.

An X-ray showed that the pains were due not to polio but to Perthes Disease which resulted in the virtual seizing up of the hip joint. A fall could have caused the problem but nobody, including Bruce, could ever be sure just which bump caused it. Twelve months earlier on his uncle's farm at Ngaruawahia he had fallen from a horse and hit a fence post on his way to the ground. He had also been involved in an accident when things got out of control in a race down a long hill in Remuera.

Whatever the cause, the result was a month in the hospital and then almost three years in the Wilson Home for Crippled Children. There were very real fears that he might never walk again. His legs were in casts and he lay on his back in traction for months. His tenth and eleventh birthdays came and went before he was allowed to leave his wheelchair and try walking on crutches. He said later that in his eagerness to get mobile he pounded around the hospital grounds building up the foundation for the broad shoulders that were to be so characteristic of him. The only lasting effect of the disease was a limp since his left leg was 1½ inches shorter than the right and he wore a shoe with a built-up heel to compensate. He had kept up his schooling in the Wilson Home, and he spent a year at home taking correspondence courses before he was allowed to face the hurly-burly of school once again in 1951. Rugby, basketball and other contact sports had been ruled out by the doctors, so Bruce took up rowing instead. By the end of his first year engineering course at Seddon Memorial Technical College he was heading his class in applied mechanics, chemistry and engineering shopwork.

22   Before this, it had been mentioned over lunch in the Mc-

Laren kitchen that perhaps it wasn't such a good idea to be using the family car for weekend competition, and with three growing children Les could understand the position. He decided to buy a car that he could use purely for racing, and to this end he tracked down an Ulster Austin Seven. The car had seen better days but it was a racing car, albeit a 1929 racing car, and in remote New Zealand this resulted in a price of 110 Pounds for the stripped car. The previous owner had pulled the car down to give it a complete rebuild but had lost heart. Parts of the car were starting to rust in boxes where they had been carefully placed for hopeful reassembly. The enormity of the task he was undertaking must have come to Pop on the way home as the little chassis swayed at the end of the tow rope and his twelve-year-old son sat among the boxes of bits and pieces on the back of the workshop truck wondering if his father really knew what he was letting himself in for.

The rebuilding took a year. Since replacement parts for the 1929 racing Austin were unobtainable Les made do with second-hand standard Austin Seven parts which he modified to fit. During the evenings and weekends Les always had an eager watcher-cum-helper in Bruce as the Ulster finally took some sort of shape. Even when it was finished the car was scarcely impressive, but it was reborn, hand-built, and because his father had performed this mechanical miracle there wasn't a better racing car around as far as Bruce was concerned.

The Ulster was elegant in a miniature sort of way, almost ridiculous when you compare the specifications with the sports cars that Bruce was to build under his own name later. The tiny 747-cc 4-cylinder engine had an aluminum crankcase with a 56-mm bore and a 76-mm stroke. The compression ratio was 6.0:1 and at 5000 rpm it developed 24 bhp. Oil pressure seldom rose above five pounds. The car had a three-speed gearbox with factory-quoted speeds of 28 mph in first, 50 mph in second and 72 mph in top. Suspension was by a semi-elliptic spring across the front and cord-bound quarter-elliptics at the rear. Steering was by worm and wheel. The spidery wire wheels were 19 inches in diameter. The wheelbase was 75 inches, track was 40 inches and the whole car weighed about 950 pounds.

In England the Ulster Austins had put up formidable performances in their class, and a very young Bruce McLaren was to learn the basics of racing in the tiny cockpit.

When the Great Day arrived and Les fired the little engine for the first time, Bruce eagerly awaited his father's report at the end of his first test run down the road. He couldn't believe

A youthful Bruce McLaren with the spindly little Ulster Austin Seven.

it when his father returned shaken, saying that, far from be-
having like a Grand Prix car, it was almost uncontrollable. The
steering was lamentable, the brakes were a joke, it handled like
nothing on earth and the first thing he was going to do was
place an advertisement in the *Auckland Star* to sell it. Bruce was
appalled. He pleaded with his father and eventually won his
case. The Ulster could stay providing Bruce maintained it himself. He had more than a year to wait until he could go for his
driving license, but Les was obviously well aware that he was
providing Bruce with the best possible way of gaining practical
experience in engineering.

Bruce booked a driving test after his fifteenth birthday and
borrowed a friend's Morris Minor to get his license. Next on the
McLaren list of motoring ambitions was his first competition
event and this turned out to be a hillclimb at Muriwai about 25
miles from Auckland and close to the beach where the McLaren
family had a weekend home. Some of the early beach races had
been held on the Muriwai sands and Bruce never forgot this
important link in his career. When he bought a new luxury
home in Burwood Park near Walton-on-Thames in Surrey, a few
months before his death, he named the house "Muriwai."

Les McLaren was in the hospital when Bruce made his first
competition appearance on the shingle hill, but he had issued
stern instructions to try and curb his son's enthusiasm. That
evening Bruce visited his father in the hospital with the news
that he had won his class with a best climb of 72 seconds and
had beaten another boy called Phil Kerr who was racing an
Austin Nippy.

Before the event Phil—later to become Jack Brabham's manager and eventually joint managing director of Bruce's racing team in England—had heard about Bruce and his Ulster through friends at school. "There was a competitive element prior to the hillclimb because I think we were both wondering how good the other one was and what sort of car he had. This was on a very junior scale, I must admit, but nevertheless there was a definite competitive element," Kerr recalls.

From then on Bruce and Phil were allowed to work on their Austins in the McLaren garage with Pop or the shop foreman Harold Bardsley always prepared to aid with advice but not with assistance. They reasoned that it was better to explain to the boys how the job should be done and let them do it, rather than to move in and do the job for them. They were right. With the urge for competition upon him and the pressing need to stay faster than Phil, Bruce moved ahead with modifications on the Ulster. The car had arrived on 19-inch wheels and these were replaced with 16-inch disc wheels at the rear and 17-inch wires in front. The rear springs were flattened to cope with the oversteer, and the front spring was turned upside down to lower the car but when the king pins started to chew out, a front axle from an Austin Big Seven was fitted and the problem was solved.

The single Zenith carburetor had been replaced by twin SUs on a McLaren-built manifold and Bruce's times up the Muriwai hill had been clipped to 47 seconds. This was enough to keep Phil behind him in the Nippy, but Bruce was less complacent the day he loaned Phil the Ulster and Phil equalled the McLaren times.

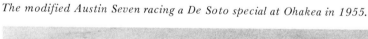

The modified Austin Seven racing a De Soto special at Ohakea in 1955.

During 1954, when perhaps more effort was being put in on the Austin than on homework, Bruce's marks at Seddon Tech started to slump and there were some terse teachers' comments on the end-of-term reports, but in his final year he was back on top of the class again and was a school prefect as he had been for the past couple of years.

In January that year Bruce saw his first major race when New Zealand staged its first Grand Prix and Bruce and Phil were crowd marshals. "We took the easy way out," Bruce remembered in his book, *From the Cockpit*. "We sat down to watch the race while the crowd behind happily sorted themselves out."

Until this time Bruce and his father had been sharing drives in the Ulster but late in 1954 Les bought one of the first production Austin-Healey 100s, a car which had been raced by Ross Jensen. Preparation of the two Austins continued side by side, with the Ulster now tuned enough to be unsuitable for driving to school—by parental decree. When the cylinder head cracked on the Ulster, Bruce set about making a new one, using a head from a 1936 Austin Ruby sedan, filling the combustion chambers with bronze and carving them out again with a rotary file. The new head was a success as Bruce proved by returning regular times under 20 seconds for the standing-start quarter mile, with a top speed of 87 mph through the flying quarter.

In August 1955, with university looming the following year, Bruce decided to sell the Ulster and buy a car he could use on the road and compete in as well. With 280 Pounds from the sale of the Ulster and 30 Pounds he had borrowed, he invested in a Ford Ten Special but he was never happy with the car and was relieved when a later opportunity came to race his father's Healey.

The McLaren-Kerr struggle advanced from the Austin Seven class up to the Ford Ten category since Phil had bought a Buckler sports car and another friend, Colin Beanland, had a tuned-up Anglia sedan. Colin was to accompany Bruce to England in 1958 while Phil continued his accountancy studies, and several years later Colin rejoined the McLaren team, eventually settling in America as manager of McLaren Engines, Inc. in Detroit.

Bruce started work on an engineering degree at Auckland University's engineering college at Ardmore, near the site of the first Grand Prix races. He was passing all his subjects, but he was having to apply himself more as the work intensified and he had less time to work on his cars. It must have occurred to him that he might have been better off to leave the university and work in his father's business (which would also mean more time to work on his cars) but he continued at school.

Bruce's father had entered the Healey in the sports car race which supported the 1956 Grand Prix but when doctor's orders made it apparent that Pop would not be able to make use of his entry, Bruce begged his father to let him take his place. Gearbox trouble in practice meant Bruce's first all-nighter before the race and a blown head gasket caused his retirement but he slept through the Grand Prix later in the afternoon happy in the knowledge that he had driven in his first major race. And one of his competitors had been Stirling Moss in a Porsche! As Pop's health improved they struck a family bargain: Whoever was fastest in practice would drive the Healey in the race. At the time this must have seemed like a fair bargain since Pop's experience could presumably be relied on to counter Bruce's exuberance. But the young McLaren's talent started to show through. On the Ohakea airfield circuit where Bruce had raced the Ulster previously, he was seven seconds faster than his father in practice and their bargain was effectively scrapped. Pop concentrated on being team manager after that.

The following summer they planned to compete in all the

Bruce in 1956 with the mediocre Ford 10 special he raced only briefly.

international races with the Healey which was getting faster and faster. The engine had been pulled down and fitted with Chrysler pistons and exhaust valves, and Buick cam followers. The ports were opened out and a special double exhaust system was fitted. A full-length under-tray helped top speed, and to compete with the disc-braked Healey 100S which was now being driven by Ross Jensen, the 100-4's drum brakes were ventilated with cooling holes and scoops on the back plates.

Ken Wharton's fatal crash in the Ferrari Monza in the sports car race took the edge off the start of the 1957 season at Ardmore but Bruce finished 5th behind a D-type Jaguar, Jack Brabham in a bob-tailed Cooper that Bruce was soon to buy, an Australian special called an Ausca, and Ross Jensen in the 100S. At Levin Bruce was 3rd, at Wigram a valve dropped through a piston, at Dunedin he was 3rd again, but on Invercargill's Ryall Bush road circuit where the Healey was getting up to 130 mph, the engine finally poked a rod through the side.

Back in Auckland, Bruce returned to college at the start of the term and tried to take his mind off the broken Healey. That was when the center-seat bob-tailed 1.5-liter Cooper that Brabham had driven came on the market. The Healey and the unloved Ford special were sold to effect the deal—probably helped with a slice of Pop's savings. It was Bruce's first Cooper drive and he reveled in the whole new scene. After a couple of small events at the end of the summer the car was completely stripped down to its tubular chassis. The McLaren racing program had now progressed well beyond Austin Sevens and Ford Tens and Phil and Colin were able to do little more than marvel at the detail on "real" racing cars and help with a polishing rag on bodywork and magnesium rims.

With the Ford gone Bruce was pedalling his bicycle to college and he was reaching the stage where he had to choose between a career as a motor engineer or a civil engineer. It was really a choice between working on engines or bridges and there seems little doubt that he would have settled for the motor side if it had been left to him. The "Driver to Europe" scheme effectively saved Bruce from the decision.

He had stayed in touch with Brabham by letter during the year, sorting out the occasional impenetrable problems that had cropped up with the sports car, and Jack suggested that a deal could be arranged whereby he brought a pair of single-seat Coopers to New Zealand for the 1959 season, one to be driven by Bruce. The Cooper sports car was sold to Merv Neil, the final university examinations were over, and Bruce settled down to

The Austin-Healey 100-4 helped move Bruce into more important races.

await the arrival of the single-seat Cooper. He spent his spare time working with Phil and Colin as they helped their friend Merv Mayo complete his Buckler sports car, little knowing that the choice of "Driver to Europe" was to lie between Bruce, Phil and Merv.

In fact Bruce's first real single-seat drive was at the wheel of a supercharged 3-liter Maserati 8CLT which had been built for Indianapolis but never raced there. The car had been bought from the estate of Freddie Zambucka by Frank Shuter who planned to try for the New Zealand speed record and Bruce's job was to make the Maserati a runner. He spent hours cleaning the jellified dope fuel out of the system, but the shattering bark of the exhaust when he finally fired it up was worth all the trouble. A track test at Ohakea was memorable for the abundance of power that brought wheelspin up to 140 mph, and the vagaries of the handling. Bruce was impressed, but glad to hand the Maserati over to its new owner and get down to the Auckland wharves to check the unloading of the two Coopers, a 1960-cc Formula 1 car for Jack and a smaller 1750-cc Formula 2 car for himself.

After a few follow-my-leader laps on Jack's tail at Ardmore, Bruce was waved past and Jack sat in behind to see if his pupil had cottoned to what he had been trying to teach in the previous laps. Bruce was rather nonplused when Jack ticked him off later for hanging the tail out too much. That, he thought, was just a bit strong—especially coming from Brabham who used the tail-out oversteering slide as his trademark in the early Cooper days!

Following orders Bruce came home 2nd in the first race heat on the morning of the Grand Prix at Ardmore, and with plenty of willing helpers he set about preparing the car for the race that was to launch him on his career. The rear of the car was raised on the quick-lift jacks and Bruce was running the car with the rear wheels spinning so that the transmission and engine would be warmed up for the start. Nobody believed the clunk from the transmission—until the second clunk. Bruce switched the engine off and ran to tell Jack that something terrible had happened to the gearbox. There was less than half an hour to the start of the race when Jack arrived back lugging a spare transmission and the McLaren crew started desperately unbolting the broken gearbox to fit the new one. It seemed like an impossible task. The local organizers did their bit by delaying the start of the Grand Prix with a fake search for oil on the back of the circuit, but they finally had to put the grid under starter's orders and flag it away. Behind the pits the final bolts were tightened on the Cooper, Bruce hastily buckled on his helmet, oil was dashed in, and he was wheelspinning his way out on to the track to take up the chase. He had half a lap to make up.

Later in his career, Bruce was to repeat this ability to perform near miracles under stress. In situations where last-minute problems had set him back, or if he was angered, he could turn on fantastic performances. In 1963 he brought one of the first Downton-prepared Mini Coopers to New Zealand and he qualified it on pole position for the sedan race. Just before the start he was told that he would have to start from the back of the grid because the drivers of some of the larger-engined cars had protested that they would run the little Cooper down before the first corner. Irate, Bruce drove like a man possessed, threaded his way to the front of the field in two laps and led the race until overheating slowed him to 2nd behind a 3.8-liter Jaguar. At Mosport in Canada in 1967 a leaking fuel bag in his M6A Can-Am sports car delayed his start and he set off 50 seconds after the field. He fought his way through the pack to place 2nd behind team-mate Denny Hulme. It was difficult to arouse Bruce, but when his fuse was lit he was very definitely hot property!

At Ardmore in 1958 he must have felt near to tears when the transmission clattered so close to the start of the Grand Prix,

Bruce bought this center-seat Cooper sports car from Jack Brabham.

but the urgency of the chase seized him and when he drove onto the track he was the local hero out to make good. He was up to 8th place when the engine started to misfire; in his haste he had forgotten to change from the soft warm-up plugs they were using when the gearbox failed. Seven minutes dragged by as the plugs were changed and Bruce saw all his hard-earned placings being lost. He went back into the race a very lonely last but he was starting to get the feel of the car now that the heat was off, when the transmission started to tighten up and he called back at the pits. His race was over. The bellhousing studs had loosened, the oil had drained out, and the gears were ruined.

So, it seemed, were his chances of winning the "Driver to Europe" scholarship. It looked as though bad luck had spoiled his big chance and he would have to resign himself to his engineering studies. So near and yet so far. When it was announced that night at the prize-giving that despite his misfortunes that afternoon, Bruce was to be the first driver to be presented with the award from the New Zealand International Grand Prix Association of a trip to Europe with introductions to racing teams and a grant to cover expenses during the season, Bruce was stunned. The world started going round again.

He asked Colin Beanland if he would come with him as a sort of companion mechanic. When Colin protested that he was a clerk in a wholesale spare parts business and hardly a racing mechanic, Bruce smoothed it all out and said it would be simple to learn as he went along.

The McLaren entourage went south again that summer towing the Cooper behind a new 2.4-liter Jaguar, and after a broken ring gear at Wigram, he collected a pair of 2nd places at Dunedin and Teretonga behind Ross Jensen's 250F Maserati. Jensen was the winner of the New Zealand Gold Star that season and he certainly deserved it with immaculate drives in the "Grey Lady," as the equally immaculate 250F was known. Inclined to be loud about most things, Ross, today running a flourishing BMW dealership in Auckland, had no peer on New Zealand tracks that season. At Teretonga the drifting sand caused odd traction problems similar to those at Zandvoort, and Bruce countered these by fitting Michelin X road tires to his Cooper!

It was during this period that I became acquainted with Bruce. Knowing that he was competing in the hillclimb at Clellands, some 20 miles from my hometown of Timaru, I introduced myself at Teretonga and took full advantage of my new acquaintance with a top driver by billing him highly in the preview of the hillclimb I wrote for the *Timaru Herald*. I was then working in the Australia and New Zealand Bank and borrowing time on the bank's typewriter to tap out freelance columns on motoring for the local paper.

Bruce fell somewhat short of my estimation in the hillclimb because after filling the Cooper's differential with plumber's lead to lock it, he snapped a halfshaft on his second run and he ended the afternoon with a best time of 55.3 seconds which was worth a class win ahead of a Triumph TR2, but only 3rd fastest of the day behind Morrie Stanton in the fearsome Stanton Special which had a supercharged Gypsy Moth aircraft engine mounted amidships, and Dick Campbell in a Mark 9 Cooper 500. Further down the results it said that one E. Young (Austin A30) had finished 2nd in class behind a Cooper-Anzani with a time of 62.9sec for the hill. It was the first and last time that my name appeared in the same list of results as Bruce McLaren's and my last competition appearance. Banking and later writing were far less wearing on the nerves and the pocket.

That night Bruce and I went down to the local dance in his father's Jaguar and I introduced him to Pat Broad. Bruce asked if he could escort her home but she explained that she was sorry but she was going on to a party. We toured Timaru that night trying to find the party but finally gave up. The next day I tracked down Pat's telephone number and Bruce went to see her. They were engaged after the 1960 Grand Prix at Ardmore and in 1961 they were married in Christchurch.

Bruce had decided to take his 1750-cc Cooper to England with him and have the engine altered to comply with the 1500-cc Formula 2 regulations, and the car was shipped to Sydney for re-loading on the Orantes which would take it to

The big supercharged Maserati which Bruce prepared for Frank Shuter.

London. Bruce and Colin flew to Sydney on March 15, 1958, trying to look a lot more confident than they felt in their new black blazers that had been presented to them with "NZIGP Driver to Europe" emblazoned in silver letters under New Zealand's national emblem, the silver fern.

The Orantes stopped to load cargo in Melbourne and there was a letter waiting for Bruce to tell him that the NZIGP had arranged a start in a works Formula 2 Cooper at Aintree on April 15th which meant that he would have to leave the ship and fly to make it in time. He climbed down into the cargo hold and spent an hour removing his tailor-made clutch and brake pedals, the St. Christopher medal from the dash panel and his helmet and goggles.

Once again Jack Brabham was looking after his New Zealand protege and starting money of 60 Pounds had been arranged. Charles Cooper, wary of another of these bush lads arriving to drive his works cars, stipulated that Bruce had to insure the car and after paying the premium of 50 Pounds, he emerged with a paper profit from his first race. Problems with the Weber carburetors dropped him to 9th place in his first event abroad, but just being there was fuel for the 20-year-old McLaren ego.

The latest Formula 2 Coopers had coil spring suspension so Bruce decided to sell his own car to Steve Ouvaroff and invest in one of the new Coopers. He had to build it himself in the workshops. When Colin arrived on the Orantes, he and Bruce took a room at the Royal Oak, a pub just around the corner from the Cooper factory, in fact behind the workshops across a little stream. A plank across the stream solved the distance to work problem, and they soon discovered that the bar was more or less a Cooper clubhouse. They only paid rent on their room while they were actually there which was ideal as they were often away at races and they were not likely to get rich quickly on the starting money Bruce was earning. "He didn't always win," says Colin, "but at least there was some money in the bank. This didn't stay there though because he wanted to improve the car and put disc brakes on it. That meant perhaps 90 Pounds for a set. And then the big thing was the limited-slip differential. All these things cost money and there were times when we ate spaghetti for days on end simply because we didn't have much money. Often we couldn't scrape up enough for my wages, but that didn't really matter because I was there for a look around and perhaps do a bit of racing. I bought a Mark I Zephyr to tow the Cooper and we borrowed a trailer from the factory."

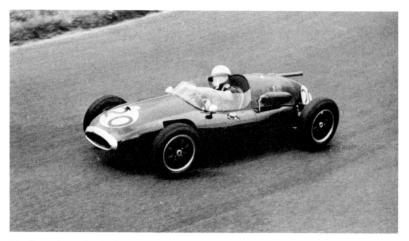

Nurburgring 1958, the most significant drive in Bruce's early career.

The idea of paying any form of retainer or expenses for a mechanic hadn't occurred to the Grand Prix Association when they started the scholarship scheme, but it was an important item and one that was taken care of in future awards. "You really had to have someone giving you a hand. You needed someone to give you pit signals. And when you're 12,000 miles from home and you're a 20-year-old kid, it's kind of handy just to have someone to talk to, if nothing else." Colin knew the score.

There were plenty of lessons to be learned in that first year. When the production Cooper tube frames came off the chassis jigs, the wishbones were bolted on, the car was assembled by hand and this meant that each car was just a little bit different. Bruce and Colin were helping to put the finishing touches to a friend's Cooper when they realised that the wheels were pointing at some odd angles. They ran a string round the car and drew this to the owner's attention. Then it dawned on them that perhaps their own car was like this. It was. They solved the problem by welding washers on to the chassis lugs where the wishbones bolted on, until the car was set up perfectly. The next race was at Crystal Palace and Bruce went sailing backwards into a bank in the rain which did bad things to their precise setting-up. Oddly enough, according to Colin, the affair with the bank didn't have a great deal of adverse effect on the handling so they were left to figure that either the Cooper was extremely strong or their setting-up was not worth the effort! **35**

A race at Brands Hatch saw Bruce come up against Ken Tyrrell who was then better known as a lumber merchant in Surrey. Ken was driving a Formula 2 Cooper for Alan Brown and he took Bruce as they were going into Paddock Bend just after the start. "I didn't even know him and I was perturbed that he should be going so much faster than I was," Bruce reported in *From the Cockpit*. "I pulled up beside him at Clearways and he left me standing. I later found he was using second and third gears and high revs, while I had been using third and fourth." Bruce got by Ken a couple of laps later and went on to win the meeting.

Tyrrell's version of the race is interesting. "Bruce had gone very well in practice and everyone was wondering who this new boy was. We knew he had won the award in New Zealand but that was about all. He really looked like a youngster then. I got a better start than he did and got out in front with him close behind. I remember thinking that he was going to have difficulty getting by, but then I imagined the commentator saying "Why doesn't that old so-and-so Tyrrell get out of the way and let this youngster get on with it?" So I moved over and let him by."

Ten years later Tyrrell was entering a Matra-Ford Formula 1 car for Jackie Stewart and in 1969 Stewart won the World Championship for Tyrrell. Tyrrell's ability as a talent-spotter and team manager has become something of a legend since those early days. In 1959 Tyrrell signed Bruce to drive one of a pair of Formula 2 Coopers that he was entering together with Alan Brown. "I thought Bruce would become World Champion because he had the ability to think about it. He wasn't going to be the world's quickest driver, but then the world's quickest driver isn't always World Champion."

Bruce ran his own Formula 2 car in several more races in England and in Europe, but the race he had set his heart on running was the German Grand Prix on August 3. The race was a combined event for Formula 1 and Formula 2 cars to make a full field on the 14.2-mile Nurburgring. Bruce's entry had been placed as first reserve since the German organizers were probably not exactly sure who he was, but John Cooper assured him that someone would crash during practice so that his place at the head of the reserve list was as good as a guaranteed start.

He borrowed passenger cars to try and put the horrors of the Ring into some sort of order and he eventually wound up with a place on the fourth row of the grid behind the 2.5-liter BRMs of Harry Schell and Jean Behra. Schell was known as one of the best exponents of the art of anticipating the starter so John Cooper warned Bruce to watch Schell's rear wheels and ignore the flag. He was 5th into the first corner with only four Formula 1 cars ahead of him. John Cooper obviously knew the score too.

By the third lap Bruce was 2nd in the Formula 2 section behind Phil Hill's Ferrari and ahead of Barth's Porsche. When the Ferrari started to run out of brakes, Bruce caught and passed it and held his lead to the finish. He went up on the victory dais and was proudly garlanded alongside Tony Brooks who had won the Grand Prix in a Vanwall. As well as winning the Formula 2 section Bruce had finished 5th overall behind Brooks' Vanwall, Salvadori's and Trintignant's Coopers and Von Trips' Ferrari.

The 1958 German Grand Prix, more than any other race that season, made Bruce's name and assured him of a Cooper drive the following season. His effort received the sort of press that Jacky Ickx's race in a Formula 2 Matra at the Ring earned ten years later. Although he might not have been aware of it at the time in the bustle to get back to England for a race at Brands Hatch the following day, he was on the threshold of a distinguished career as a Grand Prix driver and a racing car designer and builder.

At another Brands Hatch event at the end of the month McLaren must have been mildly astonished to realize that the commentator, John Bolster, was leading the crowd in singing "Happy Birthday" as they drove around on the parade lap before the race. It was August 30th, 1958 and Bruce McLaren was 21 years old.

2

GRAND PRIX RACING
WITH COOPER

JACKIE STEWART remembers his first contact with Bruce: "I had been shooting at the 1959 European Championships in North Wales and I'd gone across to see the British Grand Prix at Aintree. Reg Tanner, competition manager of Esso, was one of the people I had met while brother Jimmy was racing, and I was talking with him in the paddock when this young guy with a limp walked over to the Cooper transporter. Reg said 'That's Bruce McLaren, he's got a great future in racing.' I remember seeing him then and thinking 'Jesus - he's only 21 years of age and he's over here from New Zealand driving a Formula 1 works Cooper.' " Jackie, 19 at the time and one of the best clay pigeon shooters in Europe, was to switch to racing cars in five years. In another five years he won the British Grand Prix and went on to win the World Championship the same season.

Bruce gave spectator Stewart good value at Aintree. Brabham was out in front in the 2.5-liter works Cooper and when Stirling Moss in the apple-green BRM made a couple of pit stops Bruce found himself in 2nd place just in front of the hustling Moss. The pressure was really on and Bruce was throwing the Cooper all over the place in his efforts to stay ahead of the BRM and hold 2nd place. Caution and perhaps a tinge of embarrassment

39

The famous Aintree battle, with Bruce and Moss sharing the lap record.

prompted him to relinquish his hairily-held place to Stirling, but that didn't mean he had given up. The pair of them traded records in the closing laps and as they took the flag the BRM was just a nose in front of the dark green Cooper. McLaren and Moss shared a new lap record for the 3-mile track at 93.31 mph.

At the end of the 1958 season Bruce had fitted a special 1960-cc version of the 1.5-liter Coventry Climax engine in his Formula 2 Cooper and shipped it home to New Zealand. He won at Waimate and Teretonga and collected enough points to clinch the national championships since he was still technically a New Zealand "local" driver. His factory drive with Cooper later in the year automatically made him an "overseas" driver for subsequent races at home.

Bruce had been promised a Formula 2 drive with the Cooper team but when he arrived back in England early in 1959 he discovered that different plans had been made over the winter and the Formula 2 team was now being handed over to Ken Tyrrell and Alan Brown who were entering a pair of works-supported cars. Bruce was asked if he would mind driving in the Grand Prix team with Brabham and Masten Gregory and on his instant acceptance he was taken into the workshops and shown Jack's new 2.5-liter car and the pair of 2.2-liter cars that had been prepared for Bruce and Masten Gregory—by Monaco all three cars were fitted with the full 2.5-liter Climax engines. In addition, any weekends when Bruce was not busy in Formula 1 were now taken up with an offer from Tyrrell to drive one of the Formula 2 cars.

Only the previous year just before the German Grand Prix John Cooper, Jack Brabham, Ian Burgess, and the team secretary Andrew Ferguson had a heart-to-heart with Bruce to try and make him change his mind about giving it all away and going home to his engineering text books. Now he was very pleased he had decided to stay.

Pop and Mrs. McLaren had decided to come over to Europe to see their son now that he was a full-fledged Grand Prix driver, but they were appalled at the French Grand Prix at Reims which turned out to be a brutal race. A blazing sun melted the road surface and cooked the drivers in the cockpits. Flying stones smashed windscreens and goggles and slashed the drivers' faces. Bruce staggered exhausted from his battered car and collapsed for the 30-minute break between the Grand Prix and the Formula 2 race. When he started in the Formula 2 race he was on top of the world, literally "high" on physical exhaustion, but he realized after a few close shaves that he was not in control of what he was doing on the high-speed road circuit and he pulled in to retire as Brabham had done a few laps earlier. Bruce's parents were shocked—racing certainly hadn't been like this at Ardmore!

Following his dice to 3rd place alongside Moss in the British Grand Prix, Bruce failed to finish a race until the Formula 1

Bruce's last season as a "local" NZ driver won him all this booty.

Sebring 1959: Bruce won his first championship Grand Prix race.

circus crossed the Atlantic for the first American Grand Prix to
be held since 1916. Run at Sebring, Florida, the revived event
took the place of the Moroccan Grand Prix on the championship calendar.

The Grand Prix at Sebring was to determine the 1959 World
Championship for drivers. The battle was being fought between
Brabham with 31 points, Moss (BRM and Cooper) with 25½,
and Tony Brooks (Ferrari) with 23. If Jack won the race the
title was his, but if Stirling beat Jack *and* took fastest lap, then
Moss would be Champion. Brooks had to win and take fastest
lap with neither Brabham or Moss finishing. When the race started Moss took off in the lead with his Rob Walker Cooper ahead
of Brabham and McLaren, but when Moss's transmission failed
it looked as though the race and the title were being handed on
a plate to Brabham. Two laps from the end Jack's jinx got
him—he ran out of fuel. At the last minute he had altered the
size of the choke-tubes in his Webers making the engine run
richer and with the added effort of towing Bruce around his
fuel mileage had dropped drastically. Bruce steered past the
slowing Cooper, looking across at Jack and not knowing what
he was supposed to do next. If he won, would Jack still be
champion? Should he wait for Jack? He knew instantly that he
had no option but to race for the flag because Maurice Trintignant's Cooper was only seconds behind him and catching up

A different race car—Bruce in a Jaguar 3.8 at Brands Hatch, 1961.

fast. Bruce won the Grand Prix and Jack pushed his car across the line to take 4th place and the championship. Bruce revelled in the surprise and glory. At 22 he was the youngest driver ever to win a Grande Epreuve. He was famous.

He might have been famous but he didn't really feel very famous. He was still working hard to make a success of his career and he displayed none of the trappings of a famous racing driver. He drove a Morris Minor that he had bought from Betty Brabham and he shared a little bed and sitting room in Surbiton with Phil Kerr. This modest apartment boasted one main room that had two beds, a couple of chairs, a wardrobe and a gas fire. There was a tiny kitchen with an equally tiny gas cooker. The bathroom on the landing was shared with the other tenants. Their daily menu included a breakfast of cornflakes and coffee, and a lunch that depended on where they were and if they could afford it; the evening meal was always at Nick's Cafe in Kingston down by the coal yards beside the Thames. Their standard order was sausages, bacon and baked beans for one and ninepence (about 25 cents); they made themselves instant coffee when they got back to the apartment. By comparison Bob Cratchett had it made. On occasions they would be invited out to meals and the high point of the week, when they were not off racing, was a Sunday roast with the Brabham household.

43

Following Brabham to a 1-2 Cooper victory in the 1961 Times GP.

Bruce went back to New Zealand for Christmas and took a 2.5-liter Formula 1 Cooper with him. He finished a couple of seconds behind Brabham's Cooper in the New Zealand Grand Prix at Ardmore and while the evening's sporting papers speculated on whether Bruce had driven to team orders and let Jack win, Bruce was proposing to Pat. Three months later Pat would fly to England to tour the races with her new fiance and to act as his secretary. In the meantime Bruce had to cut short the New Zealand races and fly to South America for the Argentine Grand Prix in February. Shipping delays meant that Jack and Bruce had scarcely any practice on the Buenos Aires track and when the race started the two BRMs, the new rear-engined Lotus and Moss's Cooper were out in front of the works Coopers. The temperature was well over 100 in the shade and Bruce had taken the precaution of fitting a flask of iced orange juice in his cockpit, having learned his lesson after the roasting at Reims the season before. Innes Ireland led in the new Lotus but spun on the second lap, dropping to 6th place and then fighting back to 2nd only to break a steering arm bolt and drop back to a slowing 6th after he clobbered a curb. The BRMs had valve spring problems, Moss broke a suspension arm after hitting a curb, and Brabham's gearbox failed. Bruce was on his own out in front for the second Grand Prix in succession and he opened up a 26.3-second lead on Cliff Allison's Ferrari to win at an average of 84.6 mph.

The threat from new rear-engined Lotus called for a crash

program to design a new Cooper to defend the World Championship and the new low-line car was designed, built and tested in two months. Owen "The Beard" Maddocks had spent the winter designing a completely new 5-speed gearbox to counter the endless problems they had encountered with the Citroen-based transmission the season before, so Bruce summoned up his knowledge of technical drawings to assist in the design office laying out wishbone assemblies and other components to hasten the progress of the new car. This progress was hindered somewhat by Charles Cooper, John's father, insisting that the new car had to be designed to allow for the old Cooper rear leaf spring to be replaced if the new coil springs proved to be unsuitable. After the first day of testing the prototype at Silverstone Brabham lowered the lap record by *six* seconds, and the old leaf spring ideas were conveniently forgotten.

Light rain at Monaco turned the street circuit into a skating rink and Moss gave Lotus its first Grand Prix win, with Bruce in 2nd place. As they moved on to Zandvoort, McLaren was leading the championship, a point which was not lost on the Dutch organizers who had refused the "unknown" driver an entry the previous year. A driveshaft failure dropped Bruce from the race. Jack won at Zandvoort and continued to win again at Spa, Reims, Silverstone, and Porto to take his second World Championship. Bruce was 2nd to Jack at Spa and Porto, 3rd at Reims and Riverside and 4th at Silverstone; adding these points to his score from winning the Argentine Grand Prix and finishing 2nd at Monaco, he was 2nd in the 1960 championship with 37 points behind Jack's 43, and ahead of Moss with 19. Stirling had missed two races that season after crashing at Spa and breaking both legs.

The 1960 season was the last under the 2.5-liter formula and it was the last of the so-called Golden Years for the Cooper team. In 1961 with the 1.5-liter limit, all the British cars, with the exception of the Walker Lotus driven by Moss, were outpaced by the superior power of the V-6 Ferraris which had been developed as Formula 2 cars the year before. The British constructors tended to regard the formula change as something horrible which might go away if they shut their eyes and ignored it, and this attitude was to cost them dearly during 1961. That year Bruce was tied for 7th place in the championship and Brabham was only 11th.

Pages 46-47: Bruce (no. 14) avoided Monaco crash and won the race.   **45**

In last laps at Monaco Bruce had to drive hard to stave off Phil Hill.

Brabham decided he could do things better his way at the end of the 1961 season and left the Cooper team to build his own cars and this resulted in a touchy period at the Cooper factory because Charles Cooper maintained that Jack had taken all the team's secrets with him when he left and Bruce was effectively barred from the drawing office. This was hardly a way to encourage developments and Cooper fortunes sagged as other constructors overtook their rear-engined lead. Ferrari won the manufacturer's championship in 1961, BRM in 1962, Lotus in 1963, Ferrari again in 1964, Lotus again in 1965, and in 1966 Brabham won the championships for both constructors and drivers in his own car.

Patty had stayed in England over the winter of 1960-61 working as a beautician while Bruce went home to a mediocre series of races in New Zealand with a 2.5-liter Cooper before returning to England. Phil had bought an apartment which allowed them the luxury of a bedroom each, a lounge, a bathroom that they didn't have to share with everyone else in the building and a kitchen big enough that they didn't have to go outside to turn around. Phil can remember these bachelor days well. "Bruce never became domesticated and never showed any likelihood of becoming that way. Housework was beyond him and although we were supposed to be taking it in turns to keep the flat tidy, I always seemed to have to do it. On a weekend

Bruce won the non-championship 1962 Reims race convincingly.

when Bruce would be away racing, I would get the place all sorted out spick and span, but within five minutes of Bruce's return the whole place would be a shambles. He would walk in the front door and there would be a trail of clothes and suitcases and shoes and packages of things he'd bought while he was away. This trail would go across the lounge and into his bedroom where he would open his suitcase and then there would be a trail of clothes from his bedroom to the bathroom. It was turmoil and yet he always seemed to be quite oblivious to it all."

On one of Bruce's rare forays to the launderette he took a bag of washing which included the favorite short-sleeved blue sports shirt that he always wore when driving. It had become almost a mascot. As far as Bruce was concerned, the laundry machine was foolproof providing you remembered to put in the washing, the soap powder and the sixpence. It wasn't until he got back to the flat and started to empty out the laundry bag that he realized all the white underpants, undershirts, shirts and sweaters were a delicate shade of light blue.

"When he saw what had happened, he just couldn't stop laughing. He sat down and laughed until the tears were rolling down his cheeks and his sides ached. He just hooted and rolled about until he couldn't bear it. That's what life tended to be like in the flat."

The Morris Minor had been sold to make way for a splendid 3.8 Jaguar which Bruce had bought with the intention of shipping it home for his father. "I bought it new from the factory with high compression, a high ratio rear axle, racing suspension, and high-geared steering," Bruce wrote for a feature on road cars he had owned. "The high-geared steering was the one mistake I made with the 3.8. It was just too heavy to be pleasant on the road and it made the car 'darty' but it was great fun if you wanted to do a couple of laps round Goodwood between testing sessions. It was one of the most reliable cars I've ever owned in direct contrast to the E-Type that came next. It was one of the first E-Types and when it was brand new it was a positive joy, but I made the mistake of fitting a rear end that was too high. I opted for the 2.9 Le Mans axle ratio because I figured that with this sort of car you could cruise quite happily at 120 mph, but when I tried doing that across Europe I found that I didn't really want to go that fast after all."

At the end of the 1961 season Bruce and Patty flew back to New Zealand and were married in November in Christchurch. They had a brief honeymoon in Fiji and returned to run the

Down Under in 1964, with "Pop" McLaren enjoying Bruce's success.

Bruce and Timmy Mayer side-by-side at Teretonga in the Coopers.

series of races in New Zealand and Australia with a special 2.7-liter low-line Cooper that Bruce had bought from Tommy Atkins, and he had hired Tommy's chief mechanic, Harry Pearce, to look after the car. He had a series of minor placings with a jet dash back to England in between to check progress on the new Formula 1 car for 1962.

In Melbourne after he had finished 3rd behind Brabham and Surtees in their Coopers, Bruce offered me a job as his secretary back in England. He said he wasn't sure quite what I would do, but he would think of something. He had been under the impression that I was going back to England anyway, but when I told him I had a job lined up with a newspaper in Hobart, Tasmania, he offered to advance me the cost of the air fare against my first year's wages. I accepted his offer and flew back to England via Sebring with Bruce and Patty and worked during 1962 for 6 Pounds (about $15) per week sharing a small flat with Wally Willmott, a mechanic from my hometown who was to become Bruce's first permanent mechanic.

The new Cooper with the Climax V-8 engine and new 6-speed gearbox arrived just in time for the Dutch Grand Prix at Zandvoort which opened the championship in 1962, but the plaudits of the press were strictly reserved for the new monocoque Lotus 25. Stirling Moss had been lucky to escape with his life when his Lotus 24 crashed at Goodwood in the Easter Monday meeting and this new Lotus with Jim Clark at the wheel was to be the dominant combination of the decade.

Bruce (no. 7) led off at Sandown Park but victory went to Brabham.

Bruce won the Monaco Grand Prix after Clark's Lotus and Graham Hill's BRM had failed and he won the non-champion-ship Formula 1 race at Reims but it was six years before Bruce was to win another Formula 1 race—and then it was to be in his own car.

After a 2nd place in the South African GP that finished the 1962 season Bruce was placed 3rd in the World Championship with 27 points behind Hill, who won the title with 42 points, and Clark with 30 points.

The 1963 season was notably mainly for a series of accidents. Patty set the ball rolling when a water skiing boat capsized in Australia and she was hit by the propeller as she was swimming away. The bones in her ankle and heel were badly smashed and she spent weeks in plaster and months in pain. Before the season had started in Europe, John Cooper crashed in a mysterious accident with an experimental twin-engined Mini on the Kingston-by-Pass, and Ken Tyrrell stepped in to assist Charles Cooper in looking after the Formula 1 team. Bruce rounded off the trio of accidents when his Cooper went end-over-end at the Nurburgring and he was rushed unconscious to the hospital on the hillside behind the little village of Adenau. When he came to he had two very sore legs, a black eye and absolutely no recollection about what had happened. Back in England he hobbled into the workshops and winced when he saw the twisted broken pile of junk that had been his racing car. Piecing together the bits, they came to the conclusion that the right rear wishbone had broken.

Bruce was hiding his growing frustration with the lack of development at Coopers and his own lack of success. People were beginning to comment on the dimming of the McLaren star, and there were those who blamed Bruce for the Cooper lack of success. This was a particularly difficult time for him. He felt that he knew what had to be done, but it was becoming increasingly difficult for him to have his suggestions acted upon. There was a new formula for the 1964 series of races in New Zealand and Australia which limited engine capacity to 2.5-liters and race distances were set at 100 miles. Bruce wanted to build a pair of special Coopers and enter them as works cars in the new-style Tasman Series, but Charles Cooper blocked each approach that Bruce made. The McLaren idea was to build a pair of slimline lightweight cars to take advantage of the regulations, but Charles argued that a regular Formula 1 car fitted with a 2.5-liter engine could do the job. There was also a problem of entries for Timmy Mayer, Bruce's choice for second "works" driver because Down Under he was unknown, and Charles said that if there was to be any doubt about the validity of the entries he would cancel the whole operation.

At this stage Bruce decided to do it on his own and after discussions with Teddy Mayer, Tim's brother, they agreed to share costs and run under Bruce's own colors. Necessity bred Bruce McLaren Motor Racing Limited, and racing artist Michael Turner designed a team badge with a kiwi as the main motif. The Coopers became more McLarens as the building program progressed. The bulky side-tanks of the Formula 1 Coopers were not needed on the short Tasman races, so the tubular spaceframe was wrapped in steel sheet which helped to stiffen the chassis and acted as the body sides. The fuel was carried in a seat tank and a couple of smaller top tanks. The Cooper top rear wishbones were replaced with top links and radius arms and the McLaren Cooper was ready to race.

Brabham had also built a pair of special cars for the Series so it was a full-scale battle between the McLaren and Brabham camps. Denny Hulme won Levin for Brabham, but Bruce won the New Zealand Grand Prix on the new Pukekohe track outside Auckland and Timmy was 3rd behind Denny's Brabham. Bruce had been trying for eight years to win his hometown Grand Prix and at last he had succeeded. He followed this with wins at Wigram and Teretonga after torrid battles with the Brabhams.

Luck left the little team in Australia. Jack won at Warwick Farm with Bruce 2nd and Timmy 3rd. At Lakeside Timmy was starting to display the sort of polished prowess that had prompted Ken Tyrrell to sign him for Formula Junior and later a place in the Cooper Grand Prix team for the coming season. He led the race until his engine blew up, and Bruce finished 3rd

The reward for Bruce's private venture: the 1964 Tasman Cup.

behind Brabham and Tasmanian John Youl's Cooper. In practice for the final race of the Series at Longford in Tasmania, a fast 4.5-mile track over public roads strongly reminiscent of Reims, Timmy's Cooper became airborne over a bump just before the braking area and smashed into a tree. Timmy was killed instantly. On race day Bruce started sorrowfully from the back of the grid in no mood to go racing for the Tasman title, but he finished 2nd to Graham Hill and won the Tasman Championship.

The die was cast. He had proved to himself that he knew enough about racing now to build his own cars and run his own racing team. Racing was beginning to get exciting again. The old challenge had returned. In his book *From the Cockpit* he outlined his mounting enjoyment as his Tasman Coopers took shape for the 1964 Series. "The first essential for success in racing is enthusiasm. Not just mild, but burning enthusiasm. To succeed in motor racing or in any sport it must be the most important thing in your life.

"This goes for many things other than motor racing in particular or sport in general, because if it isn't the most important thing to you, there are a dozen other people to whom it *is*. Those are the people you have to beat.

"You must eat, live and think motor racing. The more you think about it and plan, the better you will do. 'Scheme' is probably a better word than 'think'. Stirling Moss used to think about motor racing more than anyone else I know and John

Surtees comes a close second. Jack Brabham is another for whom his sport is everything.

"When I get wound up in a project, whether it is one of Cooper's new Formula 1 cars or building my own cars for New Zealand and Australia, everything else is made secondary to it. Everything. I often force myself to go to sleep when trying to worry out a problem, or I am stuck with it all night. I decided long ago that solid sleep is one of the first essentials when trying to work hard. It is more a question of attitude of mind than anything else. The people who succeed in racing are those who would do so in any walk of life.

"First comes natural ability—and there are hundreds with it—but there must always be the dedication to want to apply it, continue applying it and keep improving it.

"Motor racing is unlike some other sports, in fact it is sometimes argued that it isn't a sport at all because one uses machinery and its efficiency is the important thing. This is true, of course, but it is common knowledge that with any good piece of equipment, be it a good gun, a good yacht, or a good racing car, one person or one crew will do better with it than others—and here lies the big difference between one competitor and the next.

"I like to feel that the combination of driver and car is important. I'm sure Jack Brabham feels the same way and that's why he is building his own car. By winning with one's own car, both other drivers and other cars have been beaten.

"The usual ambition once a person becomes serious about motor racing is to be a works driver. This is the pinnacle of GP racing, but one can go beyond it, full circle. The normal beginning is driving one's own car; when driving my own Formula 2 car in 1958, my big ambition was to become a works driver for the Cooper factory. Now I enjoy nothing better than running my own cars again."

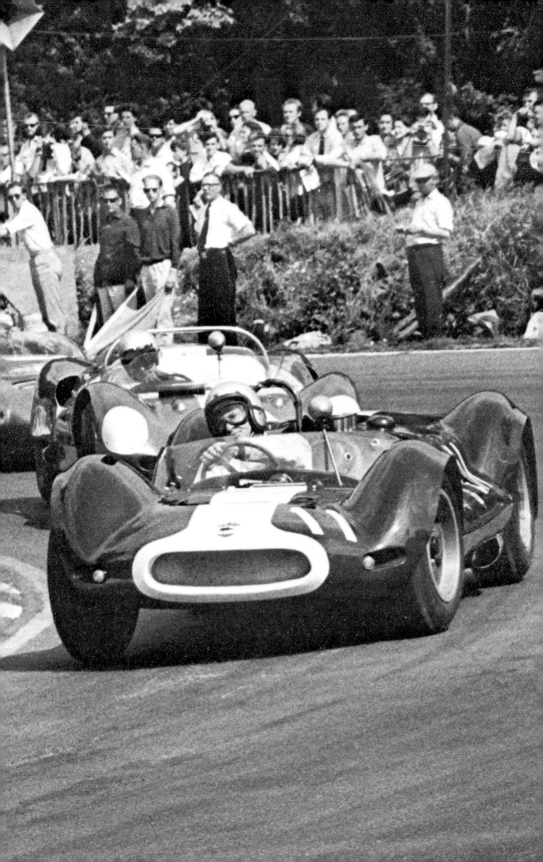

THE ZEREX SPECIAL
& THE FIRST McLARENS

IF YOU WERE to blame any one man for the McLaren involvement in American sports car racing, it would have to be Briggs Cunningham, the wealthy sportsman and sports car lover who tried for years to win Le Mans with his own Cunningham cars. His first effort was in 1950 with a Cadillac sedan and a Cadillac-powered Cunningham sports car that looked as though it had been styled by the designer of a World War I tank. The French called it "Le Monstre." The sedan was 10th that year and the monster was 11th. The following year Cunningham returned with the new C2R Chrysler-engined cars and one was lying a safe 2nd behind the Walker-Whitehead C Type Jaguar with four hours to go when engine and transmission trouble dropped it to an eventual 18th place. In 1952 Briggs himself drove a C4R into 4th place after being at the wheel for 20 of the 24 hours. In 1953 a Cunningham C5R finished 3rd and was fastest car down the Mulsanne straight at 154.8 mph. A C4R was 3rd in 1954.

Briggs bought racing cars the way other people shop in super-markets. He had to have one of everything on the shelf. In 1960 at Laguna Seca Bruce was invited to drive a development of the Jaguar D-Type that was eventually to become the production E-Type. It was his first sports car race in America and he finish-

Sebring 1962: Giampiero Dall'ara, Briggs Cunningham, Roger Penske and Alfred Momo look on as Bruce starts practice in the Cooper-Maserati.

ed 5th which came as something of a surprise to the Cunningham crew who frankly hadn't expected the car to even qualify on the tight Monterey circuit.

Briggs ordered a copy of the 1961 works Formula 1 Cooper to be painted in the American racing colors and delivered to the American Grand Prix at Watkins Glen for Walt Hansgen to drive, but unfortunately Walt wrecked the car. Roger Penske, whom Bruce had met after the Monterey race, bought the wrecked Cooper and had it rebuilt for Formula Libre racing. Teddy Mayer rented the Cooper for brother Timmy to race and Tyler Alexander looked after it.

At Sebring in 1961 Briggs asked Bruce to drive for him again sharing a rear-engined V-12 Type 63 Birdcage Maserati with Hansgen but it failed in the race with engine and transmission problems. Bruce was entered to drive this car again at Le Mans that year, and he would have if Walt hadn't parked it in a sandbank in the early stages of the race.

The Cunningham entry at Sebring in 1962 was a special Cooper Monaco fitted with a 2.8-liter 4-cylinder Maserati engine and Bruce drove it with Roger Penske. The car led early in the race until it slowed with electrical problems. At that race Roger talked with Bruce about his plans for fitting a sports car body on his Formula Libre Cooper to contest the professional races at Laguna Seca and Riverside at the end of the season. Roger

Bruce beat Jim Clark's Lotus 30 at Silverstone in 1964 with the ex-Penske Zerex, still fitted with the 2.7-liter 4-cylinder engine.

even asked Bruce if he would join him in the venture, but Bruce had his own plans. Roger had permission from the race organizers to build his sports car as a central seater, and with what was essentially a Grand Prix car with a 2.7-liter Climax engine, he had a 200-pound weight advantage on the works Coopers and he won both the big-money races in California that season. The car had been christened the Zerex Special for commercial reasons.

The people he beat, including Bruce in the works Cooper Monaco, argued later that the car was hardly within international regulations governing sports car racing (shades of the Chaparral 2J in 1970!) and for 1963 Roger had to alter the Zerex by cutting a slice out each side of the tube frame and inserting curved piping to make room for two seats, thus complying with the rules. As Bruce mentioned later, a master plumber would have been delighted with the tube bends but they gave the chassis one of the lowest torsional rigidity figures ever. Penske won the Guards Trophy at Brands Hatch with the legalized Zerex and then sold the car to John Mecom and drove for the Mecom team.

Sports cars using big American V-8s had started to become competitive and the "little" 2.7-liter Zerex with its Climax engine was parked and almost forgotten under a dust cover in the corner of Mecom's big workshops. A 3.5-liter aluminum Olds-

The Zerex gets the Oldsmobile V-8 and becomes the Jolly Green Giant.

mobile F85 V-8 engine sat in a crate beside the Zerex waiting for an engine swap when someone had the time.

So in a roundabout sort of way it was Briggs Cunningham who brought Bruce into American sports car racing, it was Briggs who bought the original Cooper that was to become the Zerex, and Briggs who brought Roger and Bruce together when the Zerex was about to take shape in the first place.

Bruce had entertained ideas of building a Zerex type of sports car before he went out to New Zealand at the end of 1963 since this would enable him to use his supply of Climax engines which he could otherwise use only on the Australasian races. In fact he had built a prototype tubular chassis. At that stage the fiercely defended McLaren pet theory was that a good, reliable lightweight car with a Climax engine was still the equal of all comers, but his colleagues Tyler Alexander and Wally Wilmott had been to Nassau and had seen just how competitive the big American-engined sports cars were becoming and they were not at all keen to support Bruce.

They finally settled on a compromise, buying the Zerex with the spare Oldsmobile engine. The car arrived in England with Tyler just three days before the Oulton Park race in April 1964. Wally and Tyler sweated to fit the regulation luggage trunk and spare wheel in time before the race, but the car retired with no oil pressure after all their work. At Aintree and Silverstone it was a different story and Bruce beat Jim Clark in the Lotus 30 and Roy Salvadori in a Cooper Monaco powered by a 5-liter Maserati engine.

The day after their win at Silverstone the Zerex was stripped and chopped up. The entire section of the frame from just behind the front suspension to just ahead of the rear suspension was scrapped and a new McLaren-designed tube frame was welded in. This was far stiffer than the willowy Zerex chassis and it had the sophistication of the water and oil flowing through the chassis tubes. Bruce left Wally and Tyler with a wire model of the chassis and went down to Monaco where the new Formula 1 Cooper with inboard front suspension broke a front upright in practice and Bruce wrecked it. He drove a 1963 Cooper in the race and retired early with an oil leak. From there he went to the Nurburgring to drive the new GT40 Ford in its first race with Phil Hill. They were 2nd fastest in practice and ran 2nd in the race to the works Ferrari at one stage but were eliminated when the suspension broke.

Back in England the new chassis for the Zerex had been completed and the Oldsmobile engine had been installed. Due to lack of time, as well as space and suspension geometry requirements, they had decided to use the "old faithful" Colotti Type 21 5-speed transmission from Bruce's Tasman Cooper.

With the Oldsmobile engine, the Zerex won first time out at Mosport.

Bruce and Tony Hilder examine scale model of first McLaren car.

There was no time to fabricate a proper exhaust system so the car was flown to Canada for the Mosport race with eight stub exhausts poking up through the tail.

The car had three names in all. The chassis had been completed on a Sunday morning, so Bruce decided that it should be painted there and then. The fact that there was no paint available and no hardware shops likely to be open on the Sabbath was of little consequence. I was dispatched to find a can of paint and I eventually returned with a can of garden-gate green unearthed in a handyman's shop that was just on the point of closing. The color was appalling, but it was paint and when we had finished the frame gleamed bright green. It cried out to be called the Jolly Green Giant. The car was also the Zerex Special re-framed and re-engined, but for various reasons Bruce decreed that it should be officially known as the Cooper-Oldsmobile. He was involving himself in a very political situation because he was still number one driver in the Cooper team and yet he was ·actively engaged in building a sports car that was to beat the factory-built Cooper Monacos. Charles and John Cooper could not help but be reminded of Jack Brabham's project to build a Formula Junior car which had preceded his leaving the team and it must have seemed obvious that Bruce was about to do

62

Bruce testing the first real McLaren, the M1A, at Goodwood in 1964.

exactly the same. To have called the revised car a McLaren would have meant instant repercussions within the Cooper team and Bruce was most reluctant to upset his relationship and jeopardize his Formula 1 drive. The idea of a McLaren Formula 1 car was then only a remote possibility on the horizon for the little team, and Bruce was also aware that an alternative Formula 1 seat might be rather difficult to find. So officially the car was a Cooper-Oldsmobile when Bruce won with it at Mosport in June.

Bruce drove the Cooper-Olds to another win in the Guards Trophy at Brands Hatch at the end of August, but between Mosport and Brands he had been working hard transferring the team from the incredibly slum-like conditions in the tractor shed at New Malden to what I had hopefully described in a press release as "a spotless new 3000-square foot racing workshop." Looking back now, the new premises in Belvedere Works, behind the shopping complex that was just being built at Feltham, were only slightly less slum-like than the tractor shed. But a thorough clean-out and a carpentry job created offices for management (Bruce, Teddy Mayer and myself) and design staff (Eddie Stait and later Robin Herd), a workshop area where the Tasman Coopers and the sports cars were prepared, and a proto-

The M1A led the Times GP at Riverside but water hose blew off.

type shop closed off at the end where the GTX Ford was to be built.

While Bruce was winning the Guards Trophy an all-new sports car—a real McLaren—was nearing completion. It was a spaceframe development of the Cooper-Oldsmobile, but it used stressed magnesium sheet in the cockpit area to strengthen the frame. The side members were set low to clear the exhaust system of the Oldsmobile which was being built by Traco Engineering in Culver City, Calif. It was now enlarged to 3.9 liters and giving 340 horsepower. The F85 engine was the ill-fated early attempt by General Motors to use aluminum instead of cast iron for the cylinder blocks, but complications in the casting processes proved costly and the idea was scrapped. Teddy was offering good prices for F85 engines from scrap yards and Traco was re-working them into racing shape.

The new McLaren used Cooper wheels, uprights and steering arms, and a Hewland Gearbox. Fitted with the engine from the Zerex the McLaren M1 lowered the Zerex's record at Goodwood by a clear 3 seconds.

The car was painted black with a silver stripe (New Zealand's sporting colors) and it was the fastest car on the track at Mosport in September but a throttle linkage broke and after a long pit stop Bruce came out again to hammer the lap record and finish 3rd. In England Frank Nichols of Elva Cars had called at the Feltham factory suggesting an association between McLaren and Elva to build production versions of the sports car for sale, and a deal was eventually worked out with Peter Agg and John Bennett of Trojan, Elva's parent company, to build McLaren replicas. They were to be called McLaren-Elvas.

At Riverside Bruce qualified the black car 2nd to Gurney's Lotus 19 and blasted off into a lead that in three laps had put him 9 seconds clear of the field. Then a water hose blew off. He lost four minutes in the pits and had climbed back up to 3rd place when the hose blew off again. At Laguna Seca another water hose blew off. Before Nassau the car was painted an orangey red in place of the sombre black, and Bruce finished 2nd to Penske's Chaparral.

It became apparent to Bruce that it was much more difficult winning once he had put his own name on the nose than it had been when he was driving the Cooper-Olds. Jack Brabham had also discovered that it was an uphill slog once his name was on the car. But for both men, their perseverance was to pay off.

Bruce's Formula 1 record in 1964 was scarcely worthy of notice, his best finishes being 2nd at Monza and Spa. Looking back over Bruce's record he seemed to do well at these fast

Bruce, Teddy Mayer and Eoin Young pose with the 1965 Tasman Cooper.

1965 Tasman season was unrewarding; here Bruce runs wet Wigram event.

tracks. At Monza he was 3rd in 1961, 1962 and 1963 and 2nd in 1964. At Spa he was 2nd in 1960, 1963 and 1964, 3rd in 1965, and in 1968 he won the race in his own car.

Bruce took a pair of Coopers down under to defend his Tasman title in January and February of 1965, with Phil Hill as number two in the Cooper Bruce had used the previous season. A new car based on the 1964 Formula 1 Cooper with inboard front suspension had been built for Bruce with the engine bay altered to take the 4-cylinder FPF Climax engine in place of the Climax V-8. Both cars had Hewland gearboxes and both were set up to take 13-inch wheels with Dunlop tires.

The McLaren contract with Firestone meant a last-minute switch to 15-inch wheels all around since Firestone was making its first appearance in European-type racing and only had 15-inch Indianapolis tires available. Phil's car stayed in England to test tires and was flown out to New Zealand at a cost of 1880 Pounds just in time for the New Zealand Grand Prix. The new tires made both cars almost unmanageable, and it was not until the final race of the series, the Australian Grand Prix at Longford, that Bruce managed to get sorted out and come up with a winning combination. It was Firestone's first Grand Prix win.

Chris Amon was signed on as second driver with the McLaren team in 1965 to run tires tests for Firestone with the original

McLaren sports car and also to get sports car drives in the American races. Bruce had always maintained that Chris had an enormous amount of natural talent if only he could be taken in hand and disciplined. Reg Parnell had been grooming Chris for greater things but after Reg's death at the end of the 1963 season, Chris had been roaming around in the racing wilderness "going to seed." He had learned about racing with a 250F Maserati when he was 17, and Parnell had brought him into Grand Prix racing in Europe two years later but at the end of Chris's first season overseas Reg had died. With Bruce in 1965 Chris learned about test driving and tire development and was later to become one of Firestone's best test men.

Chris drove the original M1A sports car to win at St. Jovite early in 1965 while Bruce was racing to 5th place at Monaco in the Cooper Formula 1 car, and after Bruce burned his neck when the engine caught fire during practice for the Martini Trophy at Silverstone, Chris took his place, started from the back of the grid and won the race.

Silverstone was the venue for the epic dice between Surtees in the Lola T70 and Bruce in the M1A that resulted in the narrowest of wins for Bruce. He was running new rear rims that were twelve inches across and reckoned these to be nearing the ultimate in rubber rollers. But five years later the McLarens had 20-inch rear rims!

Bruce led both heats of the Mosport sports car race in June but he retired both times with a broken transmission. Tyler had changed gearboxes between heats, but the same thing happened

McLaren trails here but Bruce beat Surtees after Silverstone battle.

Racing driver's wife: Patty McLaren keeps lap chart of Bruce's car.

again, so Tyler trailered the car down to his home in Boston and altered the car to take the German ZF transmission in place of the Hewland. A few days later Bruce had a hectic dice with Jim Hall's Chaparral at St. Jovite and won.

Back in England the designers were already working on the M1B, a sports car that was to have a new and more efficient shape evolved by artist Michael Turner, working with Tyler and Robin Herd. It had a blunter nose and a sharper cut-off on the tail. Tyler applied all the techniques he had learned in aircraft building to the ducting inside the nose of the new car making a proper integral structure that formed the ducts and also held the radiator. To strengthen the space-frame (the M1A had been nicknamed FlexiPower) Herd mounted a production chassis straight from Trojan to the most substantial piece of iron-mongery in the workshop—the steel-cutting guillotine—and with

Phil Hill subbed for Bruce, drove M1B to a close 2nd place at Kent.

a piece of channel-section wrought iron he made an enormous cantilever, hanging weights on it to take deflection measurements, adding tubes or cutting them out until he had a chassis that was 20 percent stiffer than the M1A and was no heavier.

The first race for the M1B at St. Jovite resulted in oily and ignominious retirement in practice when the Oldsmobile blew up in a most comprehensive manner, wrecking the transmission as well. Before Mosport a new 4.5-liter engine had arrived from Traco and with this installed Bruce finished 2nd to Hall's Chaparral. The GTX Ford that McLaren had developed was ready for this race but it soon became obvious that it was better suited to the long distance endurance races than the shorter sprints.

Phil Hill stood in for Bruce at Kent finishing 2nd in the first heat and was leading the second when he somehow jammed his heel and bent the throttle which meant a pit stop to free it.

Bruce was back at the helm for Riverside, a race that he dearly wanted to win, and he was fastest in practice but on the starting line he kept putting the car in and out of gear waiting for the starter to make up his mind and when the flag finally dropped Bruce found himself lurching away in third gear by mistake. This botched start fried the clutch and after 12 laps he pitted with a puncture. He hurtled back into the race in one of his typical McLaren hell-bent pursuits, a full lap and 20 seconds behind leader Hap Sharp's Chaparral. It suffices to say that he finished 15 seconds behind Sharp and right on the exhausts of Jim Clark's Lotus, having made up more than a lap!

Chris finished 5th at Riverside in the GTX which by this time had been christened "Big Ed" after another Ford project that had been less than a roaring success.

The 1965 season might have been short on concrete results for Team McLaren, but it was a significant season for developments. The GTX had been completed by Gary Knutson and raced in North America (it was to win the Sebring 12-hour race in 1966), Robin Herd had joined the design staff and a Formula 1 prototype car had been built, plans were being made to move to a larger factory at Colnbrook and Bruce was about to leave the Cooper team after eight years.

Although there had been some uncomfortable situations between the Cooper organization and Bruce's own racing activities, he was very much aware that he had learned everything about racing during his years with the team. He was also aware that he had been given his big chance with Cooper, and he left

No luck again at Riverside; puncture kept Bruce down to 3rd place.

The noisy but ineffectual 4-cam Ford-powered M2B in 1966 Monaco GP.

the team with genuinely mixed feelings.

He wrote in *Autosport:* "The heat of Grand Prix racing is something like the heat of battle—it either welds people together or breaks them apart. In the eight years I have been with Cooper I have to think very hard to remember a cross word between John and I. In motor racing that's something of a record—perhaps eight years with a Formula 1 team is something of a record too.

"When I started to race with John, I was very young and I blush to think of the stories that he can and is liable to tell you of those early days when I was very much a green Kiwi. With Cooper I learned a lot about racing cars and racing people, and I spent those formative years from 20 to 26 with people like John and the men around him—Brabham, Salvadori, Ken Tyrrell—and Charles Cooper who started the whole story with the car he built for John. It's due in part to the influence, the example and the success of these people that makes it possible for me to attempt Grand Prix racing with my own team."

His own team that November was like a bunch of one-armed paper-hangers, preparing for Formula 1 and the newly-named Can-Am sports car series in 1966 as well as the move to Colnbrook. The office door had a sign on it that read "DON'T KNOCK—WE DON'T HAVE THAT SORT OF TIME!" and it was literally true.

To try out Robin's advanced design ideas in metal, the M2A—the prototype Formula 1 car—was completed in September. The monocoque was made of Mallite which was a sort of sandwich with aluminum sheet as "bread" with a filling of balsa wood. It was riveted and glued together and as Robin said later, it was strong enough to have transported a tank over rough territory. For those test miles in 1965 the chassis was fitted with a wet-sump, 4.5-liter Oldsmobile V-8 which was presumed to provide the amount of power and torque that would be available from a 3-liter Formula 1 engine the following season. This car was used for extensive Firestone testing and was later fitted with the first of the McLaren-built 4-cam Indy Ford engines de-stroked to 3-liters for Formula 1.

The car had been built and tested several times before rumors of its existence leaked out to the press. It was easy to deny the existence of a Formula 1 car because the M2A had a 4.5-liter engine and was strictly a tire-test vehicle and it was also important to deny any ideas of a McLaren Formula 1 car while Bruce was still driving for the Cooper team. The cloak-and-dagger routine on the telephone had its serious side too.

The M2B was the real 1966 Formula 1 car for Bruce, while a second car was planned for Chris to drive later in the season. The expected power of the Ford fell far short of the target figure and with barely 300 horsepower Bruce qualified 10th

In Italy trying out the 260-bhp Serenissima V-8 in the M2B chassis.

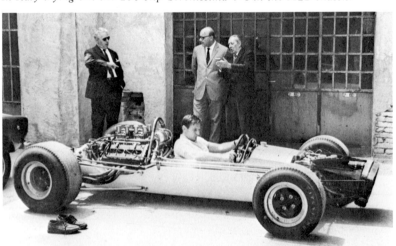

fastest at Monaco. He made a fantastic start, helped probably by the weight of the engine over the Firestones and in the opening laps he was up to 6th place before an oil union came loose and he pitted with oil pouring everywhere.

Bruce was to suffer yet another year of Formula 1 frustration, now working to make his own cars competitive and losing out badly as his engines let him down. The Italian Serenissima 3-liter V-8, hastily fitted in time for Spa, gave up in practice when the bearings failed, but at Brands Hatch in the British Grand Prix Bruce scored his first point in his own car when he finished 6th. The Ford was worked-over and refitted for the United States GP where he finished 5th, but at Mexico the engine failed again. They had gambled on the Ford and failed. Brabham had gambled on the Repco version of the F85 Oldsmobile and won, in spades.

At Le Mans in the middle of the season Bruce and Chris shared the winning 7-liter Ford GT after running a copybook race to team orders. The year before Chris had shared a Ford with Phil Hill and had led on the opening lap until joined by Bruce in another works Ford and together they led the race 1-2 during the opening hour. For 1966 the two drivers were in the same car and Ford orders were to take it easy. Chris takes up the story: "I think they considered Bruce and I were reasonably reliable drivers and not likely to get carried away and race with our own team, so we weren't told much before the start. Bruce

Bruce and Chris Amon won photo-finish 1966 Le Mans race in Ford Mk 2.

Amon (no. 2) and McLaren (no. 4) lead off at start of St. Jovite race.

and I talked a lot about what we would do in the race. We were
fairly certain that Dan Gurney would go fast at the start and if
this happened we knew Ken Miles would go after him, so Bruce
and I decided to hang back. We knew we couldn't afford to get
very far behind, but at the same time we couldn't afford to get
involved in a race with our teammates.

"That is actually what happened in the race of course.
Gurney took off and Miles chased him and at one stage we were
a lap behind. But I think this paid off the next morning when
both Gurney and Miles had troubles with their brakes—largely
because they had gone a lot faster than we had the night before.

"We started off lapping around 3 minutes and 35 seconds
whereas Miles and Gurney were lapping at around 3:33. By
about two o'clock on Sunday morning it looked as though the
Ferrari challenge had failed and we received strict slowing-down
instructions. We found 3 minutes 40 seconds comfortable, but
just after dawn orders came to slow down to 4 minutes, which
was close to half a minute slower than we were capable of
lapping and it took me something like ten laps of concentrated
effort to slow down to this speed. I found that we could do this
by saving about 800 revs on the straight, 800 revs through the
gears and barely using the brakes at all. This became very mo-
notonous. When you're going hard the time seems to pass quickly but when you are just cruising around the spells take forever.

We had to stop for fuel every hour and a half but the spells seemed to take five times as long as that.

"Bruce reckoned that he never liked sleeping at Le Mans because he had always been woken in the past by someone telling him the car had broken. I never did get to sleep properly in 1966. The most sleep I had was about three quarters of an hour somewhere around eight o'clock on Sunday morning, but surprisingly I didn't feel tired during the race.

"It was the first time I'd seen the dawn at Le Mans and I must say it was a very pleasant sight to see the sun start to come up and to know we had the night behind us. But when I looked at my watch and realized that we had another eleven hours to go! The sun came up around six and it looked as though it would be a good day, but later in the morning it clouded over and started to rain. The car had been good when it rained during the night. But in the rain on Sunday afternoon with all the oil and rubber about, the track was extremely slippery. This meant that even going through slow corners in first gear with the throttle off we were going too fast and we had to disengage the clutch going through Mulsanne, Arnage and Tertre Rouge..."

They won the race in the hotly disputed photo finish from the Ken Miles/Denis Hulme car, Bruce maintaining that he had driven slowly side by side with Miles on that last half of the last lap but that Miles had been hanging back and Bruce wondered if Ken would jump him on the line. Their teammates Denny and Chris were being interviewed on television as the two cars came

Victory in Mosport race was not followed by Can-Am successes in 1966.

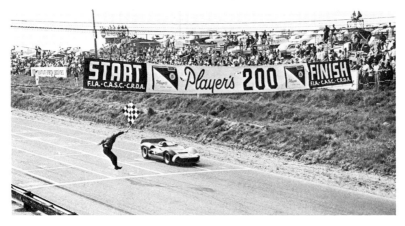

Fuel injection trouble spoiled yet another Times GP for Bruce.

up to the line and suddenly the interviewer found himself alone with his microphone. The excitement had been too much for the co-drivers and they were running to the finishing line!

Amon's chance for a McLaren Formula 1 drive faded with the horsepower curve of the 4-cam Ford and after showing impressive pace in the Can-Am series he signed to drive for Ferrari and led their Grand Prix team for three seasons, before switching to the British March team and then the French Matra team for 1971.

For the first Can-Am series in 1966 it became obvious to the McLaren team early in the season that their 5-liter Traco-Oldsmobile engines were going to be no match for the 6-liter cast iron Chevrolets in the Lolas driven by Hulme and John Surtees, and after the opening races in Canada Bruce switched from the aluminum engine to a 5.4-liter cast iron Chevrolet which weighed 200 pounds more than the Oldsmobile but gave 100 extra horsepower. After the first western Can-Am race in the fall the capacity of both McLarens was upped to 6 liters, but this didn't bring race wins. Both Bruce and Chris were pacemakers but they weren't winners. Bruce tried Hilborn fuel injection at Laguna Seca and both cars were so fitted for Riverside but in the heat the injection system gave trouble and for the final race at Las Vegas they were back on carburetors and Bruce finished 2nd to series winner Surtees.

The 1966 season had been the first year for the new Grand Prix formula and the first running of the Can-Am sports car series. The McLaren team had expected to do well in both

Bruce borrowed Eagle V-12 from Gurney while awaiting BRM engine.

fields, but by the end of the season they had little to show for their efforts.

"One would have thought that after a very dispiriting year like that everyone would have been so depressed that they would have wanted to give up," says Robin Herd, "but the result was completely the opposite. Everyone was ten times more determined .to do better the following year. It seems strange that when you are successful it's difficult to be determined but when you're unsuccessful determination comes very easily."

The 1967 season was another lost year in Formula 1 for Bruce. The BRM V-12 engine had been promised in time for the first Grand Prix but it didn't arrive until the Canadian Grand Prix in September. To fill in time Bruce drove one of his pretty little M4A-Cosworths in the early Formula 2 races and built up a special M4B Formula 1 version by fitting a 2-liter Tasman BRM V-8 in place of the 1600-cc Cosworth FVA unit. At Monaco Bruce was up to 2nd place with this car when the battery went flat and he finished 4th, at Zandvoort he spun the car into a fence on the first lap, and the car was finally gutted by fire during Goodyear tire tests at Goodwood. Dan Gurney gave Bruce drives in one of his V-12 Eagles in the French, British and German Grands Prix but engine trouble put him out of each race. The McLaren M5 monocoque had been waiting in the workshops since the beginning of the year and when the V-12 engine arrived Bruce did 30 miles around Goodwood with it and went straight to Canada. For want of a nail this particular

The BRM V-12 engine gave the M5 a front-row start in Italian GP.

McLaren horse lost the Grand Prix—they had decided to run the car without the alternator to save weight and the battery went flat. The car handled extremely well in the rain despite its lack of testing and Bruce was up to 2nd place behind Denny Hulme until the rain eased and Jim Clark went past into 2nd place again with the Lotus 49. Another rain shower would have meant a McLaren advantage again but the drained battery was causing the V-12 to lose its edge and the oil pressure was also starting to sag. Before the race ended Hulme had stopped for a visor to combat the rain and Clark's engine had failed. For want of an alternator the car just missed having a victorious debut.

At Monza the McLaren-BRM qualified on the front row of the grid with Clark and Brabham, comfortably faster than the works H-16 BRMs, even though Bruce's BRM V-12 had been developed purely as a customer engine and was meant as a sports car unit. The McLaren was painted red—normally Italy's racing color—and during practice the Italian organizers had been pressing the crew to paint the car the British green in accordance with the international regulations. When they realized that the McLaren was the only red car on the front row of the grid their protests stopped. Bruce was in 4th place when a connecting rod broke in the engine. At Watkins Glen a water hose blew off and in Mexico Bruce finished 13th and last after chronic problems with overheating.

Bruce's last race in the M5-BRM was the discouraging Mexican GP.

CAN-AM DOMINATION

T HE LACK of success in the 1966 Can-Am races and the late delivery of the BRM V-12 engine that crippled the 1967 Formula 1 program had a direct bearing on the overwhelming success of the M6A Can-Am sports cars for 1967. It was, in fact, the turning point for Team McLaren fortunes.

Design and building had been completed on the Formula 1 and Formula 2 cars and there was time for long involved discussions on an ideal Can-Am car between Robin, Bruce, Teddy, Tyler and Wally. They analyzed the reasons for their lack of success in the past, talked about the better points of their opposition and went deeply into the most intimate details of the new sports car before a line was ever put on paper. Seeking the optimum in aerodynamics, they experimented and worked on the full-size M1B in a wind tunnel. There were a lot of reasons for the instant success of the new car.

It was the first McLaren monocoque sports car, it used Goodyear in place of Firestone tires, the ZF had been replaced by a Hewland transmission, Lucas fuel injection was fitted for the first time to the 5.9-liter cast iron Chevrolet engine, and Denny Hulme had joined the team. The M6A was also the first McLaren to be painted the now familiar orange.

The first car, M6A-1, was completed and ready for testing at

Bruce had to walk home but Denny won Elkhart Lake Can-Am in M6A.

Goodwood on June 19, 1967, more than three months prior to the opening race in the Can-Am series. The car covered over 2000 miles of testing before its debut at Elkhart Lake. The best testing time at Goodwood early that season stood to John Surtees in his Lola at 1 minute and 16 seconds and the best lap by the M1 had been 1:18. During the M6A's afternoon at Goodwood, running on a 200-mile destruction test without the body, Bruce lapped at 1:16.2 in the new car.

"For a completely new car the M6A wasn't really new," Bruce said. "With the exception of the drive-shafts everything else was a development of something we had done before. The basic layout of the rear bulkhead was identical to that of the M5 Formula 1 car. The idea of tying the side-stress boxes into the front engine mounts came from the 2-liter BRM-engined car. The front suspension was a mixture from the production sports car and last year's Formula 1 car. The scheme for the Lucas fuel injection on the Chevy engine came mainly from the M4A Formula 2 car. Our design philosophy? Simplicity, light weight and—a rider that I stressed fairly hard—strength." The ideas might not have been new but they were proven developments, well tested before the series started.

"You've got to demoralize 'em right away," Denny said when he came back from slicing 10 seconds off the old lap record in practice at Elkhart Lake, and then Bruce went out to chop a further tenth of a second off his time and take the pole. They were two seconds faster than the next man, Dan Gurney in his Lola.

"Denny charged off into the lead from the rolling start with my car tucked in behind him," Bruce said. "I did precisely three laps. I'd lost oil from an oil cooler leak. I didn't know whether to cry, shoot myself, hurl rocks at the Lolas, or what. Eventually I settled for walking back to the pits, where I sat getting more and more nervous inventing problems that might cost Denny his lead, and biting my nails down to the wrist. But this time Lady Luck was with us—believe me, she's the best pit popsy a team could have!"

At Bridgehampton Denny won again with Bruce 2nd. At Mosport they finished 1-2 again, but the results didn't begin to tell the story of the race. Bruce started half a lap down on the field, and Denny had finished with smoke pouring from a smashed fender that had punctured the tire!

Bruce almost missed the race. "An hour before the race the mechanics went to lower my car off its jack stands when the leak appeared. The car had been sitting with full tanks since early morning. If we'd found the leak ten minutes earlier it wouldn't have been dramatic—ten minutes later and it would have been like, forget it. Fifty gallons is an awful lot of fuel. Getting it out of the tanks involved filling every vehicle we had around and some that weren't ours. When we got to the stage of pumping it out faster than we could empty the cans into the trucks and cars, we simply tipped it over the fence. By the time we had installed a new rubber fuel bag, filled the tanks and got the engine running, the race had started. Just 40 seconds earlier, to be precise! This was just the exact gap that could be made up without going completely crazy. I made it to 2nd place with just ten laps left. Denny was well out in front but two laps from the flag he had an incident at the hairpin and ploughed off the road, folding the left front fender in on the wheel. The fiber-

First Can-Am win for Bruce came in 1967 on twisty Laguna Seca circuit.

glass cut the tire and it went flat, but Denny limped in with smoke pouring from the demolished front end to win. Another lap and I would have caught him."

Bruce was wistful about not catching Denny because he had yet to win a Can-Am race and Denny had won three in a row. Laguna Seca was to be Bruce's race, but he almost cooked in the cockpit and halfway through the race he slowed beside the pits and the mechanics tossed a bucket of water over him. Revived, he continued on to win but his hands were blistered and his lips and mouth were badly sunburned where he had pulled his face-mask down to gasp for air.

Riverside made it two in a row for Bruce but he had to work hard to win the prize money and the pace car. Gurney led for the first two of the 62 laps while Bruce battled with Parnelli Jones' Lola-Ford. An unintentional result of this tussle was Denny's retirement. Jones ran over one of the rubber tires that marked the course, knocking it out in front of Denny damaging the nose of the McLaren. Denny raced for the pits and the crew pulled the smashed fiberglass clear of the wheel, but the officials black-flagged him and his race was over after only two laps.

Bruce finally won at Riverside after race-long battle with Jim Hall.

McLaren F1 debut was victorious; Bruce (no. 2) won Race of Champions.

With Jones now behind him Bruce's next challenge came from Jim Hall in the Chaparral and the pair drove hard, swapping the lead while lapping tail-end traffic, each man giving his best. This was real racing with McLaren out to beat Hall, and each man out to prove the Can-Am car he had produced. As the white and orange cars came nose to tail up from Turn 9, Denny watched from the pits and wondered whether Bruce would be able to stand the pace in the desert heat.

"Bruce had been really whacked at Laguna Seca and I was sure that he was starting to tire and Jim would get the jump on him, but ten laps from the end Bruce perked up and it was all over as far as Jim was concerned."

As they flew to Las Vegas for the final race of the 1967 championship Bruce led Denny by three points. Bruce took pole position in practice but on race morning he came in after a few warm-up laps and the mechanics found oil foam puffing out of the engine breather. It was too late to change engines—there wasn't even time to take the heads off—so they crossed their fingers and slurped in as much gasket sealing cement as they could find. It looked as though Bruce had lost his chance for the title before the race had started.

It was a moment he remembered well. "When the race started I could barely see for oil. I let Denny by and hoped the oil problem would cure itself but then I saw Denny's left rear tire starting to go soft. Within a couple of laps I had to stop

85

Leading here, Bruce won 1968 Belgian GP after opposition dropped out.

too—by that time the oil was cooling the engine and the water was lubricating it! Denny had changed a wheel and charged out again a lap behind the leaders. All the previous hot shots—Gurney, Jones and Hall—had dropped out and Mark Donohue was leading from Surtees and Mike Spence. There was a chance that Denny could catch them. For an hour or more he was catching them at a second a lap, but then his engine blew spectacularly right in front of the grandstand in a spray of water and a cloud of oil smoke.

"If Denny's engine had held together and he had finished in a place he could have been Can-Am champion for us in addition to already being World Champion in Formula 1 that year driving for Brabham. As it turned out, I won the Can-Am Championship from Denny with both of us standing in the pits as Surtees took the lead on the last lap to win. It's not the way I would have chosen to win the title, but I really couldn't complain. In the six Can-Am races our team collected six fastest laps, qualified on the front row six times, took five pole positions, and won five races."

During the 1967 Can-Am series Robin Herd went to some of the races, but he was working on the design of a new Formula 1 car rather than a development of the sports car. This was to be the M7A. Structurally it bore quite a resemblance to the monocoque M4A Formula 2 car which was elegant if not particularly

7-liter M8A gave Bruce a repeat victory in Times GP at Riverside.

successful. The M7A was in fact designed to take a chassis-mounted wing but it didn't race with a wing until the middle of 1968 after Ferrari and Brabham had used wings at Spa. Herd copied the Lotus layout by using the Ford-Cosworth V-8 as a stressed member of the car and in its original test form the M7A weighed just 30 pounds over the Formula 1 lower limit. When the design was finished, Herd left the McLaren team to join Cosworth Engineering.

Gordon Coppuck was now chief design engineer, later being joined by Jo Marquart. In the Spring of 1968 they started the design of the M8A Can-Am car which followed the thinking behind the M7A single-seater in that the engine was a stress-carrying part of the car. This was more difficult because while the Ford-Cosworth had been designed to take stresses, special mounting arrangements had to be made for the 7-liter aluminum Chevrolet that the team was to use in Can-Am racing during 1968. They were starting the new season with the best engines for both categories of racing and they were to make good use of them.

Bruce was now very much the manufacturer and business-man as well as a successful racing driver. He had moved from the apartment in Surbiton to a new split-level home in Wey-bridge with Patty and baby daughter Amanda and the Jaguar E-Type had been replaced by a Mercedes 220S coupe.

In a weak moment during negotiations for the BRM V-12 engine the year before Bruce had agreed to drive a 2.5-liter BRM in the 1968 Tasman series and this turned out to be a disaster. The cars were hopelessly uncompetitive and Bruce, normally placid and unwilling to criticize other people's cars publicly, was saying in the Auckland newspapers how poor his chances looked for the Grand Prix.

The V-12 was said to be giving 330 horsepower, equal to the Tasman version of the Ford, but Bruce offered to eat every horse that the V-12 was giving in excess of 300. In an attempt to track down fuel pressure problems Bruce lapped Pukekohe with a fuel pressure gauge sprouting between his legs. "Most racing cars I've driven have had this sort of thing mounted on the dash panel," was the McLaren comment.

Bruce gave BRM its only win in the series in pouring rain at Teretonga where most of the drivers went off the road. Bruce had smashed the nose of the BRM during a preliminary heat, but it was repaired in time for the race and for once he benefitted from the gentle torque and motored home to win. The next major win for BRM came when Pedro Rodriguez won the Belgian Grand Prix at Spa in June 1970, a week after Bruce's death.

At home—he had now made up his mind that England was to be "home" for the foreseeable future—Bruce had the new power of the Ford Formula 1 engine to look forward to. Denny had now officially joined the team and their first Formula 1 race with the M7As was the Race of Champions at Brands Hatch.

McLaren cars side-by-side at Monza; Denny went on to win the race.

Bruce won and Denny was 3rd. The next event was the International Trophy at Silverstone where Denny won, Bruce was 2nd and Chris Amon was 3rd in the Ferrari. It was an eventful race because Denny had dropped back at half distance when a stone smashed one lens of his goggles, but he retook the lead and won, driving with one eye shut! Chris had been challenging Bruce for 2nd place but with only a few laps to go the strap of his goggles broke and he dropped back wrestling with his spare pair, leaving the two McLarens a safe 1-2.

Team McLaren had won the two opening races of the season but it wasn't a happy time for the Grand Prix circus. Jimmy Clark had been killed at Hockenheim and it wasn't the same without him. Bruce had been roped into driving the new F3L Ford prototype in the BOAC 500 sports car race at Brands Hatch, but after he fought his way into the lead the car quit and he set off for home along the A25. On the way the news came over his car radio that Jimmy had been killed in the Formula 2 race in Germany that afternoon.

"I was stunned," Bruce wrote in his *Autosport* column. "Jimmy ranked with, perhaps even out-ranked, Nuvolari, Fangio and Moss, and I think we all felt that he was in a way invincible. To be killed in an accident with a Formula 2 car is almost unacceptable. But tragically it's true."

This was the way the motor racing world accepted the news of Bruce's own death in his testing accident two years later. Bruce didn't dwell on sentimentality or talk about the risks of his occupation, but when Jimmy was killed Bruce was moved to

Dan Gurney got return favor with McLaren ride in late-1968 GP events.

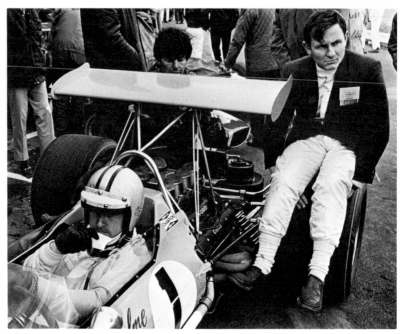

After two straight McLaren GP wins, Watkins Glen was a disappointment.

put his thoughts on paper.

"Too often in this demanding sport, unique in terms of ability, dedication, concentration, and courage, someone pays the penalty for trying to do just that little bit better or go that little bit faster. And too often someone pays the penalty for being in the wrong place at the wrong time when a situation or set of circumstances is such that no human being can control them. However, that's the way it is. We accept it, we enjoy what we do, we get a lot of satisfaction out of it, and maybe we prove something, I don't know."

The first European Grand Prix in 1968 was on the new Jarama track just outside Madrid in Spain. Denny had driven the BRM-engined 1967 car earlier in South Africa and finished two laps behind Clark and Graham Hill in the Ford-engined Lotuses. With the Ford-engined McLaren M7A Denny was 2nd to Hill in Spain, and at Monaco he was 5th after stopping to change a driveshaft. Bruce's season had been dismal. He was in New Zealand with the BRM while Denny was in South Africa, in Spain he had been in 3rd place when his engine started spewing oil 13 laps from the end and at Monaco he was out of the race on the opening lap after spinning on oil and crashing.

But he made up for it at Spa by winning the Belgian Grand Prix. As he crossed the finishing line and took the flag Bruce was delighted with his performance—but he thought he had finished 2nd! He wasn't aware that Jackie Stewart's Matra had stopped on the last lap for more fuel, and that he had actually scored the first championship Grand Prix win for his own car. He braked hard after crossing the line and steered through the gates at the bottom of the pits when Cyril Atkins, one of the BRM mechanics, came up and started talking excitedly to him. Bruce couldn't hear what he was saying. "You crossed the line number one!" he shouted, but Bruce stared blankly at him. "My number was 5—I wasn't quite sure what he was talking about, but then he shouted 'You've won! Didn't you know?' I didn't, and it was about the nicest thing I'd ever been told."

At Colnbrook Gordon and Jo were completing the new M8A which was in effect an M6A that had been chopped off behind the rear bulkhead. Jo had been detailed to handle the design of the front end which required on a tidy-up of the Herd M6A work, while Gordon did the more complicated mounting of the engine, and then the rear suspension, which was attached to the Hewland transmission.

The lightweight 7-liter engines were being developed by Gary Knutson and Colin Beanland in workshops in Los Angeles, but they were to experience trouble with their new dry-sump modifications and although Team McLaren's orange cars won four of

First lap at Edmonton—M8Bs lead Amon's Ferrari and Surtees' Chaparral.

the six races in the series, they were less than happy with the engines. The aluminum engine weighed about the same as the cast iron version they had used the previous season but it was putting out an extra 100 horsepower.

The M8A was four inches wider than the M6A, and because of the dry-sump mods the engine sat five inches lower. The Hewland had been altered from a 5-speed to a 4-speed because a very low first gear wasn't required with the Can-Am rolling starts.

At Elkhart Lake Bruce qualified on the pole and finished 2nd to Denny. Bridgehampton was won by Mark Donohue in Roger Penske's M6B, Denny and Bruce finished 1-2 at Edmonton, John Cannon won the wet Laguna Seca race in his aged McLaren Mk2 (the production version of the M1B), Bruce won Riverside from Donohue (Denny finished 5th after stopping to have crash damage repaired), and once again they went to Las Vegas still not knowing who was going to win the championship. Denny had a 3-point lead over Bruce and Mark who had equal points for 2nd place. Qualifying saw Bruce on the pole ahead of Denny and Jim Hall with Donohue 4th. Poor Mark's car refused to start as the field fired up for the pace lap. Bruce wrote, "Someone said there was white smoke coming out of the exhaust pipes as Mark's engine churned over—and someone else said there was white smoke coming out of Roger's ears!"

The field bunched as they came up to the starting line and in the drag race to the fast right-hand sweep of the first corner

Denny pulled ahead of Bruce. Mario Andretti tried to follow Denny through from the outside but as he swept across the line he caught the nose of Bruce's car and spun him into the sand on the inside. Instantly there were cars spinning in all directions, crashing into each other and bouncing off the guardrail on the outside of the corner as they ploughed blindly through the dust and sand. Miraculously nobody was hurt and as the sand settled cars were sorting themselves out and picking their way through the debris. Chris Amon's Ferrari had gone straight ahead into the desert and stayed there with the fuel injection hopelessly clogged with sand.

On the inside of the track Bruce was getting himself sorted out with the front of the car badly battered. "I had stalled the engine and before I came to a stop I snicked the lever into low gear, let the clutch in and the engine started. That was a surprise. When I drove back onto the track and pointed it at the first corner it went through with no drama and I was even more surprised. The brakes worked and everything felt fine, but it had been a very bumpy ride for a few seconds and I felt sure something had to be bent. I continued around and stopped at the pits yelling at the boys to have a pull at the wheels. We had

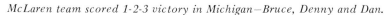

McLaren team scored 1-2-3 victory in Michigan—Bruce, Denny and Dan.

93

The familiar order as McLaren M8Bs dominate 1969 Laguna Seca Can-Am.

a spare body available but from where I was sitting everything looked okay so I charged out again.

"But right away I knew I had made a mistake. As soon as I got up to any sort of speed the nose shell started to lift so that at the end of that lap I came back into the pits, they lifted the shattered nose shell off, dropped the new one on, tied it tight with tape and rubber cords, and I charged off. It was the *third* time I'd started this race." He had to start a fourth time when he was black-flagged for having no mirrors on the new nose, and he finally finished the race drastically slowed when a brake seal blew out and he lost all the brakes. In the closing laps he was cruising past the pits shouting an unintelligible message to the crew. They didn't know he was without brakes until he came in after the race and almost wiped everyone out because he couldn't stop!

In the race Jim Hall broke both his legs when his Chaparral flipped over the back of a car that suddenly slowed in front of him. Denny won and took the 1968 Can-Am title with Bruce 2nd. Team McLaren had taken pole position in all six races and McLaren-built cars had won all six, but it wasn't until the last couple of races that they had managed to get on top of their engine problems.

In Formula 1 they were on the crest of a wave. At Monza Bruce had qualified 2nd fastest to Surtees' Honda and started from the middle of the front row with John on one side and Chris Amon's Ferrari on the other. Bruce made a perfect start with the tachometer needle firmly on nine-eight and grabbed a handy lead in the opening laps. On lap 8 Amon had taken Surtees for 2nd place but then the Ferrari slid wide, hit the guardrails and somersaulted backwards into the trees while Surtees smashed into the guardrails trying to dodge the spinning Ferrari. Chris was saved by his seat harness.

Bruce was caught a few laps later by the usual Monza bunch of slipstreamers and he dropped back to retire finally with an oil leak, but Denny took over to trade blows with Stewart's Matra until Jackie's engine blew and Denny led for the remaining 28 laps.

In the Canadian Grand Prix at St. Jovite the McLaren team turned in a Can-Am type performance, finishing 1st and 2nd

McLaren family: Bruce and Patty with daughter Amanda in new home.

with Denny leading over the line and boosting his championship score to equal Graham Hill's for the lead. The race really belonged to Amon's Ferrari which had equalled Jochen Rindt's pole position time and led for 72 of the 90 laps, dropping out with a broken transmission when almost a lap ahead of Denny's McLaren. But it proved the old motor racing maxim: To finish first, first you must finish.

Dan Gurney had been driving a third McLaren at St. Jovite and he led the works cars early in the race until forced to retire with overheating. Dan drove his rented McLaren again at Watkins Glen and was running 3rd until a puncture two laps from the flag dropped him to 4th. Denny had crashed and Bruce had run short of fuel with a blocked tank breather.

Denny stood a chance of retaining his championship title if he won at Mexico City but that chance vanished when his rear suspension snapped coming into the pit straight and he crashed into the barrier, skidding down past the pits on three wheels and climbing out hurriedly as a blaze around the engine was doused by fire-fighters. Bruce came in 2nd to Hill's Lotus as Graham clinched his second World Championship in what had been a black year for Lotus with Jimmy's death.

Denny had finished 3rd in the championship and Bruce was 5th, but in the Constructor's Championship McLaren cars were 2nd on points behind Lotus. When they got back to England there was a surprise waiting for Bruce. He was awarded the Ferodo Trophy "for his tenacity of purpose in making and developing cars which have won Formula 1 Grand Prix, and Group 7 cars which have dominated the Can-Am championship." In his reply on behalf of the team after receiving the celebrated golden spike from the chairman of Ferodo, Bruce said "I would like to think the company couldn't have done the job without me, but I know that I certainly couldn't have done the job without them."

Bruce's eloquence came as a surprise to some, but he had been getting plenty of practice as a "star" in America and he was certainly a better known personality there than he was in Europe. Jim Kaser, the man mainly responsible for setting up the Can-Am series as Director of Professional Racing for the Sports Car Club of America, gave McLaren the man as much credit for the success of the Can-Am series as he gave McLaren the driver and McLaren the car-builder. Bruce worked hard to ensure the success of the series but at times he was over-working himself and this showed. "I remember how tired he used to get," says Kaser. "He would really run himself down with a very ambitious program and I remember him dragging himself off airplanes and getting out to the Can-Am race that weekend, trying to grab some sleep, and then on Monday morning he was on a jet again going back to England. But he was the nicest guy. He could really relax alongside the motel pool to get away from the pressures of the moment. He was a nice guy when he needed to be in front of the television cameras or the Press, but he was just the same anywhere else, and that's the sort of thing you remember about an individual—what he was like when he wasn't up front, when he didn't have to turn it on."

As the team grew and the cars became more and more successful, Bruce's schedule became busier and busier. Although his leg sometimes bothered him when he was tired, and occasionally he talked of having an operation done on the hipjoint, he was immensely strong and was able to stand the strain of the constant travel probably better than Denny or Teddy. One eye was quite a bit weaker than the other, to the point where he would fake the eye test at the track medical examinations, covering the weak eye with his right hand to read the chart and then using his left hand to cover the same eye and read the chart again. He wasn't able to fake the Indianapolis medical this way, but on that day his eye was strong enough to pass their test. When he was tired it seemed to be worse, but few people were aware of it. He had the ability to relax completely and sleep anywhere which helped to conserve his energy, and he also worked out on a trampoline in his garden whenever he had a chance.

For 1969 the M8B Can-Am car was an updated version of the M8A with a high wing mounted to the rear uprights, and the Formula 1 car for Bruce was updated to M7C and followed the design of the M10A Formula A/Formula 5000 car with a full monocoque instead of the open-topped "bathtub." The spate of accidents with wings early in 1969 resulted in the sudden wing ban at Monaco in May and this accelerated development of 4-wheel-drive cars in the Lotus, Matra and McLaren camps. At Cosworth, Robin Herd was designing a completely new car around 4-wheel-drive, but it was destined never to race. In fact the 4-wheel-drive program was a dead-end road for all concerned, and for Lotus and McLaren it resulted in a season of lost development with all the design and developments efforts wasted on 4-wheel-drive cars.

Bruce finished 3rd in the 1969 World Championship behind Jackie Stewart, driving a Tyrrell-entered Matra, and Jacky Ickx, driving for Brabham. His best placing was a 2nd behind Stewart

in the Spanish GP at Barcelona after the Team Lotus wing accidents had demolished the cars of Hill and Rindt. Stewart was the king that season, winning six of the eleven Grands Prix.

Denny finished a lowly 6th in the world title standings but he scored a convincing win in the final race of the season at Mexico. It was a mixture of determination and supreme confidence. Denny had qualified beside Stewart on the second row of the grid and he passed Brabham on lap 6, Stewart on lap 8, and on the tenth lap he took Ickx for the lead which he held to the end.

It was the last race of the Sixties and it was more than

significant that a youthful Bruce McLaren had won the first race of the decade in Argentina and one of his Grand Prix cars had won the final race in Mexico. The decade had seen the switch from the factory drivers to the driver/constructors with first Brabham, then Gurney and McLaren and later Surtees deciding that they could build better cars themselves.

The Can-Am series that season had gone pretty much according to what people felt was the McLaren Plan. They won all eleven races, with Bruce taking the checkered flag in six and winning the championship for the second time.

The team had the 1970 M15 Indianapolis car ready for testing in November 1969, and the 1970 M14 Formula 1 car was being built alongside it, being an improved version of the M7 and its derivatives with a better suspension layout. In 1970 McLaren Racing were to be the only team taking part in Can-Am, Indianapolis, and Grand Prix racing, and Bruce had considered phasing himself out of the chore of driving every weekend. He had decided to drop Formula 1 personally and concentrate on development but he wanted to stay in Can-Am racing. At Watkins Glen in 1969 Bruce talked with Jochen Rindt, Jackie Stewart and Chris Amon to see if one of them could

A better view than from a Can-Am cockpit—Bruce with Amon and Young.

99

drive with Denny in the McLaren Formula 1 team. Jochen was sorely tempted to sign with McLaren for 1970, but Bruce didn't want to run three Can-Am sports cars and, Jochen said, "They would have been keeping me away from the bread."

It would be pleasant to think that if Jochen had signed with the McLaren team, both he and Bruce would be alive today, but the sad fact is that Bruce reveled in testing and so the accident, in the new M8D or some later car, was almost inevitable.

Before the South African Grand Prix in March 1970 Bruce rented an air-conditioned Ford Fairlane and drove Patty, Amanda, my wife Sandra and me up to the Kruger Park game reserve for five days of relaxation, cruising along the dusty roads and watching the wild animals in their natural surroundings. The fact that Bruce collected us from the Johannesburg airport, loaded our cases in the trunk, tossed his coat in on top and then slammed the lid just as he remembered the car keys were in the coat pocket served to indicate that five days of McLaren hilarity lay ahead. Away from the pressures of the factory Bruce liked nothing better than to enjoy himself doing new things or flopping about in a swimming pool. The project for that week was to teach Amanda to swim. His enthusiasm was infectious and Amanda was soon trying a few solo strokes.

At the end of that week Bruce drove the new M14A at Kyalami and was overhauling Jackie Stewart's March when the engine blew. Denny finished 2nd behind Jack's new Brabham. At Jarama Bruce was 2nd, but at Monaco he clipped the chicane and was out with damaged suspension after 20 laps. Then he was jet-hopping back to Indianapolis for the qualifying weekends.

Before he left Monaco he sat around the pool at the Metropole Hotel and talked about his plans. He was getting slightly disenchanted with Grand Prix racing, he said, and he went on to rationalize the thinking behind his talk of phasing himself out of Formula 1.

"I consider that I could be a good racing driver or a good engineer. I feel I could be a better racing driver than I am and I could be a better engineer than I am, but I could be a better engineer than a racing driver and the company is going to be dependent on its cars and on its engineering more than on its drivers."

Patty McLaren accepts Bruce's Seagrave Trophy from Lord Camden.

Bruce was by no means selling himself short as a driver, though. At the end of the previous season he had won the British Racing Drivers' Club Gold Star for most points scored during 1969, and his total exceeded that of World Champion Jackie Stewart.

When he had time to appreciate it, Bruce was enjoying life in a manner that he thoroughly deserved. He had moved into a large modern home in a private park, and in the lounge a selection of his trophies reminded him of his progress. Trophy shelves flanked the chimney. There was the International Trophy for winning the hectic duel with John Surtees at Silverstone in 1965 with his first sports car. Behind it stood a model of a 158 Alfa Romeo with its detached left front wheel propped beside it. A silver serving dish with a McLaren badge inset recorded five years of successful association with Trojan building the production McLarens. A color photograph of Piers and Sally Courage and their family looked over three silver Can-Am medals and the replica of the Tasman Cup that Bruce won in 1964.

On a shelf below was a silver plate won at Solitude, Germany in 1961 with the Formula 1 Cooper, a photograph beside it showed Bruce hooting with laughter at some joke as he hauled his Nomex mask off at Brands Hatch in the pits, and there were Auto World models of the M8A and the winged M8B standing with five gold Can-Am medals and a silver cup from winning a Formula Vee race at Nassau. On the other side of the chimney was the 1968 Ferodo Trophy closely watched by a photograph of Amanda as a baby, then two Martini gold medals and the B.R.D.C. Gold Star.

In pride of place was to be the Seagrave Trophy—at the top of the plaque were the words "Imagination, Courage, Initiative." It had been awarded to the right man. The only pity was that he never lived to receive it.

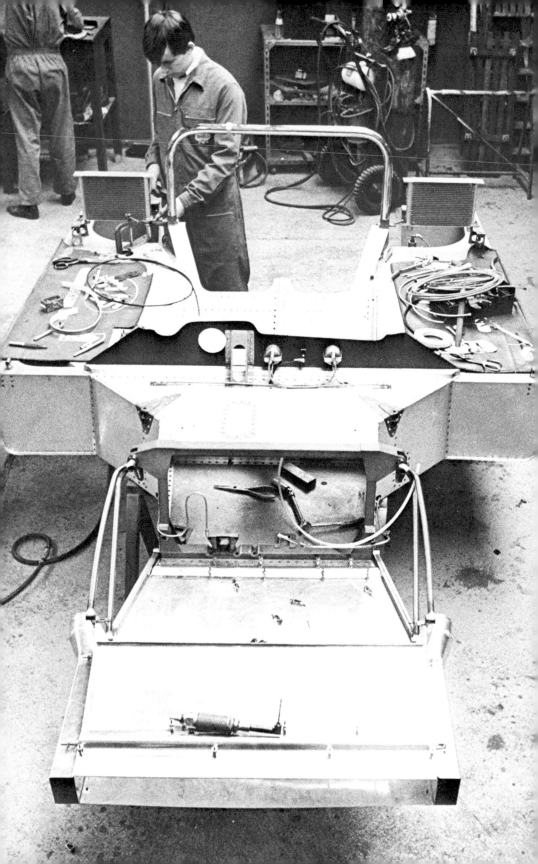

DESIGNING THE McLARENS

I
N THE FIELD of detail design in motor racing the fact that the Dzus fastener had not been properly closed on the oil tank flap in the nose of the Zerex Special was probably as significant as the apple falling on Isaac Newton's head. Bruce was testing the Zerex at Goodwood late in 1964; soon after leaving the pits he realized that the small flap had come undone. He decided to stop and fasten it next time around. As he powered through the tight Lavant right-hander and picked up speed entering the straight he mused absently on the fact that the forward-hinged flap was being forced *up* and open as he went faster instead of being flattened shut by the force of the air-stream over the sleek nose of the Zerex. That inconsistency set the McLaren mind in gear and by the time he had reached the pits he wasn't looking for a screwdriver—he wanted a pair of tin snips! He expounded his new theory to the mechanics and soon he had hacked a sizable hole in the nose of the car where the oil tank hatch had been. This tin snippery did little for the looks of the car, but in his first fast laps Bruce realized he had accidently stumbled on the answer to several of their high speed handling problems.

At the time there were very few applications of aerodynamic theories being applied to racing cars and a smooth wind-cheat-

The tidy spaceframe of the McLaren M1A under construction in 1964.

ing shape that looked right was regarded as the optimum. The
Zerex, with more power available from the 3.9-liter Oldsmobile
V-8 which replaced the 2.7-liter 4-cylinder Coventry Climax
engine, found itself with the problems of understeer and instability at high speed because the nose was getting light. Air taken
in through the nose was passed through the core of the radiator
and left to find its own method of exit under the car, and this
caused a pressure area that lifted the nose at high speed. When
the flap opened in the nose of the Zerex and Bruce realized that
the air pressure coming up from inside the nose was greater than
the force of airstream he knew he was on to something important. The larger hole he hacked in the nose was a crude forerunner of the distinctive "nostrils" that have been a feature of
all McLaren cars since then, and are now also common to almost all other racing cars.

Bruce had the three years of studying for his engineering
degree in Auckland as a base of theory, and he built on this base
with years of practical experience in the motor racing field. To
begin with he learned about racing from his father, but when he
met Jack Brabham he moved into the big league. Jack helped
him when he first arrived in England in 1958 and it was Brab-

ham's coaching and coaxing, together with McLaren's own racing talent, that earned him a spot in the Cooper Formula 1 works team in 1959.

From Cooper and from Brabham, Bruce learned that development on an established theme was often better than innovation for the sake of innovation. Brabham pursued this theory when he left the Cooper team, building straightforward, workmanlike cars with Ron Tauranac. These set few standards in advanced racing design, but they were race winners and they sold well to private teams. As an example of the Brabham refusal to follow the herd, they continued to build space-frame cars for eight years, ignoring the aluminum monocoques in use by all other teams, until they finally brought out the monocoque BT33 in 1970. Ron Tauranac used to maintain that the fastest thing about a monocoque was Jimmy Clark.

The first McLaren sports cars were very obviously Cooper-based with McLaren ideas superimposed, and it was not until Robin Herd joined the team, bringing with him advanced—and not always practical—theories from the Royal Aircraft Establishment, that the true McLaren stamp was evident in the cars they produced. Their first Formula 1 car, the M2B, was so bundled up with all the accumulated ideas on how to go Grand Prix racing that it was almost a complete failure. The reason the M2B was disastrously uncompetitive was the dead weight of the 3-liter version of the 4-cam Indianapolis V-8 engine, but in other areas the GP car also ignored the McLaren principle of developing an established theme. The lesson was learned well.

Looking back, Herd remembers that when he joined the team early in 1965 McLaren design was very much influenced by Jim Hall and his Chaparrals. "Jim was going through a phase of being a really outstanding designer and constructor while our emphasis tended to be more on the elegance of the chassis structure rather than on the design of a really quick racing car. I now find this rather surprising because Bruce's sense of values in relation to the design and engineering of a racing car was first class. He never, after our first few months together anyway, lost sight of the immediate aim which was to design a car which crossed the finishing line first. On our initial design we erred from this and tended to go towards technical ingenuity and bullshit rather than race-winning engineering."

Herd had left Oxford with an engineering degree and had been hired first by the Royal Aircraft Establishment to work in the National Gas Turbine Establishment at Farnborough as a scientific officer on the Concorde project. As a racing car de-

The chassis of the M1B, with its strength-giving alloy undertray.

signer Herd was green when he arrived to work for Bruce. To begin with they operated very much like a Y with Bruce and Robin on opposite sides, pooling the knowledge from their different fields and joining at the fork with a cohesive design. Toward the end of 1965 the McLaren design team was joined by another refugee from Farnborough when Gordon Coppuck arrived. Gordon had been a leading draftsman at the N.G.T.E. and had worked with Herd. When Robin left to join Cosworth Engineering at the end of 1968 Gordon became chief designer.

"Bruce was very good at vehicle dynamics," says Gordon. "This is the theory of why vehicles do certain things—vehicles generally, and not just racing cars. Whereas most racing drivers could tell you whether the car was oversteering or understeering, Bruce understood about centers of gravity, moments of inertia, things of that nature, and he could apply them. This was of great benefit to the firm. I don't know where he learned it, or whether he just evolved it himself. I don't think he would have learned it at school because it isn't taught in schools. He most likely evolved it by applying a basically good education and a good mind."

Referring to the Y approach, Robin recalls that Bruce had a big influence on the way he carried out his detail design but he also feels that to a degree he changed Bruce's thinking. "Bruce's designs would tend to be very easy to make, sound, reliable, perhaps not very light, and I think it's fair to say not particularly elegant, whereas mine were the other way around. Between us we made up for each other's deficiencies by our experience and ability, such as it was then. Bruce gave me an immensely free

Robin Herd called the M1B one of the best looking sports/racing cars.

The M2A chassis being test-fitted with the M2B's cam Ford engine.

hand in the design and when I talk to other people—perhaps about the way Maurice Phillippe works with Colin Chapman at Lotus—I realize just how good Bruce was in this way, although perhaps I didn't fully appreciate it at the time. He had the experience I hadn't got and he really was a super bloke to work with."

Herd maintains that although he and Gordon looked after the detail design and Bruce would come by every couple of weeks between races to check and maybe change something, Bruce could have carried out this detail design himself but was prevented from doing so purely by lack of time. "If he changed something it was always for a valid reason. He did have one or two idiosyncrasies, but eventually one got to know what these were, and we avoided incorporating them in the design."

Herd's background in advanced design spurred the interest and development of the McLaren team in the field of aerodynamics, and they began experimenting with the wings and adjustable tail-fins back in 1965. The Oldsmobile-powered M2A Mallite-chassis racing car, used as a test vehicle for Firestone and as a prototype for the 1966 Formula 1 car, was taken to Zandvoort in November 1965 and a simple sort of wing was tried on the back. With the wing fitted Bruce immediately chopped three seconds off his lap time around the Dutch circuit, and with the wing removed his times fell back by the same three seconds. All evidence of the wing was then destroyed as the team determined to use it was their secret weapon for 1966. "Indeed, if the Indy Ford engine had lived up to expectations you would have seen the M2B McLaren with a wing on the back," says Herd.

When the Ford-powered car was used for tire testing at Riverside early in 1966 the car was meant to carry an advanced form of adjustable wing mounted above the transmission. It was designed so that the angle could be altered to suit the amount of downthrust required, but engine trouble curtailed these wing tests. The fact that Dan Gurney was sitting on the pit wall during much of the testing also had a negative effect on the display of new ideas before such an interested spectator.

Herd outlines the basic theory of aerodynamics as applied to racing cars: "Our ignorance of aerodynamics is vast, but this is where the biggest gain in racing car design is going to come. If we only had a bit more knowledge and some sensible research were done we could improve the aerodynamics enormously. We're after low drag so that we can gain acceleration and maxi-

Some of the staff of the then-small McLaren organization gathered around the M2B chassis. From left to right: Eoin Young, Howden Ganley, Bruce, Bruce Harre, Colin Beanland, Chris Amon and John Muller.

Bruce Tests the M2B-Ford Formula 1 car at Riverside early in 1966.

mum speed, but we also want negative lift which has the effect of pushing the car down on the ground increasing the cornering force and traction in proportion to the force between the tire and the road. This force between the tire and the road comes from two factors: the first is the weight of the car, and the second is the aerodynamic downforce on the car. If you can use aerodynamics to increase this downforce you can increase traction in braking and cornering immensely."

For an example of early efforts at aerodynamics in racing, Herd points to the streamlined Cooper tried at Reims in 1959. "I'm sure Brabham would never dream of using a body like that now on one of his cars. Unfortunately they tried something that was a sensible experiment and it didn't work so they said that the basic idea was wrong and scrapped the whole thing. The basic idea wasn't wrong. What was wrong was the detail interpretation of the idea. The particular body shape they tried was wrong. You know, I look at a photograph of that car now, and I think 'Jesus, poor Jack must have had the fright of his life.' "

The McLaren M1A, the very first McLaren sports car built late in 1964, had an attractive body shape with low drag, but it was like a mobile wing the wrong way up and it developed a tremendous amount of lift. It was quick in a straight line, but it was not very quick around corners. The M1B sports car of the following year was essentially a revised and improved M1A and one of the big gains with the 1965 car was the new body shape which had been styled by the motor racing artist Michael Turner to the aerodynamic requirements of the McLaren designers. Herd rates the McLaren M1B as one of the most attractive body styles ever on a 2-seater sports/racing car.

Aerodynamic experiments in a wind tunnel told only half the story, because a wind tunnel cannot reproduce road conditions. The ride height varies considerably in cornering, braking, accelerating and at full speed, and this has a big effect on the aerodynamics. "We tried wind tunnel work on the early sports cars," says Herd, "and we came up with a whole string of answers most of which were wrong in terms of the car's performance on the track. In order to obtain realistic data we went down to Goodwood with the M6A and set up a series of pressure tappings over the internal and external surfaces of the car, and I rode as a passenger to record the appropriate readings."

In another test at Goodwood, Herd rode facing backwards over the tail, sprawled out from the cockpit so that he could watch the behavior of the rear suspension through holes in the body, trying to trace the problem with the handling. During this test, Robin's legs slid across Bruce's left arm pinning it in the middle of a corner and they spun down the road. Robin, facing backwards, could do nothing about the situation except hang on for dear life. "Looking back on this incident I am surprised to recall that as the car got steadily more out of shape I had a feeling of calmness rather than terror, and having enough time to convince myself that if Bruce couldn't get us out of this situation, nobody could. It was fascinating to see the combination of throttle bursts, steering movements and brake applications that sent us spinning harmlessly down the center of the track. When the car stopped we both looked at each other and started hooting with laughter. I'm not sure now whether I was laughing from amusement or sheer relief."

Although the actual design of the McLaren cars was put on

Robin Herd, Bruce and Teddy Mayer examine model of M4 Formula car.

The "whoosh-bonk" spaceframe chassis of the M3 sprint/hillclimb car.

paper in the drawing office by Robin Herd and Gordon Coppuck, the initial design discussions, when details of a new car or a development of a previous model were hammered out, were long involved conversations between the designers and Bruce, Teddy, Tyler and Don Beresford who was in charge of contruction of the new cars. With the design and the building program completed, the development of the new car then depended very much on the test driver and his ability to iron out the bugs.

Test driving was something Bruce reveled in for it was, to him, an enjoyable extension of all his engineering training combined with the pursuit of what had started out as his hobby—racing. The McLaren talents as a tester did not benefit only his own team. When Ford decided to go racing with the GT-40 that grew from Eric Broadley's original mid-engined Lola GT, Bruce was retained as a development driver and he worked with the company during much of the project. In 1966, co-driving with Chris Amon, he won the Le Mans 24-hour race in one of the 7-liter Ford Mk IIs that he helped to develop. Roy Lunn, then in charge of the GT-40 program, remembers the early tests on the car when Bruce and Phil Hill were driving for Ford. "There was a real contrast between them. Phil would come in and say *everything* was wrong with the car, but Bruce was such a nice guy that he didn't like to criticize the car, so you had to dilute everything Phil said by a factor of 10, and accentuate everything Bruce said that was slightly derogatory about the car by an equal factor. Bruce went from that stage to being a very objective guy in every respect of testing. He would come in with the car after a test run and tell you exactly what had happened, and what's more he could tell you what to do to put it right. He was just a wonderful combination of driver and engineer and car builder and he could also communicate with you. I think

Bruce's first sidetank experiment on an M7A in 1968 Spanish GP.

M7B, here also with biplane wings, was a specially-built sidetank F1.

that was the reason for the success of his cars. He had all three talents and minimum communications problems because they were all locked into one guy. The problem we had was that if we were designing and building a car, we weren't capable of driving and testing so we had to rely on the test driver to communicate back. Bruce was able to communicate back—he could tell you that you had a problem and also how to cure it."

Chuck Mountain, who also worked on the Ford racing project, agreed. "That was beautiful. So many guys go out and have a problem and they have difficulty enough in just defining it, but Bruce could perceive the problem, define it, and have half a dozen solutions by the time he pulled back into the pits. He'd pick up the most uncanny things—things that were just so remote that you wouldn't think a guy had the ability to feel or recognize them, but you would check into what he said and make a change, and sure'n hell he was right!"

In 1964 when the GT-40s went to Le Mans for the first time, Bruce's car developed an electrical miss on the last night of practice when he was up around 160 mph on the straight. The engine would mysteriously drop 300 rpm and the technicians checked and double-checked and by the time they had finished, practice had ended and there was no further chance to try the car before the race. Bruce offered to drive Lunn back to the hotel and garage at La Charte about 20 miles from the circuit, so that he could satisfy himself that the problem had or hadn't been fixed. As Lunn recalled, "It was about 11:30 at night going across the rolling French countryside and it was the most hairy ride I've ever had in my life. By the time he got it up to 160 miles an hour he leaned over and shouted 'Can you hear it missing?' Hear it missing? Man, I was hearing angels singing!"

Bruce's 1966 Le Mans win was his high point in the association with Ford, although he could never come to terms with the enormity of the whole operation which descended on Le Mans like an invasion and won the race by overpowering it after unsuccessful early attempts. Bruce loved the story of the 1964 race when Phil Hill made a panic pit stop on the very first lap with a misfiring engine. Phil, never one to stand quietly about in moments of tension, was shouting his problem to the team manager while the engine cover was being hinged back. He felt sure the problem was a blocked jet, and since there was a different expert for every aspect of the car, the call went out for the

Bruce always took a hand with detail design, as here on M8A chassis.

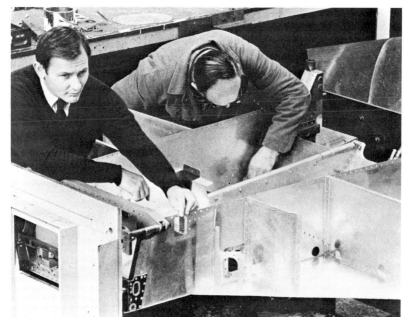

117

carburetor man. He was nowhere to be found, until a shrill little voice was heard from the balcony above the pits. The carburetor man's work was apparently presumed completed when the race started and since there hadn't been enough pit passes to go around, he had been relegated to the grandstand!

As far as the Ford men were concerned, Bruce's best race was the Le Mans he didn't win in 1967 when Dan Gurney and A.J. Foyt came home 1st in their Mk II. Lunn takes up the

M6GT was to be for Group 4 but became prototype for possible road car.

story: "Gurney and Foyt have to be, from my point of view, the worst development drivers when it comes to setting up a car, and to have the two of them in one car both with different ideas of how the car should be set up—! They got the car really screwed up on the two days of practice and it got progressively worse." Mountain said Dan and A.J. almost had reached the point of deciding to go out and blow the car early in the race. Lunn continued, "They had got their car to go progressively slower and slower while Bruce meanwhile was doing his normal routine improvements and had the fastest qualifying time in the car he was sharing with Mark Donohue. Their car was beautifully set up, so what we did was to take the Gurney/Foyt car back to the garage and set it up exactly the same as Bruce's car. By the time they got into it at the beginning of the race, they'd never driven *that* car—it was set up completely different and of course, they went on and won the darn race!"

The ability to test drive, to be able to analyze the behavior of a racing car at competitive track speeds, comes only from experience, and experience was something Bruce had a lot of.

Robin Herd likens test drivers in racing cars to test pilots of new airplanes. "They are just as crucial to the success of the project, although this is seldom appreciated. Unfortunately there is no recognized training for a test driver and it is therefore not surprising that those who are good are also very rare. The driver has to be sensitive to the car's behavior although there are several factors which make this difficult. It's amazing, for instance, how easy it is to become accustomed to even the most unpleasant faults in a car if you drive it for some time. You have this pointed out when someone new drives your own road car. Further, for each driver there appears to be certain aspect of the car's performance to which he is almost blind, so to some extent it pays to have several people test-drive a new car because you will usually learn something from each one."

After a day of testing a McLaren at Goodwood the results would be examined in some depth during the drive back to the factory in Bruce's Mercedes or Ford Zodiac with Teddy, Tyler and Robin (or later Gordon) all sharing in this rolling development session. These sessions were a most enjoyable phase of testing, Robin remembers. "We'd go through what we had run during the day and then we would analyze what the car was doing in all aspects of its performance, why it was doing this, whether it was good or bad or adequate, and what we could possibly do to improve it. It was in these head-scratching drives that we really found some big improvements in performance

119

Designer Jo Marquart and Bruce study 4-wheel drive unit for M9 F1 car.

and these were inevitably reflected in later designs."

Bruce's pet theories were something of a family joke within the team, and his "whoosh-bonk" cars were typical of the McLaren tenacity to follow an idea through in the face of what he considered to be ill-founded opposition. "If Bruce had one of his theories, even if it was crazy, he was able to make it happen," Tyler recalls. "Everyone had a lot of faith in him and he was able to instill enthusiasm for these projects."

The title "whoosh-bonk" came from Bruce's enthusiastic assurance of the short time the cars would take to construct: "You take the suspension off the sports car—whoosh—knock up the chassis and—bonk—there's the car!"

It was probably Patsy Burt and her garage and racing manager Ron Smith who prompted the hurricane building program on the "whoosh-bonk" cars that went down in the McLaren list as M3s. In fact they were single-seat space-frame versions of the M1 sports car, just as the later M15 car for Indianapolis was in effect a single-seat version of the M8 Can-Am car. The new cars, Bruce enthused, would find an unlimited market among hill-climb and sprint specialists such as Patsy, who held most of the ladies' sprint records and a lot of hill titles. When others in the company failed to mirror his optimism, Bruce pressed on alone. "It was a classic of Bruce's cigarette-package designing," according to Gordon. "Neither Robin or I had anything to do with it. Bruce literally designed it on scraps of paper and picked out the suspension based on the previous year's sports car. He took these sketches to John Thompson in the workshop and he joined up the points under Bruce's supervision. It all happened in a fortnight. There were no drawings, and in fact we still don't have any drawings of the M3! After we had built three—one for Patsy Burt, one for Swiss hillclimber Harry Zwiefel, and one for MGM as a camera car for their film *Grand Prix*—we thought perhaps someone else might want one and so we would do a drawing of the chassis as it was. We had a designer draw the chassis as a 'moonlight' job, and he had no sooner finished the drawing than the cleaner crumpled it up and threw it in the wastepaper bin, so we never did get a proper design drawing!"

Bruce's other pet theory was the side-tank M7C—a version of the M7 Formula 1 car which he had fitted with pannier fuel tanks between the wheels, extending as wide as the regulations would allow on either side of the monocoque. Tyler remembers how it started. "I believe it all stemmed from a discussion Bruce had with Colin Chapman about sports cars, and Chapman reckoned that perhaps one of the reasons that a sports car handled better than a single-seater was that the weight was spread out more instead of having all the weight in the center of the car. Bruce had also thought about this and since he respected Chapman's opinion he seized upon this opportunity to build a single-seater with sports car characteristics. He did some initial testing with this car and it did prove to be better, but the practical applications of the thing didn't work out because it made the car too heavy and we had to abandon the project. The idea, I think, was right, and we did prove it to some extent with the M15 Indianapolis car, getting the weight low and spread out between the wheels."

Bruce's favorite project was the road-going version of the ill-fated M6GT which failed to get homologated as a Group 5 GT car—of which 50 were required to be built—even though a batch of 50 neat-looking bodies had been made to fit the basic M6 monocoque Can-Am chassis. Building his own road car was a project that had interested Bruce as an ambition to be achieved when the company was well under way with the racing program. It was a five-year-old, off-and-on project, but early in 1970 he organized the building of one of the M6GTs for use on the road in an effort to find out what problems would have to be overcome in a proper mid-engined road GT car. The result was, literally, a semi-civilized Can-Am car that was anything but easy to climb into but was bliss to drive or ride in once you were installed. Even with a standard 5-liter Chevrolet V-8 in the back it would accelerate to 100 mph in around 8 seconds, and of course the handling was fantastic. One problem was that the car was so low that other traffic often had difficulty in seeing it coming up behind. Bruce loved the GT, but he wasn't blind to its shortcomings. In fact he had started work on an alternative design at the time of his death, spurred on by an artist's very stylish impression of what the McLaren road car could look like.

Gordon and Bruce had long discussions about the M6GT and about the problems they had discovered running the car on the road. The radiator outlet duct in the nose, for instance, while proving to be an ideal windshield defroster on cold mornings, generated a lot of noise and they had decided to delete the duct on the next version of the McLaren road car. Entry and exit across the broad side-tanks was another feature that was scheduled for a tidy-up. "Another problem," said Gordon, "was that it had odd-sized wheels, with small ones in front and big ones at the back. It handled beautifully, but it meant that we would have to find out which were the best rim sizes so that we only needed to carry one spare wheel. At that time there wasn't room for a spare anyway, and that was another problem. I was really surprised with how comfortable the car was when I borrowed it for a weekend. Quite incredible when you considered that it was basically a racing car."

Bruce had built up an intimate relationship with Robin and their designs were very much joint efforts, and for this reason Bruce was very hurt when Robin left to join Cosworth. He felt that Robin was taking with him all that Bruce knew in the building up of a racing car and a racing team. Strangely enough it was the same sort of hurt that Bruce had not understood Charles and John Cooper feeling when Jack Brabham left the Cooper team at the end of the 1961 season. Although the Coopers maintained that Jack had taken all the company's racing knowledge with him, Bruce always felt that Jack had done a tremendous amount for the Cooper team in return and there should have been no recriminations when he left.

Gordon noticed that after Robin left, Bruce was reluctant to take him into his confidence on design matters because he had a sneaking suspicion that since Gordon had followed Robin from the National Gas Turbine Establishment to McLaren, he might well follow him from the McLaren team to Cosworth. When Bruce realized that Gordon had no intentions of leaving the

The first McLaren assault on Indy started with three cars for two drivers—
Chris Amon and Denny Hulme. Here, from left, are designer Gordon
Coppuck, Chris in car, Denny, Bruce, Tyler Alexander and Teddy Mayer.

team, he soon started building a close liaison again with his designers. Jo Marquart, a Swiss-born designer who had come from Lotus to the McLaren team, joined Gordon on the design team when Robin left at the end of the 1968 season.

Gordon had been working in Robin's shadow, and the first car he really designed was the M10A car for Formula A and Formula 5000 racing. "That was actually my project and Bruce was very communicative and very helpful. Obviously he knew what he wanted, but it was one thing for him to come and say what he wanted straight out, and another thing to discuss it and evolve what seemed to be the best solution to the particular problem. I'm sure he was pleased with the result of the M10 and by the time we were doing the M15 Indianapolis car I did that more on my own with more of my ideas on it than I'd been used to having. We used the expression that by then I was McLaren-orientated. I believed that the way in which we were developing was the right way for us. It wasn't a question of just going along with what Bruce thought about any particular design feature—I really believed that for us it was the best way to do it."

Designing is probably the least glamorous side of a racing team from the outsider's point of view, but in the world of design there is a certain amount of contained excitement in bringing a racing car concept into being via the drawing board.

Gordon doesn't find his job dull. "The thing that strikes you about racing is the speed with which drawings are turned into parts. In the Gas Turbine Establishment, I'd been used to people coming up with drawing office queries fifteen months after I'd done the drawings, and I couldn't remember anything about them. In racing, drawings become parts within a week, and that's so much more satisfying from a drawing point of view without considering the excitement of motor racing itself.

"I must confess that I don't find racing in itself as exciting as perhaps the spectators do. It's exciting to me if it's an exciting race and we are directly involved in the action, but winning a race at a canter doesn't thrill me and *not* winning a race doesn't impress me either! I think it's important for designers to go to race meetings at sufficient intervals to be aware of how the team is doing in racing. It's very easy not to go to races and keep getting secondhand stories that aren't true, whereas if the designer is there he will know at first hand what has happened. Someone should certainly be in direct contact with people who have been to every race. To remain competitive you must have detailed knowledge of what happened last Sunday. The team manager should tell you what developments have taken place, and the chief mechanic should tell you what problems have arisen, both with our cars and with parts similar to ours on other cars."

Bruce's overall concept of a car was important to the designers and to the discussions of concept that were held either formally in Bruce's office or informally over a dinner that Patty had cooked at home. Like most motor racing wives, Patty had to sit at the edge of long involved conversations, keeping vague track of the topic and avoiding inane remarks.

"Bruce knew how the car should be and how it should be laid out," says Gordon. "He was also very good when it came to difficult details on the car. When we were doing the M8 Can-Am car we came across a particular difficulty where we couldn't get a sanitary solution for the point where the tubes joined the bellhousing at the rear of the engine. Bruce could sit and work over a problem like that, while we were getting on with the rest of the design. If something looked right, Bruce maintained that it usually *was* right, but he always followed this up by saying that if it looked wrong it was wrong. We will certainly miss Bruce's development work on a car. Having taken the car from the drawing office and made it and then taking it down to Goodwood to test, he could quickly put his finger on any bugs that needed sorting out. He was able to translate these problems to us and communicate well. You could talk to him and understand what he meant and this communication between the driver and the designer (and this was probably even stronger between Bruce and Tyler as chief mechanic) was very strong. That's where I've learned all I know about racing."

6

RACING ENGINE DEVELOPMENT

THE DECISION to use the Indianapolis Ford V-8 in 3-liter form for their first Grand Prix car in 1966 cost the McLaren team dearly during the first two seasons of the new formula. They had based their development program around the Ford engine, but when it failed to meet hoped-for requirements the Grand Prix project virtually lost its drive for two years. And during those two years the Brabham team used the engine the McLaren team rejected—the Oldsmobile F85 with its aluminum block—to win two World Championships. In 1968 the Ford Cosworth engines were made available to teams other than Lotus, and the McLaren team was back on even terms with its engines but they had lost two years of development while they switched from one stop-gap engine to another. They lost the early advantage in tire technology gained during their initial testing with Firestone in 1965 and they also lost the development work on airfoils—done in secret during 1965 and planned for use as a "secret weapon" in 1966, two full seasons before the airfoil wings first appeared on the Ferraris and Brabhams at Spa in 1968.

At 7 o'clock one night in April 1965 Bruce called a meeting in his office at the Feltham factory and with Teddy Mayer, mechanics Tyler Alexander and Wally Willmott and designers

Bruce had great hopes for the 4-cam Ford-engined M2B Grand Prix car.

Robin Herd and Eddie Stait, he discussed opinions on an engine for the new 3-liter formula the following year. It was obviously important to start early and to have a proven engine ready to race while other teams were perhaps struggling to sort out a new power unit.

They talked about the new BRM engine but it seemed wise to let BRM deal with its own teething troubles. They decided the Maserati V-12 would probably be less than competitive and anyway it seemed that the Cooper team had lined up an exclusive deal with the Italian factory. The 2.7-liter Coventry Climax engine? Not enough power and not enough scope for development. A 3-liter version of the Oldsmobile engine they had been using for sports car racing? The job of engineering a conversion on the stock-block engine would be prohibitively expensive, and they weren't sure that the block was strong enough to stand the higher rpm in 3-liter form.

The 4-cam Indianapolis Ford presented itself as the best choice because it was a pure racing engine and as such could be developed, and there was always a chance that the Ford Motor Company would take an active financial interest in a team that was preparing to go Grand Prix racing with a Ford engine for the first time.

"We were never under the delusion that the engine was a potential winner without major engineering changes, but we had a feeling that we might be able to pressure or coax or lead Ford into doing something about the engine for us if we were to take the initiative. But although we did get some back-door advice, Ford never did get involved in any overt operation with us," says Teddy Mayer.

In 4.2-liter form, running on gasoline, the 4-cam Ford was giving a reliable 470 bhp, and it was felt that with the reduction in capacity to 3-liters there would be a safe 335 bhp with a pleasant torque curve to start with, and more power to come with the higher revs that could be used with what was really a sophisticated racing engine.

In the light of more recent developments in the engine field, however, it is now apparent that the basic design of the heads on the Ford was wrong for the application but expert opinion at the time deemed that the engine could be made to give the required horsepower in 3-liter form. Klaus von Rucker, who had worked on BMW and Mercedes racing engines, was appointed as a consultant to look into the possibilities of the Ford, and engineering work started in England.

Gary Knutson soon found that progress was lagging on the engine project and the whole operation was shipped to the workshops of Traco Engineering in Culver City, California. Five 1964 Indy engines were bought from Ford. Early in 1966 the Formula 1 Indy Ford engine ran in the McLaren Mallite-chassis single-seater for the first time during Firestone tests at Riverside but valve problems cut the testing short.

Work continued at the Traco shop where the McLaren engine men tried to sort out the several problems, and Bruce received a

129

Inside the test room Bruce supervises running of the 3-liter Ford.

graphic note from Wally Willmott: "We had decided to try dropping our valves somewhere else so we set up a cylinder head in one of Jim Nairn's (an engineering shop next door to Traco) big machines and coupled it up with oil pumps, splash shields and loving care. The first test ran for five minutes at 10,500 revs, then broke a valve spring, just about deafened all in Mr. Nairn's shop and started to eat up his big machine. The last two items didn't appeal to Mr. Nairn's sense of humor so we had to revise our test rig somewhat. The gobbling of the machine was fixed quite easily but the noise factor meant we could only run at night after everyone had gone home. The final result was that in the next four days and nights we worked from 10 a.m. to 5 p.m. at Traco then from 5 p.m. to 3 a.m. at Nairn Machine Co. In these four days I saw more broken valve springs and learned more new words rude and technical than I had picked up in the last five years. The final outcome of the whole deal was that we now had a valve that had done around 1,800,000 ins-and-outs, and a valve-spring set-up that lasts for 1¼ hours at 10,500 revs. This doesn't sound like very long but it is 10,500 revs that kills the springs and when you think of the number of times that an engine reaches or holds these revs even at Reims, it isn't bad."

The engine certainly looked impressive in the chassis with the big-bore injection bellmouths sticking up four on each side of the engine, and the drainpipe-like pair of exhausts coming out the center of the vee and sloping down and back. It sounded impressive too. At Monaco the ear-splitting blast of noise was almost beyond comprehension as it bounced off the buildings in the Principality. But the performance was dismal. It had proved to be unbelievably heavy, unreliable, and the peak horsepower of just 300 bhp was only available in a very narrow rev range. The team had been hoping to start the season with at least 330 bhp. An oil fitting came loose after 10 laps, and Bruce's race was over.

Count Volpi, head of the Italian Serenissima company, was aware of the desperate straits of the McLaren team and he offered them the use of his 3-liter V-8 sports car engine. It was giving only 260 bhp, but it was an engine and it *did* work, so the team set about altering the chassis to take the Serenissima engine with its side exhausts necessitating the removal of the part of the monocoque that extended alongside the engine. At Spa chronic bearing problems retired the McLaren before practice was finished. With these doctored, the car finished 6th in the British Grand Prix at Brands Hatch to earn Bruce his first championship point in his own car, but he was really only marking time and using the Serenissima to develop the chassis while work progressed on the Ford engine in America. The Ford reappeared for the U.S. Grand Prix at Watkins Glen where Bruce finished 5th, but when it blew during the race in Mexico a final curtain was drawn over the unhappy saga of the first Ford

Last attempt to extract usable horsepower from Ford was in U.S. GP.

Temporary replacement for 4-cam Ford was Italian-built Serenissima V-8.

engine in Grand Prix racing.

While the McLaren team wrestled with the overweight, underpowered Ford and all its problems, Jack Brabham had taken the aluminum Oldsmobile engine to Repco Engineering in Australia and convinced them that their engineering work to convert the Oldsmobile into an overhead-camshaft 3-liter Formula 1 engine would be made more than worthwhile by the international prestige and publicity gained for Repco when the Brabhams won races. Jack had to call his cars Repco Brabhams, but his gamble paid off. When Jack won the world title in 1966, the Repco gave around 290 bhp and in 1967 when Denis Hulme won the championship in a Brabham he had around 330 bhp—the figure the McLaren team had been working for in the winter of 1965.

In 1967 Ford of Britain announced that they had financed Cosworth Engineering to the tune of 100,000 pounds (approximately $240,000) to follow up the 1.6-liter Formula 2 engine with a 3-liter V-8 engine for Formula 1. Used exclusively in the works Lotus 49s that season, the engine won first time out at Zandvoort with Jim Clark driving, and he also won the British, U.S. and Mexican Grands Prix that year with the Lotus-Ford. In 1968 the Ford Cosworth DFV V-8 was made available to other teams, including McLaren Racing, and it became the power unit that dominated Formula 1 until Ferrari found form with the flat-12 in 1970.

Keith Duckworth, designer of the Cosworth engines, defined

the requirements of a racing engine, writing in the authoritative annual *Autocourse* in 1966 while he was still working on the design of the Formula 1 V-8:

"The primary function of a racing engine is to propel the car in which it is fitted across the finishing line ahead of all the other cars. The function of the racing engine designer is to produce an engine which has the best combination of power, weight, size, accessibility and fuel consumption. The power

Like most F2 cars, McLaren M4A used Cosworth FVA 4-cylinder engine.

M4B had BRM V-8, ballast and sidetanks in order to run as Formula 1 car.

must be usable over an adequate range, the weight must be as low as is consistent with reliability and the overall lay-out must be well suited to the general configuration of the car. Accessibility is probably less important in an engine built for works use than in one which is for sale to customers, but even so such things as the plugs and the rest of the ignition system should be easy to get at. Fuel consumption is possibly one of the most important features of all, for it governs the shape and size of the car and its consequent starting line weight."

With the Ford-Cosworth engine reserved for Team Lotus in 1967, the McLaren team decided to use the 3-liter BRM V-12 which was being developed ostensibly for sports car customers because the BRM Formula 1 team was running the complex H-16 engines. Delivery was not expected before mid-season, so a 2.1-liter version of the 1.5-liter BRM V-8 from the previous formula was fitted into one of the pretty little McLaren M4 monocoque Formula 2 cars. This car, which was 4th at Monte Carlo, was the McLaren works entry until just after the Dutch Grand Prix when it was gutted by fire during tire tests at Goodwood. While waiting for the BRM V-12 to arrive, Bruce drove one of Dan Gurney's 12-cylinder Weslake-engined Eagles.

The M5 chassis waited in the workshops until the BRM V-12 engine finally arrived just before the Canadian Grand Prix.

M5 was designed for BRM V-12 but late delivery spoiled development.

Bruce ran the car until the end of the season but because of the late delivery of the engine it was very much an interim car as design work progressed on the M7A Formula 1 cars to take the Ford-Cosworth V-8 which the team has used since.

Bruce had learned the basics about engines after school in his father's garage in Auckland. He put this knowledge to practical use on his Ulster Austin 7, the Ford Ten special that followed it, his father's much-modified Austin-Healey 100-4, and finally a string of cars with Coventry Climax engines that started with the bob-tailed 1500-cc Cooper sports car he bought from Jack Brabham in 1957 and ended when the 2.7-liter Climax engine was taken out of the Zerex special in 1964 and replaced with the 3.9-liter Oldsmobile V-8.

Bruce won the "Driver to Europe" scholarship in 1958 driving a single-seat 1750-cc Cooper-Climax, he won his first Grand Prix at Sebring in 1959 in a works 2.5-liter Cooper-Climax, and he won the Monaco Grand Prix in 1962 with a 1.5-liter Cooper-Climax. He had a close working relationship with Walter Hassan and Harry Spears at Coventry Climax and when a special 2.7-liter version of the Formula 1 4-cylinder was built for Jack Brabham to use in the Cooper at Indianapolis in 1961, Bruce was able to use some of these engines in the Tasman Series. He also worked with the Climax engineers on a short-stroke version

135

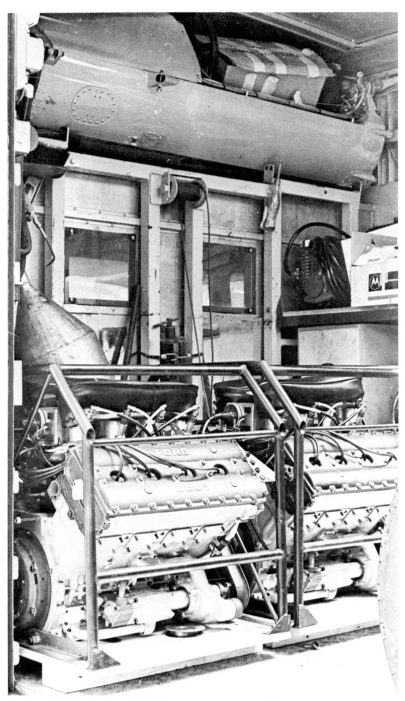

136   *Cosworth DFV engines in McLaren transporter with extra monocoque.*

of the FPF 4-cylinder engine when the Tasman Series was limited to a maximum of 2.5-liters on pump fuel in 1964. For 1970 the Tasman regulations were opened to allow 5-liter pushrod engines in addition to the 2.5-liter racing engines.

The horsepower figures and prices of the Coventry Climax engines in the early Sixties make interesting reading. The 1960 Mark 2 version of the 2.5 FPF 4-cylinder engine gave 240 bhp at 6500 rpm and cost 1750 Pounds (about $4900). When the formula changed in 1961, the FPF engine in 1.5-liter form gave 150 bhp at 7200 rpm and cost 1500 Pounds ($4200). The first of the 1.5-liter Climax V-8s, the FWMV, gave 180 bhp on carburetors at 8500 rpm and cost 2500 Pounds ($7000) in 1962, but for 1963 a short-stroke version of the V-8 was developed using fuel injection and the horsepower rose to 200 bhp at 9750 rpm and the price doubled to 5000 Pounds.

When the Ford-Cosworth DFV V-8 was first offered for sale in 1968 it was giving 410 bhp at 9000 rpm and cost 7500 Pounds ($18,000)!

Bruce was not at all convinced that there was no substitute for cubic inches when they talked about going sports car racing in 1964, but it soon became apparent after a few races in England with the Zerex that the extra horsepower and torque of the Oldsmobile was badly needed. In fact the 3.9-liter aluminum Oldsmobile weighed little more than the 4-cylinder Climax engine and in Traco trim it gave 300 bhp. The Oldsmobile was eventually enlarged to 5-liters with 380 bhp during 1965 but Bruce was fighting a losing battle against the Chaparrals with their 6-liter aluminum Chevrolet V-8s. These aluminum Chevrolet engines were strictly "back door" units for Jim Hall's team, and Bruce's only alternative in the horsepower race was to fit a cast iron Chevrolet—something that offended his ideals of a sports car being light and compact.

In 1966 the team was really hurting for horsepower that the Traco-Oldsmobile patently did not have, and for the St. Jovite race in June they fitted a 5.4-liter, 480-bhp cast iron Chevrolet, and with a bonus of an extra 100 horsepower, Bruce won the race. Why had he stuck to the Oldsmobile for so long? "I guess we were wrong," Bruce wrote in *Autosport* after his win in Canada. "In the early stages of sports car racing, development of tires and transmissions hadn't reached the stage where 500 bhp could be reliably used. Now it has."

Bruce was still suffering a 100-pound weight handicap over the aluminum Chevrolets in the Chaparrals, but he was surprised at the performance of these American pushrod passenger car

Cosworth V-8 made McLarens competitive in F1; this is Hulme at Monaco.

engines. "These Chevy engines are damned good," he wrote at the end of the 1966 season. "At 5.4 liters our engines are twice as big as the 2.7 Climaxes we used to use and which were and still are very good engines. The Climax gave about 240 bhp with twin overhead camshafts and as much racing experience as could be crammed into it, and yet these Chevys of ours are giving 480 bhp and they are common, garden-variety pushrod engines with single camshafts, and you can buy them (if you happen to live in the U.S.A.) just down the road for a few dollars. They are strong Mothers and we've found them to be pretty reliable. It certainly makes you think twice before down-rating some of this Detroit Iron."

The capacity of the Chevrolet was soon increased to 6 liters with stronger connecting rods and a new fuel injection system which put the power up to 527 bhp. As Bruce commented, they now had race-winning potential—all they wanted was some race wins. But the wins still weren't forthcoming and John Surtees won the first Can-Am Championship in 1966 with his 6-liter Lola T70.

The story was different in 1967. The sophisticated M6A used the 6-liter engine again, modified by Gary Knutson, and the cars won five of the six Can-Ams with Bruce taking the title. For 1968 the long-awaited aluminum 7-liter Chevrolet blocks were made available to the McLaren team for the first time, and they were fitted into the M8A. This was an advanced design that set a Can-Am trend with the monocoque halting abruptly behind the cockpit and the engine acting as a stressed member of the chassis. The M8As won four of the six Can-Ams in 1968 and this time it was Denny Hulme's turn for the title.

An engine building shop had now been set up in the Colnbrook workshops in England to defend the McLaren title as King of Can-Am, and when Gary Knutson left to rejoin Chaparral, an employee of Traco Engineering, George Bolthoff, was hired to take his place.

The team had decided that using engines modified by Traco or Bartz was more expensive than setting up their own engine facility. There was also a problem in that any power modifications discovered by the McLaren team immediately found their way into other customer's engines. "We felt that it would be better if we did our own engines and used our knowledge solely for our own benefit," said Teddy Mayer.

There were problems, however, in preparing American engines for an American series of races from a workshop in England. Supply lines were extended so much that delivery became difficult and on occasions almost impossible.

In England it was hard to find a machine shop familiar with American V-8 engines or equipped to handle them. "Even small jobs that you can do easily in the States, you couldn't do *at all*

4.5-liter Oldsmobile V-8 powered first McLaren single-seater, the M2A.

in England. They had no equipment to handle V-8s, whereas in the States the V-8 is the average engine and there are a lot of shops that can handle custom work," says Bolthoff.

So the decision was taken to set up an engine shop for the team in America and a new company, McLaren Engines Incorporated, was formed at the end of 1969 and a factory building was rented in the city of Livonia on the outskirts of Detroit. Detroit was chosen because of its proximity to the engine suppliers and also because it was a central point for the Can-Am races on the East Coast and the mid-west, as well as Indianapolis which is a 5-hour, 250-mile drive from Detroit. Also there were daily freight flights from London to Detroit and a telex message flashed to the parent factory could get a part delivered in Detroit within 24 hours.

Colin Beanland was made general manager of McLaren Engines, while Bolthoff looked after the engine building and race preparation. In one corner of the 4500-square foot building they installed a Heenan & Froude dynamometer in a specially built test cell adequately soundproofed to drown the bellow of a revving Can-Am engine to a muffled rumble. Half of the building is given over to space where the Can-Am cars are prepared between races. The Indianapolis cars and engines are also prepared in Detroit.

Bolthoff, 37, came into the engine building side of racing through dragsters. He ran a double-A gas dragster with a 392-cubic inch Chrysler V-8 bored and stroked to 465 cubic inches and fitted with a 671 supercharger. It ran 197 mph, with a 7.97-second E.T. which was a world record for the class when Bolthoff ran professionally between 1963 and 1965. He was working with Traco when he heard through the grapevine that Gary Knutson was leaving the McLaren team, so he telephoned Teddy Mayer in England and applied for the job the instant it became available.

With the strip, check and reassembly jobs completed on the 4-cylinder turbocharged Offenhausers for the Indianapolis M15 McLarens, Bolthoff joined Lee Muir and John Nicholson in the building of the 1970 Can-Am engines.

When the engines arrive from Chevrolet they are the absolutely bare 430-cubic inch aluminum blocks as sold over the counter or fitted as an option in the Corvette. The other parts are mostly stock from Chevrolet, and they are then modified as necessary. The blocks are treated very much as raw material and they are extensively reworked. All the dimensions are checked, the blocks are line-bored to ensure accuracy, and the deck surface is machined to true it up. The rough edges of sand casting and aluminum flash are all removed in the process.

"We do porting work on the stock heads and then we fit special aluminum-bronze valve guides that we make in England. The valves are stock. Chevrolet has a high performance valve that's about the best thing you can buy. Wherever possible we stick with standard Chevrolet parts where they work, because there's no sense in trying something tricky that may not work.

"The manifolds and rocker covers are all made in England, but we do the hand work on them here. We have to port the manifolds and set up the butterflies and throttle assemblies. The manifolds are McLaren Racing designs, but the fuel injection parts are all from Lucas.

"The main problem with adapting the engine to fit the Can-Am car is in the re-routing of the oil system to fit the headers. The headers come down very close to the block and we have to modify the oil inlet lines to get the engine into the car physically."

The engine is fitted with a dry-sump oil system because the high lateral g load during cornering would interfere with oil pick-up on a normal wet-sump engine. Doing away with the standard oil sump also allows the engine to be mounted lower in the chassis.

The 465-cubic inch (7.5-liter) engines use the 430 ZL-1 Corvette aluminum option block fitted with a crankshaft from a 427-cubic inch engine that is standard in the Corvette and other Chevrolet models. This standard crankshaft is nitrided as are the camshafts before they are installed in the racing version of the engine.

"We see about 675 bhp from a good 465-cubic inch engine. I think in its basic 430-cubic inch form as a Corvette option it's rated at about 450 bhp or maybe less because Chevrolet is a little conservative about rated horsepower, on the Corvettes especially. I imagine that if you took a good Corvette and gave it a sharp tune-up you'd get close to 500 horsepower out of it."

The 675-bhp engine weighs 460 pounds in racing trim and Bruce eagerly rated it as a better power unit on a horsepower-per-pound basis than any other racing engine, including the 3-liter 4-cam 32-valve Cosworth V-8 Grand Prix engine that weighs 360 pounds and gives 430 horsepower. Bruce had invented a weight-to-power ratio for a Reynolds Aluminum news release, but it was still a fact that the aluminum pushrod Chevrolet stacked up better than the pure racing engine.

The engine test cell cost around $30,000 to install, with the

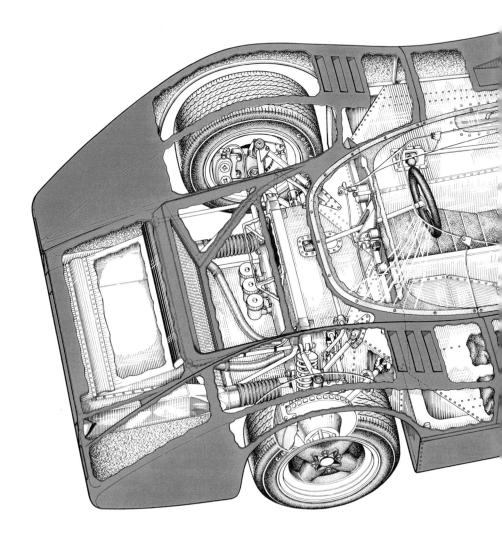

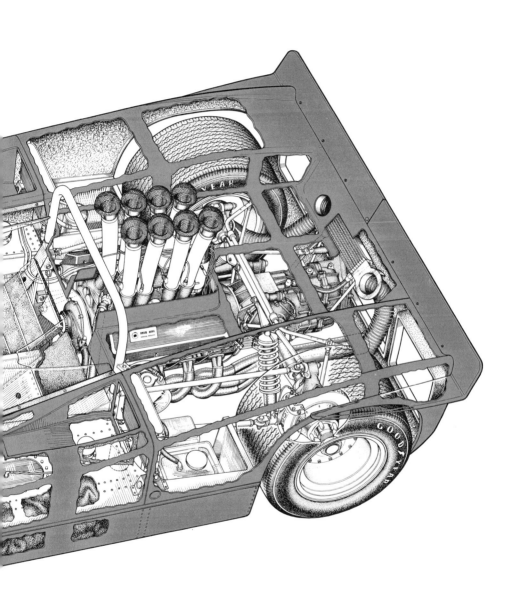

McLAREN M8A

dynamometer the most expensive single item at $8500. In fact
the dynamometer itself is a small part of the installation and it
needs many accessories. An accurate tachometer, and efficient
water system and a quiet exhaust system are required. The
McLaren installation has a large pair of industrial silencers
twelve feet long and three feet in diameter mounted on the
roof.

The dynamometer absorbs engine torque in water wheel effect; the more water you put into it, the more torque it absorbs,
and it is controlled by running water in and out of the water
wheel. The torque is read out directly on a scale, and then the
torque is converted with the rpm figure into horsepower.

Bolthoff explains the dyno procedure with an engine fresh
from a rebuild. "The dyno more or less simulates the installation in the car. You start it and run it until it warms up. With
these aluminum engines you have to torque the heads down and
set the valves while they are hot—we call this a hot torque and
valve-set operation. It takes about ten or fifteen minutes before
the temperatures get up to 180 degrees F for the water and 200
degrees F for the oil. As the temperatures rise the block grows
about ten thousandths of an inch in all directions which means
that all the valve clearances change. If you set the clearances
with the engine cold they get way out as the engine warms up,
so this is why we have to do the settings with the engine hot.

"We have a 2½-hour run-in cycle. We start out at 2500 rpm
with a light load and eventually end up at about 4500 rpm with

a fairly heavy load on it. You get the load by adjusting the amount of water inside the dyno. This is done with a hydraulic and electronic control system. When we've got it warmed up and run in, we check to make sure it isn't going to leak oil in the race car, we take a quick horsepower reading and if it's reasonable we take the engine off and put it in the car.

"If we don't have time to run the engine in on the test bed, we have to do it in the car, but this is difficult. With the dyno, we can walk round the engine while it's running and check for oil leaks; at the track you can tell that there's an oil leak but because the airstream blows it all around the engine it's hard to pinpoint exactly where the leak is."

Bruce impressed George with his knowledge of the entire system of the car and the engine, and he always took a practical interest in developments. In design discussions he would raise a practical point that might have escaped notice. George designed the ram stack adapter with a curve in the casting allowing the use of a straight pipe which can easily be changed to alter the ram stack length. "I was going to put the fuel injection nozzle straight in at 90 degrees to the butterfly shaft, but Bruce made the suggestion that if the nozzles were swung round by 45 degrees, the body could be made to fit in much closer to the engine. He could pick up things like this quickly because he saw the car as a whole, and not as separate units joined together."

Chevrolet V-8 engine, here in M8A, has been ultra-successful in Can-Am.

145

Despite disclaimer, the materials have been put to very good use!

Throttle linkages were Bruce's pride and joy, and he used to work for days perfecting a set of linkages for the Weber carburetors on his Tasman Coopers. The linkage on the Can-Am engines was Bruce's design. "That was one of his pet things. We tried to make a super zoomy linkage to the metering unit and I worked for a couple of days on a prototype thing to make it sanitary. I thought is was really nice until Bruce came over and looked at it and started shaking it and moving until he just about broke it off. He didn't like it and that was the end of it. I hadn't given it quite the test he had! Denny is like this too. He bends and twists things and if they give, then he's right."

Teddy Mayer says there is as much work in building the pushrod Chevrolet into a Can-Am engine as there would be in modifying a Chevrolet passenger car to go racing. "There is so much detail that needs changing or modifying or uprating or updating or checking or blueprinting or servicing, that it gets to be a monumental sort of task. Because the block and heads and crankshaft are available from a production line, those parts are reasonably cheap, but after that the expense is about equal with a Formula 1 engine. Our Can-Am engines cost about 5500 Pounds (over $13,000) each, compared with a Formula 1 Ford Cosworth at 7500 Pounds."

The per-race maintenance cost on the Formula 1 engine works out at about 500 Pounds ($1200). The Ford-Cosworth gives 430 bhp but this figure is not guaranteed, nor is it average, according to Mayer. "The horsepower that you race with is whatever comes out after the engines have been rebuilt. Even specialists like Cosworth don't always know why a particular engine gives ten or fifteen or even twenty horsepower more

146

than the engine built alongside it on the bench. They know that an engine with a peculiarly happy set of tolerances and parts and just general circumstances runs better, and they know why it should, but they don't know how the engine happens to be built like that, or often what's involved in the peculiarly happy set of circumstances. Cosworth has had problems with servicing the engines, but this is understandable with 70 engines in service and five major Formula 1 teams using them. Like a race car, an engine responds to being built and cared for by expert mechanics, and the number of expert mechanics available to Cosworth, or anyone else, is very limited. So you presume that some of the engines are being built and cared for by people who aren't as good, and like race cars they don't respond as well as if they were 'tweaked' by the best."

Before a season in Grand Prix racing the McLaren team can budget fairly accurately on an engine program. They know they will need seven engines representing an outlay of 52,500 Pounds ($126,000) to be certain of having at least four engines at a race for two cars.

Their engine budget is formidable taken in total. They have four turbocharged Offenhauser Indianapolis engines which cost $25,000 each, and they maintain six Can-Am engines which represents a total of $79,200.

This makes an initial outlay for engines to compete in Grand Prix, Can-Am and Indianapolis-type racing that totals a staggering $305,200—or more than Ford of Britain invested in Cosworth Engineering to design and build the world-beating Grand Prix engine from scratch!

7

TEAM MANAGER
TEDDY MAYER

Wᴴᴱᴺ EUROPEAN motor racing changed from its amateur standing to that of a very professional sport, there were those who strongly criticized the commercialism, blissfully unaware or ignorant of the immense costs involved and the pressing reasons behind the businessmen being brought in. Why, they argued, does racing have to be big business when it has survived for decades without the emphasis on cash support? It was very difficult for the purists to realize that *because* European racing had gone for years without being businesslike and without emphasizing the amount of trade backing it received, it was necessary to find a quick means of rescuing major motor racing from going bankrupt. Advertising was allowed on racing cars and sponsors who had supported racing for years were at last able to get some recognition for their support. It also opened the door to sponsors outside motor sport to gain publicity with the fastest and most exciting sport in the world, while providing extra backing for the growing number of teams. In America, of course, racing had always had a commercial bias and the problems that ruffled the feathers of the amateurs in Europe were regarded as faintly comical.

Bruce McLaren's racing team grew up from very humble beginnings around Bruce's talent as a racing driver, his reputation as a "nice guy," and his ability to pick the right people to work with him. Running the Zerex Special with a three-man team, however, was a far simpler operation from a cash and organizational point of view than it was soon to become when the team shifted to larger premises with a higher rent, and employed more mechanics for the McLaren sports car project. At this critical stage in the team's history, toward the end of 1964, Teddy Mayer joined the company as a director, bringing with him a welcome boost to the team's bank balance and the promise of increasing his own finances by applying his keen mind to the business of motor racing.

Edward Everett Mayer, known as Teddy and sometimes as "The Weener," had left Cornell with a law degree but his consuming hobby was motor racing and before devoting himself to tax law he decided to work at furthering the career of his younger brother Timmy who was showing a Stewart-like flair as a driver and was soon to precede Jackie into Ken Tyrrell's Formula Junior team, racing in Europe. Ken saw a good future for Timmy, but the 26-year-old American was killed during practice for the last race of the 1964 Tasman series. If he had returned to Europe, he would have driven for the Cooper team as number two to Bruce McLaren that season.

Timmy raced in America with a Formula Junior Cooper and a Cooper Monaco sports car run by brother Teddy, before he was spotted by Tyrrell. When he went to England in 1963 Teddy accompanied him. "I went over with Timmy as an observer to try and further his interests in racing, and also to see if there was any possibility of a job in racing for me."

In discussions with John Cooper during 1963, Teddy was given to understand that there was a real chance for him to be employed in some form of team management capacity the following season, but Timmy's death cancelled all those plans. To gain experience in single-seaters with comparable power to the 1.5-liter Formula 1 cars, the Mayers arranged to build a twin Cooper to Bruce's and embark on the 1964 Tasman series as a joint team venture. "After Timmy was killed I'd gone home and attended to his estate and gone up to Vermont skiing for two or three weeks to sort myself out and decide what I wanted to do."

Back in England at this time Bruce was sitting down at the kitchen table in the rented house in New Malden, Surrey, with Wally Willmott and me, working out what the tiny team should now turn its attention to. Sports car racing looked like being a field offering a chance of success. It was decided to buy the

Zerex Special from John Mecom with a view to campaigning the car in England, so Bruce telephoned Teddy in Vermont and asked him to handle the purchase. Teddy contacted Roger Penske to agree on a price and then called Tyler Alexander to collect the car and arrange its shipment to Bruce. This new connection with motor racing probably helped Teddy to make up his mind that he wanted to go motor racing more than he wanted to be a tax lawyer, so he drafted up a proposal, offering his services to the small McLaren team in a management capacity. At the time, Bruce was confident that his own men could handle the program they had currently embarked upon and he wrote back suggesting that Teddy might work in America as a McLaren agent. "I replied that I didn't think that was a very suitable arrangement because I had to become completely involved full time in racing or go back to being a lawyer. Finally we decided that it would be a reasonable idea for me to join the team, and I wrote a synopsis of the team potential as I saw it. I felt there was a possibility of it making some money after about three years, but I wasn't particularly convinced that it would be an instant success and I certainly wasn't convinced that it was an excellent financial investment. I didn't see it as a large loss either—in other words, it was a purely speculative idea for both Bruce and myself. Bruce was hedging his bets by remaining with Cooper, and I was hedging mine by not making a large financial investment. Because I was only 26, I still had the potential of going back and being a lawyer."

The Mayer family is a wealthy one living in Scranton, Pennsylvania and one of Teddy's uncles, Will Scranton, had been Governor of the state. Teddy wasn't, as popular rumour had it at the time, one of the MGM Mayers. However, he had some financial leeway in his decisions on what to do with his career and just as he had concentrated his efforts on management of a person—his brother—now he applied those intensive efforts in the management of a project—Bruce McLaren Motor Racing Ltd.

Teddy was not an instant favorite, either with the team or with the people in the racing field who dealt with the team. His approach to racing was strict and direct; he didn't believe in the casual attitude adopted by most people racing in England at that time. If a visitor was in the workshop or in one of the offices passing the time of day and with no intention of either buying a car or making a deal that was attractive to McLaren Racing, Teddy would be very likely to pass strong hints that the person should go someplace else and waste someone else's time.

The old pals network in British racing meant very little to Teddy, but Bruce was aware of how long it had taken him to meet and become accepted by the barons in the racing trade and by all the technicians, and he cringed when Teddy would deliver a verbal caning over the telephone when a piece of equipment was late in delivery. Late deliveries were part of racing in England, but Teddy wasn't prepared to accept this languid approach. If it was a business, he reasoned, it had to be run on a businesslike basis and if company A couldn't deliver on time to our specifications, then we'd try company B. Often this worked, but often it didn't. Bruce had to work at defusing his explosive new partner, but at the same time he was taking note of Teddy's business methods. It was his application of those methods that worried Bruce.

"The points that Bruce taught me first had nothing whatever to do with racing. He had been on his own and in business as an operating human being outside the sphere of influence of family and schools and education longer than I had, and he taught me first of all how to manage myself with regard to other people; a certain amount of what it took to get along with the world of motor racing rather than how to go racing or anything about the technical aspect of it. From time to time there were clashes of personality between me and other members of the team, but Bruce almost never had a personality clash with any other member of the team, except me. Sometimes he should have, and in his last two years he began to learn how to chew people out and get angry. I'd be all for firing a guy if he'd done something wrong that I considered was really stupid. I think we learned from each other that sometimes you have to be a little tougher and sometimes you have to give way a little. You must remember that both of us were very young when we started. Some of the people we were working with in our own company were older than we were, and almost everyone we dealt with in business was considerably older, so it was very difficult and we had to learn lessons as we went along."

The thing that impressed Teddy was the sheer difficulty of going motor racing properly and overcoming all the problems. He told a simple analogy that Bruce enjoyed because it summed up the urgency of racing. "If you go down to your friendly Ford dealer and order a white Ford with black upholstery, he'll tell you it will be ready two weeks from Monday, but if he phones you on the Friday before and says sorry, but it won't be ready until Tuesday, you say, well, that's fine, really, no problem. And you go down on the Tuesday and pay the full price

A younger Mayer watches Bruce take Denis Jenkinson for a lap in M1A.

for your Ford. But if we arrive at the other end of the world an hour late—not a day late—for a race, no matter whether we've had problems with a dock strike or an uncooperative customs officer or whatever, we not only don't get paid the full price— we don't get paid at *all*. In other words, in racing there is *no* excuse.

"I was always impressed by the fact that Bruce never gave up. We got involved in the same amount of problems and scrambles everyone else does in racing, but he was willing to keep plugging away at it until it was over and done with, or we had accomplished the job one way or another. He taught me that you just don't give up. You keep trying various ways. Sometimes you have to swallow your pride and try ways you really feel you shouldn't, particularly in regard to the political aspect of racing."

Teddy was more than a smart-aleck Yank lawyer come over to revolutionize racing as he soon proved to the rest of the McLaren team, because he was more than willing to work just as hard as they were. If he did things wrong it was from ignorance, not from carelessness, and he figured ignorance was something lessons and experience would put right. Before he married Sally, he lived with Tyler and Wally and me and on occasions with Gary Knutson or Chris Amon, when we rented an enormous

153

house with an overgrown tennis court and an orchard standing well back from the road in Surbiton. We called it The Castle. Nobody was keen to share a room with Teddy because of his voracious appetite for reading, and his incredible habit of falling asleep in the middle of a sentence and spending the remainder of the night fast asleep with the light on. He was slightly older than the rest of us and took a rather more serious approach to life—plenty of which was going on all round him at The Castle.

At one party after a Guards Trophy sports car race at Brands Hatch, the invitations had been written in Old English, stressing the knights and faire ladies atmosphere of our castle. To heighten the effect (to the amazement of visitors like A.J. Foyt) we had borrowed a suit of armor dummied up in fiberglass, and a couple of very real swords. The highlight of the evening came when Jimmy Clark dressed himself in the armor, donning the lightweight helmet as well as the breastplate, and Graham Hill did an Errol Flynn, leaning out over the stair-rail and proceeding to smote the luckless Jimmy around the head, unaware that the sword was real and Jimmy's armor wasn't.

In case it should be misconstrued that Bruce had the racing ability and Teddy the cash in the company, it is worth pointing out that Bruce always retained a controlling interest in Bruce McLaren Motor Racing Limited, putting his own money in and also, in effect, providing his services as a driver free. "We considered Bruce's driving as a fee which would have been earned driving for anyone, and adding that to his contributions, it made our interests in the team quite equal."

Initial sponsorship came when McLaren Racing signed a contract with Firestone at the end of 1964 for the 1965 season. The contract covered an extensive testing program in addition to sports car racing. The American tire companies were just discovering that European racing was quite different to racing they had been used to at tracks like Indianapolis, and Indy rubber was certainly not competitive with tires fielded by Dunlop who had a monopoly in Grand Prix racing at the time Firestone and Goodyear made their appearance. The alliance suited Firestone because they wanted a way into racing that did not involve a big league team until a competitive tire had been evolved. They also wanted to start racing in a field where it didn't matter if they fared badly to begin with. Bruce's specialized knowledge and regular participation in the Tasman series was ideal, and when Bruce took a pair of Coopers south for himself and Phil Hill to drive in the Down-Under summer—January and February— of 1965, the cars were shod with Indy-type

Firestones.

Race results were something less than immediate or spectacular, but the elaborate series of tire testing with Firestone gave the McLaren team a head start in the technical rubber battle that was about to begin. "It gave us an insight into the problems of rim size, tire construction and compound at a time when Dunlop were pretty much telling teams they would run, say, 7-inch rims with their only tire available. You could perhaps raise pressures two pounds or drop them two, but that was your lot. The situation became more involved when you had a choice not only of shapes, sizes and compounds, but tire companies as well. For a while we had an advantage because we had some idea from the testing we had done what was involved in why tires worked as they did. This certainly was true in sports car racing, and it might have been true in Formula 1 although we had other problems there which prevented us from pressing any advantage we might have."

This was a difficult period for the team. It was difficult financially because there was the pressure of expansion and the need for extra capital to cover purchase of equipment, cars and engines, and the hiring of personnel. It was difficult because team successes to date had been modest, and difficult because all concerned were learning the business and feeling their way carefully in a highly competitive world where competitors were loathe to offer helpful hints.

During 1965 as the team was becoming established, and looking towards Formula 1 for 1966, Teddy gained four distinct impressions of Bruce—as a man, as a businessman, as a racing driver and as an engineer. "As a man I'd come to know him quite well, possibly better during this period than in the last two or three years of his life, because we were so busy later. And possibly also because with success you start to build a slightly different image both of yourself and your business.

"I had a lot of respect for Bruce as a man. He had a great deal of patience and he had an enormous amount of confidence. Perhaps the confidence was not always entirely well-founded, but it was unshakable and this was very useful during some of the difficult times we faced.

"As a businessman, Bruce seemed optimistic. I've always felt that if you have something to sell you may have to work hard to sell it, but it will ultimately be salable. At this period (1965-66) I didn't really think we had much to sell. It needed quite a lot of money to keep even what we had going. Bruce, on the other hand, didn't seem to have a very good idea of how much money it took to do the job, and he had a fairly optimistic theory of how much we were worth.

"Bruce as a driver during this period was difficult for me to assess. He was more than sufficiently capable to do the job required in our sports cars, but he was still driving for Cooper and it was difficult to know whether his lack of real success at the time was due to the problem with the cars at Coopers, or whether it was due to his driving talent, or his unwillingness to stick his neck out too far. I think Bruce would stick his neck out if he thought we had a real chance to win, but perhaps sticking your neck out is the wrong thing to say because some race drivers drive as hard as they can whether they're 1st or 3rd or 8th or 28th. Some race drivers drive very hard if they're 1st or 2nd and reasonably hard if they're 4th or 5th, and not hard at all if they're 10th or 12th. Bruce was one of these. He drove well, dammed hard, and, I think hung it out a bit if he thought there was a good chance to win. On the other hand if he was running 5th or 6th he would set a reasonable pace for himself which I sometimes felt was below his limit, and wait to see what would happen.

"By comparison Denny falls in the category of a man who will drive reasonably hard all the time, and very very hard if he thinks there is a chance to win. He will not drive very very hard all the time, as a Stewart or a Rindt or a Clark or a Moss might, but he will drive reasonably hard all the time. Bruce wouldn't do that. This is difficult to say because you never know for sure what is going through a driver's mind and there is no sensible way that a manager can force a driver to tell whether he is driving hard. I've heard that it has been done by the Italians and by Neubauer, but it's never been my position with Bruce or with Denny to tell them how hard to drive or to tell them when they're not driving hard enough. I would only have upset them by chipping in my advice. Bruce and Denny had plenty of experience and they knew the score, but this could change with younger drivers and with Peter Revson and Peter Gethin I've tried to apply a little driver psychology and talk them into going steady or giving an all-out effort as the conditions seemed to warrant.

"At the time Bruce knew so much more about the engineering of racing cars than I did that it was difficult to know how good an engineer he was. I got the impression that he had quite a lot of practical experience but he was still learning a good deal of theoretical knowledge, and his testing for Firestone and Ford with their Le Mans cars, plus his wide reading of all the engi-

Bruce and Teddy check Denny's car during practice for 1968 Laguna Seca.

neering journals he could get his hands on, were adding considerably to his knowledge."

As a team manager in both racing and business, Teddy had some reason for his concern about the financial position. It was not a question of making more money to salt away in the company's coffers; it was a matter of gathering finance to survive. Teddy felt it was probably financial considerations that prompted them to decide on the 4-cam Indianapolis Ford engine that spelled doom to their first Formula 1 season in 1966. "I have a nasty feeling that if I had not urged the Ford engine more on financial than engineering grounds, Bruce would very probably have found some other solution to our engine problem, and it certainly couldn't have been worse than the one we actually chose."

When commercialism arrived in motor racing the cries of disgust from the purists came from those angered at the thought that the teams were earning too much money. Probably the owners of small businesses in the process of expansion were better able to sympathize with the need for extra finance than were the voluble fans with no direct interest in the racing field.

Mayer feels most teams are in shaky financial positions most of the time if their only interests are in going racing, as opposed to teams backed by a line of production cars (Lotus, Ferrari) or

157

an engineering combine like BRM or Matra. "The major reasons are that you can have large losses through accidents, either through crashes or blow-ups, at any time and these losses are probably of greater magnitude relative to the financial resources of the company than most businesses would normally hazard. Secondly, I think the whole racing business is peculiarly vulnerable financially. By this I mean racing in itself. Participating in racing alone in no way supports a first class racing effort. There's just not enough starting money or prize money to begin to support a proper team; therefore you're dependent on sponsorship, and sponsorship is dependent on the financial climate of the time, and upon the success of the team involved. So if for any reason you're unsuccessful or the financial climate is not good, the sponsorship could dry up very quickly."

Working with Bruce in any sort of management capacity was like standing by with a brake ready to apply if he looked like shooting off at great speed in any direction in pursuit of a new project. Some drivers employ managers to blame when things go wrong, but Bruce was prepared to temper his enthusiasm in the light of other opinions that he respected. Or at least listened to. To eavesdrop on a discussion of future plans or a new car between Bruce, Teddy, Tyler and the designers or mechanics directly concerned, was like overhearing a family fight as the guidelines were established. Bruce would make a point and if it was thought to be without basis or foundation it would be argued down by Teddy or Tyler and then Bruce would put the point another way. What sounded like fierce arguments interspersed with hoots of laughter, always ended with concrete and forward thinking plans and schedules being made. This "family" description occurs frequently, in marked contrast to other teams where one man's word is law.

"Bruce rarely, certainly more rarely than the converse was true, tried to impose his thought processes on me. Generally speaking, our votes were equal and we would thrash it out and come to a decision that we both thought was pretty sensible but at no time did he throw his weight around with me. The one guy in the outfit neither of us really managed to convince if he didn't want to be convinced was Tyler. If he believed he was right and you were wrong, he'd let you know until it was all over, and possibly for several years thereafter."

Phil Kerr joined the company after leaving Jack Brabham where he had helped to build up a small empire in the eight years he had been there, and became joint managing director with Teddy. Prior to Bruce's death Phil handled most of the administrative work. He would be in on policy decisions but generally speaking he never cast a vote. As Teddy says, "By the time Bruce and I had thrashed it out none of us really cast votes because it had become obvious what to do. After Bruce's accident Phil's role has changed somewhat in that on policy we now work fairly equally. We decide on how we're going to proceed on the basis of his and my information and thoughts, as opposed to Bruce's and mine.

"I butted into the technical procedure sometimes more than Bruce really liked because I was interested in it and because I felt that I would be able to do a better job with the operational procedure if I knew what was happening technically. Usually I would set out the procedure as to how we would accomplish what we wanted to do, then Bruce and I would discuss it, and in many cases I would set out both the technical and operational procedure. This wasn't because I was qualified to do so, but I liked setting out procedures, and Bruce was often busy on other jobs and didn't particularly like the job of putting things down on paper. Although he generally left operational procedures largely to me, he would correct my technical procedures a great deal and then he would proceed with the technical side and I would execute the operational procedure. It worked out very well. My role has changed somewhat since Bruce's death in that I've had to do his job in setting out the technical procedure purely because it has to be done by someone. Tyler is learning to do a good job in this area, but much of the time he is away with the Formula 1 or Can-Am teams. Now I go into the design office as Bruce used to do and say we'll run 12-inch discs and a wing on the top and radiator out the back because someone has

In back of truck at right, Teddy watches Denny's stop in 1968 Times GP.

to say, 'That's what we've got to do.' The designers will do a better job than any of us—Bruce or I certainly—could have done, but they want help in saying 'That's it.' "

Teddy carries his air of clinical business correctness to the track with specially printed McLaren Racing timing charts to record not only every lap time but every driver comment during pit stops, and every alteration made to the car. He carries his watches, his yellow foolscap legal pads, and his charts and gold Cross pens to the pits in an expensive tan leather briefcase with a combination lock. An interesting tale surrounds the first time Teddy set the combination on his new briefcase and promptly forgot it!

During long test days at Goodwood, sorting out new cars or refining current machinery, Teddy learned a lot about what is required from a driver in evaluating racing cars. He classes Bruce and Denny in different categories, both achieving results, but these results being gained by different means.

"I've given a good deal of thought to Bruce's ability as a car-sorter and development driver. This was tremendously important to the company, and intellectually it was of tremendous interest to me. Bruce worked very hard at being a development driver but I don't think that he was always entirely unbiased if he had a pet theory he wanted to prove. He was generally better at telling you *how* to fix a problem than he was at deciphering whether or not the problem had been fixed. For example, if you put a different rear tire on and sent Bruce out, he might do 50 laps and come in to say he thought it was better or thought it was worse. If you put the same tire on Denny's car he could come in after 10 laps and say the tire was either better or it was worse and he would eventually be proved right. Ultimately Bruce would end up where Denny had ended up, but Denny would never have any idea *why*, whereas Bruce would have a good idea of what was causing the problem, or what the characteristics were. Denny would just know that it was better or worse.

"Really, if you're going to a race track to race rather than test, Denny is a better sorter than Bruce was. Denny will arrive at a reasonably quick solution to the car faster than Bruce, but if you were going testing with a car that was miles out of the ballpark, Bruce would tell you what was wrong with it and how to fix it. Denny would only know that it was wrong. So obviously for the original sorting-out of the car Denny was not as valuable as Bruce.

"If you tried one thing at a time with Denny—as with most

Teddy Mayer and Carroll Smith in the pits during the Ontario USAC race.

drivers—you would eventually arrive at a solution, but with Bruce you could get there a lot faster because he could sort problems caused by aerodynamics from problems caused by spring rates from problems caused by tire size, better than Denny. It's very easy for a driver to be misled here. It's an enormously complicated problem with endless permutations and Bruce was misled any number of times, but he was very good at sorting out the problems and I think he arrived at reasonable solutions very often."

It took probably a year for the McLaren-Mayer combination to start operating efficiently, and it became obvious that even if Teddy's business methods were a little too super-efficient for England, they were very well suited to negotiations with American companies where the team looked for support and sponsorship. Their main field was sports car racing in the United States so it seemed logical to look to the relatively untapped sponsorship market in the U.S. rather than trying to plead a case with the traditional sponsors in England who were already well committed and not as interested in American racing anyway. From this logic came the Firestone contract (and later the Goodyear contract), a deal with Ford in Detroit to build the GTX which was a special open version of the GT-40 built at McLaren Racing in Feltham, and major sponsorship by Gulf Oil Corporation in Pittsburgh and Reynolds Aluminum in Richmond.

Bruce was a very important figure in these contractual discussions—while Teddy talked dollars and cents, Bruce was quite

161

frankly charming the company principals. But it wasn't a case of turning this charm on. It was there all the time. At almost any hour of the day or night the friendly McLaren grin could prompt mechanics to keep working, or just as easily impress a vice president with the man's obvious sincerity and the fact that the charm wasn't false.

"Bruce had a particularly fortunate personality and people liked him immediately. He was adept socially and he made a very good impression on everyone. As a racing driver and therefore in a sense the romantic hero of the team as well as the name which the company sported, Bruce was extremely important in negotiations for sponsorship. Everyone wants to know the principal in the act, and if the act is motor racing then the drivers have the star roles. Businessmen and engineers and mechanics may be very important and the sponsors may want to know who they are and what kind of people they are, but I think they get a bigger kick out of knowing and meeting and talking to the star. Bruce's personality was excellent in this regard and he did an extremely good job just by being himself."

Teddy believed in getting everything down on paper professionally and it wasn't unusual after protracted meetings and then a long dinner for Bruce to go to bed and for Teddy to tap away on his little traveling Olivetti using the hunt-and-peck method of typing until he had prepared a complete proposal based on the day's talks. This efficiency could not fail to impress.

As a company director, Teddy was an office tyrant, demanding that desks be spotless and uncluttered by surplus books, papers or pens. He would stomp off muttering about untidy desks and untidy minds. Because he has a very nasal way of speaking it has not always been easy for people to understand Teddy when first meeting him, and he would rage at telephone operators who were doing their best. If an operator lasted a week in the downstairs switchboard/reception office, she could reckon herself hired. Secretaries had to type faultless letters because Teddy insisted that clean, accurate well-typed letters were good advertisements for the team. The same went for efficient operating of the telephone switchboard. He carried the same necessity for neatness out onto the workshop floor, often grabbing a broom if he couldn't see the cleaner, and sweeping away the offending litter himself.

Teddy's willingness to do the work himself finally won him grudging favor with the mechanics, who were impressed that "the little grey-haired guy" would be in all day Sunday helping to crate up spares for shipment, and still be there working on schedules in his office when they were going home. In this respect he was like Bruce; both Sally and Patty counted themselves lucky if their men were home for dinner before 8 o'clock most nights. Sunday was just another day at the shop if there was a project nearing completion or a freight flight to catch.

Most Americans, as Teddy often observes, like living in America and this was one of the reasons why McLaren Engines Inc. was set up in Detroit so that they could hire and keep the top American engine men, who were often keen to get home after a few weeks in England. After some vague grumbling about Englishmen who use their baths to keep coal in, and the difficulty of finding a house with a shower or a large U.S.-style refrigerator, Teddy settled down to the English way of living. He and Sally and their children Timmy and Anne live in a large country house in the "stockbroker belt" just outside Esher in Surrey, about a half an hour by 250 SE Mercedes or MGB GT to the McLaren shop at Colnbrook. It takes the same time to get to London's Heathrow airport which is important because Teddy spends much of his time in trans-Atlantic commuting or flying to races in Europe.

8

DENIS HULME,
CAN-AM CHAMPION

THE LITTLE DROPS coursing down the side of the windscreen on the Indianapolis McLaren were whipped by the 200-mph airstream as Denny Hulme rocketed up to the braking area for Turn 3. He noticed the tiny rivulets and remembered them as the condensation he had seen streaming across the windows of a big jet airliner as it came in to land. It never occurred to him in that split second that the drops were methanol fuel leaking from a breather cap that had popped open.

When he got on the brakes, the fuel gushed forward from the open breather just ahead of the cockpit and the wind fanned the spray back over the car onto the red-hot turbocharger behind the Offenhauser engine. The car ignited in a shimmering blast of heat. Denny Hulme had only seconds to escape and the car was still traveling at 180 mph—every second the car was covering 264 feet. He knew there was fuel on the rear tires and as he braked hard he was prepared for a spin. But the harder he braked the more fuel surged out of the breather to fan the raging but invisible flames. He feared an explosion, but he was going too fast to jump.

The car was slowing as he braked desperately but his hands were already burning. The leather of his gloves had shrunk, turning his fingers into painful claws as he battled with the buckle of his seat harness. The fire extinguisher had gone off but it couldn't cope with the blaze at that speed; it registered as a brief discoloration of the air and it was gone—wasted. The blast-furnace head had welded the clear vizor of his Bell Star helmet. His flame proof overalls were starting to char. With the pain of his hands more than he could bear he wriggled out from under the specially-flattened leather-rim steering wheel and tried to stand in the seat. The speed was down to about 70 mph and it seemed like a crawl. He turned backward in the seat and pushed himself out over the rear wheel with his forearm against the roll hoop. His burning hands were useless. He hit the road backward and bounced, amazingly without breaking any bones. As he picked himself up he still had the strength to curse the fire crew on the truck chasing the runaway burning car. They hadn't realized that the driver was also on fire.

Denis Clive Hulme is a strong brave man. His father Clive had bred this family courage; for his heroism in World War 2 he had been awarded the Victoria Cross, the highest award for bravery in the British Army, Navy or Air Force.

Sitting up in the hospital in Indianapolis, the pain coming and going with the effect of the drugs and his hands, feet and left forearm caked in tacky white dressing like icing, Denny was still able to chat and laugh when Bruce and others in the team called to see him each day. The burns were extremely serious and there was the unspoken chance that he would lose some fingers on his left hand. Bruce was terribly concerned at the condition of his friend and teammate, their closeness showing through as clearly in times of trouble as it had when they had fun traveling together between races. The close relationship between Denny and Bruce grew from mutual respect of the other's ability—Bruce as the engineer and Denny as the driver.

Denny withstood the pain of his burns without a tear, but when Bruce was killed at Goodwood three weeks later, he broke down in his grief.

New Zealand is a country some 1200 miles east of Australia in the South Pacific, with an area of 103,000 square miles and a population of under three million. This comparative isolation from the world breeds parochialism and fierce independent qualities which, when added to an inborn desire to succeed, has resulted in single-minded successful men like Bruce McLaren and Denny Hulme. You could compare the country in area with England, in size of population with Paris. At home New Zealanders tend to be complacent, an attitude encouraged by their geographical remoteness from world troubles. To make their

Denny Hulme in his Cooper-Climax in New Zealand in 1960.

way in the outside world New Zealanders trade this complacency for a compensatory aggressiveness that appears in different forms. With Bruce McLaren it was a restless urge to do things better, to develop better racing cars, to rage at indecision. With Denny Hulme it is an almost animal strength, a dogged desire to win, and an unwillingness to suffer crowds, boring company, or questioning pressmen.

This thumbnail sketch of Hulme as a man with the physique and mentality of an ox does not come close to a true portrait. Behind the craggy facade the reason is probably a basic shyness which is strenuously disguised. The year he won the World Championship on the Grand Prix tracks, the thing that bothered him most about the glory was the round of speeches and public functions he had to attend. That was in 1967. Today Denny copes a little better with all the aspects of being a professional racing driver, helped probably by the fact that in 1968 he started driving full-time for the McLaren team and some of the McLaren charm rubbed off. Not a lot, but some.

Some racing drivers are born; others are made. Denis Hulme was hewn. He was born on June 18th, 1936 on a small dairy farm in the tobacco growing area of Motueka at the top of the South Island. His father was invalided out of the army after action in Greece and Crete in 1941 and came back to New

Denny, right, with the "big boys," Brabham, Cooper and McLaren, 1961.

Zealand to buy a small trucking business in the tiny village of Pongakawa, only a mile from the sea and the Bay of Plenty beaches and a few miles from Te Puke, a slightly larger township with a population of 2500. So there was no reason for Denny to be any other way than the way he is. He grew up in bare feet, sunshine and sea and spent any spare moments in his father's trucking workshops. After a couple of years in secondary school, Denny went to work for his father. Clive Hulme tells the story of noticing a strange smell in the workshop and drawing Denny out from under his welding goggles to ask him what it was. It turned out that Denny had stepped on a glowing welding spark that was burning into the sole of his bare foot and he hadn't noticed it!

He was 19 and had earned some extra cash by driving new cars down from Auckland to Tauranga for the local Morris dealer when he experienced his first sports car. It was a brand new

1500-cc MG TF and even at breaking-in speeds, Denny was entranced. From then on the beach took second place to cars. He was working so hard, driving one of the trucks and looking after servicing as well, that his father decided to give his son a surprise and bought him a new MG TF. Denny was probably more taken with the idea of top-down motoring than any thoughts of racing, but he was soon lured into the local car club. In those days anyone with a car that remotely resembled a sporting vehicle was badgered into competing. At his first hill-climb he knocked six seconds off the class record. The bug had bitten him, and in 1958 he moved up to an MGA. Early the next year the local papers carried reports that the young Auck-lander Bruce McLaren was going to Europe to race Coopers during the 1958 season, but this meant little to Denny, other than the fact that he had seen Bruce and talked with his father on a rally where Denis was driving his MG TF and the McLarens were in their Ford Pilot V-8.

His reputation as a production sports car driver grew and he saw no reason why he shouldn't try a single-seater. By now he knew about Bruce McLaren and the other "real" racing people and after the Grand Prix at Ardmore in 1959 he bought a 2-liter Cooper-Climax. Denny's habit of driving in bare feet probably stemmed from the balmy club days when they lay about wear-ing only shorts and as often as not drove just like that when it came to their turn. With the Cooper he earned his "Driver to Europe" award and in 1960 he and George Lawton (who had equalled the Hulme form in a 2-liter Cooper) were bound for England with their manager/mechanic Feo Stanton. Feo met Denny when they were both driving Clive Hulme's gravel trucks.

It was a season of mixed fortunes and tragedy when George was killed on the Roskilde track in Denmark. Denny had raced Formula 2 and Formula Junior Coopers, and had one drive in a non-championship Formula 1 race at Snetterton in a 2.5-liter Cooper. He won at Salerno and Pescara in the Formula Junior car, but these victories were small potatoes to the New Zealand public, who were reading about Bruce McLaren winning Grand Prix races and finishing 2nd to Brabham in the World Cham-pionship.

The first meeting between McLaren and Hulme had come about after the 1960 Grand Prix at Ardmore when Bruce had congratulated the winners of the "Driver to Europe" awards. Denny took Bruce at his word and called on him as soon as he arrived in England and Bruce loaned him his Morris Minor while he shopped for a car of his own. From time to time Bruce **169**

Like Bruce, Denny was a pupil of Jack Brabham in early European career.

would check on the Hulme progress among the jigs and trestles and chassis frames in the dim Cooper workshops. Denny was competing very much in the lower ranks of racing then but looking back he is able to assess Bruce's early ability in Formula 1 racing.

"I thought he was very good, although in a funny way you could compare him with Fittipaldi stepping into the Lotus 72. A very good car and a guy coming up with some good races behind him and winning a Grand Prix very early on. Jochen Rindt didn't do this. Chris Amon certainly hasn't, and there are others who have really had to thrash along before they finally succeeded. So maybe he was a little lucky. Without a doubt he was stepping into the best car around at the time. It was reliable and quick and he had Jack Brabham to guide him. He only came over in 1958 and yet he was second in the World Championship in 1960. That was pretty good."

At the end of the 1960 season, Denny made a deal with Reg Parnell for a 2.5-liter Cooper to use in the races in New Zealand during January 1961 and with this car he went home and won the National Gold Star as McLaren had done after his first season abroad.

It was Denny's inability to cope with the prevailing necessity

The first big Can-Am victory, at Elkhart Lake in the M6A in 1967.

for talking to the right people—the "old boy" syndrome—that probably kept him out of a Formula 1 drive in 1961. Denny reasoned that driving prowess should get you to the top, but he was ignoring the fact that diplomacy was usually necessary to get the opportunity to display the prowess in the first place.

Motor racing is fickle. You need someone to pay the piper, and if you don't keep dancing while the music plays, you're out of business. Denny had a foot in the door with his scholarship award and the publicity that went with it in 1960, but in 1961 on his own it was a different matter. It was uphill all the way.

He bought a Formula Junior Cooper but with a misguided sense of economy he installed a Martin-tuned Ford engine. It was cheaper than other power units that year but it was also less powerful and less reliable. With a tired Mark 1 Ford Zodiac as a tow car he hauled the Cooper around the crowded calendar of European races from Karlskoga in Sweden to Messina in Sicily.

I traveled with him that summer as someone for him to talk to, rather than as someone who helped with the racing car. Looking back ten years at the early career of one of racing's top money earners is enlightening and just a little exhausting.

Denny built the Cooper at the factory and his first continental race was the Danish Roskildering. He was traveling with the **171**

But he won! Denny finished the 1967 Mosport Can-Am with burning tire.

1961 "Driver to Europe," Angus Hyslop, who was racing a Lotus 20. Angus won the race and Denny was an also-ran with a fire in the Cooper's undertray. At Rouen in France both cars retired, and a week later the two Kiwis drove a Fiat Abarth 850 in the Le Mans 24-hour race. We stayed at a small hotel in the country outside Le Mans while Denny did an engine rebuild on the footpath outside, throwing a cover over the car and coming in for a beer when it rained. The Abarth ran without a clutch to win its class and place 14th overall. From Le Mans we headed south to Caserta in the middle of Italy where Denny started on the pole but dropped back with a bent gear selector. From there we went up to the Monza track in the royal park outside Milan a fortnight later, checked in at the hotel, unloaded the race car at the track—and discovered that the Hulme entry hasn't been received. Denny made some terse comments, trying to remember if in fact he had sent it in, and the upshot was an all-night drive over the Swiss Alps to Reims where a race was being held the same weekend. He finished 6th and then headed back to England to overhaul the Cooper.

If Formula Junior racing qualified as a circus, the Hulme entourage certainly smacked of a gypsy caravan. The Zodiac was as purchased with a vase of plastic flowers that had never been tossed away for some reason, a defunct tachometer, a row of extra instruments that all read either zero or 212, and a siren which had the miraculous effect of clearing traffic in European villages. (This siren almost resulted in the Hulme equipe being reduced to ashes in France when the overloaded electrical system went up in smoke. Denny, resourceful as ever, stopped the blaze by pulling out the fuses, which were made from half a screwdriver and a drill bit!) The rear seats were removed and the back of the car and the trunk were crammed with spare parts and gasoline cans. Standard practice after each event was to fill the racing car as well as the six spare five-gallon cans, and this was usually enough to keep the Zodiac fueled as far as the next track. Denny's headquarters in England was the Lamb Inn at Kingston in Surrey.

The next race was at Messina in Sicily and we set off in convoy with the Hyslop team on a Tuesday morning. A hundred and twelve hours and 1800 miles later we were crossing on the ferry from the toe of Italy's boot to Sicily. Angus won the race and Denny came in 2nd. "We couldn't have planned it better with a shotgun," said Hyslop's mechanic, Bill Hannah.

That winter Denis stayed in England and worked in one of the Jack Brabham garages, planning to update his Cooper and race it again in 1962. It was a dismal year for him, making 1961 look like a good time. Brabham's manager Phil Kerr could see the potential in Denny if he was given a chance, but Jack was not at all convinced. It took an accident which broke the collarbone of the regular Brabham Formula Junior driver to get Denny into a factory Formula Junior car for the first time at the end of the 1962 season and he proved his point. In 1963 he drove a works Brabham and in 14 starts he brought home seven wins and four 2nd places.

For 1964 he had a works Formula 2 Brabham, and the next

Driving short-nosed M7A Formula 1 car to 2nd place at Jarama in 1968.

year he was given occasional Formula 1 drives. In 1966 he was Jack's partner in the Grand Prix team. At Le Mans, co-driving a Ford GT-40 with Ken Miles, he finished 2nd to the McLaren/Amon Ford in the fouled-up photo finish.

Jack won the World Championship in 1966 and Denny won it in 1967. He was also "Rookie of the Year" when he finished 4th at Indianapolis in an Eagle, and driving an M6A McLaren sports car he won three of the six races on the 1967 Can-Am trail, finished 2nd to Bruce in the championship and won $40,000.

There were more than 40,000 reasons why he decided to leave Jack and join the McLaren team for 1968. Denny acknowledged the fact that the Brabham team had given him his chance to make a name in racing, but Jack was well aware that Denny had outgrown his Number 2 slot, and there wasn't really room for another driver who wanted to win—especially if it involved beating the boss to do it!

With the McLaren team Denny settled down quickly to an established routine. Bruce was the engineer and sorter-out and very quick in Can-Am cars. Denny was quick in the Can-Ams but it was recognized that he was faster than Bruce in Formula 1 races.

"Bruce was quicker than me in Can-Am and I sort of knew that he was going to be quicker. He would set his car up the way he wanted it and he was very smooth. He liked Can-Am racing. It was his one big thing and it made the world of difference. He was the hardest guy to beat in a Can-Am car and yet

Running without wings, Hulme had convincing victory in 1968 Italian GP.

he could put the same amount of effort into a Grand Prix car and get nothing like the same results. I think one of the reasons for this was that he was so smooth. If you throw a Can-Am car around you lose time, whereas the only way to get a Grand Prix car to go quick is to start hurling it around and really get it set up for fast corners. I don't think Bruce liked doing this somehow."

Other differences came in their acceptance of people. "Bruce used to like going out and meeting people. He managed to cope even when they were asking the most ridiculous questions, whereas my natural reaction was to think 'What a bunch of idiots we've got here,' and either tell them so or not talk to them at all. But that's just the way I am. Bruce could spend the whole night entertaining people and this is how he made lots of friends. He was the same with the Press. He always had time to talk with them. I've never been able to do this. For certain people in the Press, yes, but for most of them, no. There's probably only half a dozen I can sit and talk to, but the rest of them—I feel they should do their homework more and find out what it's all about. Bruce always coped with them better."

Bruce said that Denny was one of the talent-spotter Ken Tyrrell's rare mistakes. Ken never reckoned that Denny would make the grade, but Bruce also acknowledged Ken's covering maxim that a good "hungry" driver would always beat a good "fat" one. For someone who looked like missing the boat, Hulme hasn't done badly. Since he started Formula 1 racing seriously as a regular works driver in 1966, Denny has been 4th,

A furious Hulme storms out of pits after 1968 Riverside Can-Am mishap.

Winning Stardust GP in Las Vegas gave Denny the 1968 Can-Am title.

1st, 3rd, 6th, and 4th in the World Championship, and has won five Grands Prix.

In the hospital Denny had been telling everyone that he would be driving the Can-Am car at Mosport in mid-June, less than a month away. "The doctors just sort of laughed about it. I think they thought I was being a bit optimistic."

A week before the race he couldn't bend either of his hands, but with typical Hulme homespun therapy he was wandering about the McLaren workshops with a steering wheel, forcing his fingers to close around the rim. He finished 3rd in that first Can-Am race with hands raw under the bandages where blisters had burst. But to Denny that race was a gesture. He had first set his heart on Mosport to bolster his own spirits during the painful days in the hospital, but eventually he was aiming at Mosport with grim determination to "do it for Bruce." In several of his early races he had to bend the fingers on his left hand around the steering wheel and lock them there for the race, doing all the work with his right hand.

The left hand, shiny with scar tissue, still lags behind the recovery of the right hand and he favors it handling a fork or when dressing. At one stage he had to be careful even reading a newspaper because the sharp edge of the page could slice his tender hands.

Once racing drivers had to concentrate on keeping fit, but now Denny seldom has time. Apart from the occasional swim in the motel pool after a race, Denny says the workout involved in driving the cars and getting from race to race keeps him in trim. "It's difficult to say how fit you've got to be. You don't have to run a four-minute mile—it's more important to be able to pace yourself, to know your own capacity and to make it last the race. If you're strong from the waist upwards, especially the shoulders, arms and neck muscles, you're able to concentrate better. This stands out at the beginning of each season. For the Can-Am at Riverside at the end of October my neck never gets tired going round the loop at the end of the straight, but when we went there for Goodyear tire testing in January, I found that my neck was getting really sore after the layoff. It's the same at Indy. After a day's practice my head starts to ache with the strain; the next day it aches a little but not as much, and the next day it's better again. You must remember that a crash helmet like the Bell Star I wear weighs just over three pounds, and this is subjected to all the g-loadings during braking, acceler-

Denny and Bruce get relief from hot cockpits in swimming pool.

Hefting victory garland looks harder for Denny than winning races.

ation and cornering.

"The other thing I find tiring at the beginning of a season is trans-Atlantic jet travel, but here again you soon get used to it and it doesn't bother you. The more you do it, the better you become adjusted. One thing I try and do on these long flights is to eat only when I ought to be eating—every four or five hours—and not every time they put a meal down in front of me. This way I can help to regulate myself and not get caught by the time change which is the real problem. You gain five hours on the flight between London and New York, and across to Los Angeles it's nearly double that. Fortunately I can sleep on a plane."

In 1968 Denny flew back and forth between Indianapolis and Monaco like a Boeing 707 shuttlecock. He left Indianapolis on the Wednesday to qualify for the Monaco Grand Prix on Thursday afternoon and Friday morning. He arrived back in Indianapolis on Friday night, qualified his Eagle on Saturday afternoon and at 4:30 p.m. he was in a helicopter heading for the airport where a Lear jet was waiting to fly him to New York. A Boeing 707 to Milan was met at 8:15 a.m. Sunday morning by European Cessna agent Bob Williams, with a Cessna

411S for the hop to Nice, and he was sitting down for breakfast with the slightly incredulous McLaren crew at 10 o'clock on the morning of the race. He finished 5th in the Grand Prix after changing a broken driveshaft during the race, and the next morning he was heading back to Indianapolis again where he finished 4th in Eagle.

"Trips like that do get to you," Denny admits. "It's hard to say how much but you're not as alert as you should be, because all those time changes lumped together do affect you."

There are two sides to Denis Hulme. One is the side which the racing fraternity sees—the ragged grin and the wave, the thinning hair and the determination. But at home, he mellows to a slippered family man and father, with his feet up watching television or worrying about progress on the modern new home that is being built to his specifications at St. George's Hill in the heart of Surrey's stockbroker belt. At airports, Denny is inclined to buy or browse through magazines on houses and home-making, rather than the horsepower press for the racing buffs. His father talks of Denny's prowess in the family flower garden in New Zealand, but at first glance Denny gives no hint of a latent green thumb. The apartment in Surbiton that he bought when he and Greeta were married in 1963 had no flower garden, but when Denny got to work one winter it had central heating. From yards of copper piping Denis had equipped the apartment with a system that would have done credit to a qualified tradesman. Young Martin Hulme, just starting school, is an experienced racegoer.

I suppose you have to call Denis Hulme an introvert if you must put a label on him; he is nobody's idea of a swinging extrovert, hellraising racing driver. The modern successful driver is a quiet-living professional, with few exceptions. Denny drives a 3-liter Ford Zodiac Executive and doesn't aspire to anything more sporty. Transport in comfort is what he requires. He gets his speed kicks on the race tracks. He remembers Bruce, like

Only 1969 GP success for McLaren team was Denny's Mexico City win.

When he isn't in the cockpit, Denny is super-casual, as above at Monaco. Below, he talks with Linda Vaughn after being burned at Indianapolis.

Brabham, as a slightly absent-minded driver on the road. "He'd chat away going slowly for mile after mile and then suddenly he'd spurt off in a burst of enthusiasm."

I always had the impression riding with Bruce in his Mercedes that he felt he was driving down a one-way street and there would never be any cars coming the other way. His mind was invariably on other things. Denny agrees. "That's right. He'd be chattering on about his theories on the latest projects that had caught his attention, and suddenly he'd jam on the brakes and say, 'You drive. I'm going to sleep.' And he'd climb

180

Oliver gave Hulme close battles at Laguna Seca and Riverside in 1970.

over into the back seat and that'd be the last you'd hear from him!"

To Denny, accidents were generally things that happened to other people until the New Zealand Grand Prix in 1968 when his Formula 2 Brabham somersaulted after tangling with a slower car. Denny emerged battered and bruised with nothing broken except the car. The fire at Indianapolis put another crack in the cocoon of confidence that most drivers race in. If they didn't have this confidence, they couldn't race. Denny says he doesn't take risks that can be avoided. He doesn't go out to practice in the rain unless it's absolutely necessary. He likes to make a personal check on the strength of the parts that go into the suspension of his car.

For most drivers it almost comes down to a belief in their own white-knight invincibility. "It's strange. If you have a crash and walk away from it you're inclined to joke about it afterwards, and it doesn't really seem to sink in that you could have been killed. Bruce was testing the M8B Can-Am car a year before his fatal crash at Goodwood, and he went off on the opposite side of the road. The tub was destroyed. A big rock went under the car and did a lot of damage. He was annoyed at the setback to the test program while the car was rebuilt, but he never thought anything about the fact that he'd hopped out of the wreck without getting hurt. And yet he could easily have gone off on the other side of the road where the marshal's post was, a year earlier...."

Tyler briefs Peter Revson as he takes Denny's place in Indy car.

9

TYLER ALEXANDER & THE MECHANICS

RACING MECHANICS, whether they admit it or not, are a special breed of people. They have to be. The hours involved are as long as it takes to get the job done, and social life has to be put to one side. Dedication to the job in hand is everything. The glitter soon wears off the foreign travel if the only touring you do is driving between the hotel and the track—and then that's usually after dark. It is a special job requiring special people to do it.

Bruce McLaren started his racing team off with his own personal mechanic, Wally Willmott, a New Zealander who came to England in 1962, having served a standard five-year apprenticeship as an auto electrician in Timaru and having raced his own Ford-engined special and a Cooper-Norton 500. Wally was groomed as Bruce's personal mechanic and they established a considerable rapport between them which showed clearly in the impeccable standard of the small McLaren operation that visited the Tasman series with special Coopers. Bruce always maintained that the closest cooperation with key staff was important to a close-knit competitive racing team. When Tyler Alexander joined the embryo McLaren racing team following the death of "his" driver Timmy Mayer in one of the McLaren team Coopers during practice for the 1964 Longford race in Tasmania, Bruce made the American and the New Zealander an equal pair in his growing team.

The problem with forming close relationships in any form of business, as Bruce was to find out, is that the other party often does not place similar importance on the association. It may be important to the job at hand, but it doesn't always seem imperative to maintain the close liaison. To Bruce, it was always imperative if the job was to be done successfully. And this was why he took it as a personal blow when Wally Willmott left the team to get married and live in Australia in 1968, and when designer Robin Herd left to work with Cosworth on the 4-wheel-drive Formula 1 car in 1968 and eventually to design his own Formula 1 car, the March.

The intercommunication of ideas between Bruce and Tyler was probably the most lasting liaison in the team and Tyler was elevated to chief mechanic, engineer in charge of the racing operations in all fields the team entered, and finally a director of the company.

McLaren Racing is the only team which currently competes in Grand Prix, Can-Am and Indianapolis-type racing but from a mechanic's viewpoint, Grand Prix training is the best background. Tyler explains, "We've got a better team in Can-Am racing because a lot of the people that work on our Can-Am cars used to work on the Formula 1 cars. The thing about Grand Prix racing that makes you a better mechanic is that it is so intensely competitive. You can't slow at all. You've got to try to be smarter. You've got to keep thinking about it. It's very hard work but it's so competitive that you develop a very competitive spirit about the whole thing and with this competitive spirit you develop a very competitive attitude. If you miss by a second because someone's forgotten something, you don't make the race, but in Can-Am you can miss by ten seconds and still get in the race.

"It's difficult to explain . . . if you're good you're good. If you're not very good or you're not as good as the other people in the team it shows up, and there are always a lot of people who are willing to work harder and take your place.

"Formula 1 cars are easier to work on than Can-Am cars, but in Formula 1 you have to work much harder and faster. Taking it as a vehicle, a Can-Am sports car is more work and we probably do more on the Can-Am cars between races than we do on Formula 1, but with Formula 1 the competition is so keen and so competitive that you've got to do things quickly and be sharp. Really on the ball. You can't mess around trying to make up your mind what to do when something goes wrong on the morning of a Grand Prix. You've got to say, 'Do you think that's going to be better? Well, try it. Quick. Now!' Because when you operate like that it could mean half a second somewhere in the race.

"If you're a good Formula 1 mechanic, you're pretty good at almost anything, but Indianapolis is a completely different deal. It's another kind of motor racing and patience is something you need there more than at any other race. The best thing about Formula 1 is that you can get on with it, but at Indy everything is such a long drawn-out process. Some of their rules are justified because Indy is a very dangerous place. You go very, very fast in a confined area, much more so than on any Grand Prix or Can-Am road circuit. The difficult thing for a mechanic is that in any other form of racing if you have a problem in practice you drag out your toolbox and get after it, but at Indianapolis you have to pack everything up on the pit front and drag the car away to the garage area and do a 15-minute job in two hours. At a Formula 1 race there's no way you could take that long because you just wouldn't make the race."

Like racing drivers, some of the better mechanics seem born to it. They have the special blend of tolerance and talents that are required to keep them on the job and on the rails working under tension and strain for much of the time. But good racing mechanics can also be made with proper training. Care, thoroughness and dedication are the main requirements. Tyler Alexander studied aircraft engineering when he left school and this instilled thoroughness into him as well as teaching the technical skills of welding, fabricating sheet metal, and the practical side of engineering as applied to building airplanes. Inadvertently it was the ideal background for a modern racing mechanic in an era when design in racing became closely linked with airplane principles.

"If someone were to ask me what was the best training for a racing mechanic I'd tell them to go to an aircraft engineering school. You learn to be a lot more careful and precise because when one of those things quits in the air you don't just get out and fix it. You have to make sure that it doesn't quit. After a while you develop the attitude that it's not so much knowing what's wrong when it goes wrong (although it does help!) as doing it right in the first place so that it doesn't go wrong."

This sort of training is probably better for a racing mechanic than the more usual garage apprenticeship, Tyler points out. "Alastair Caldwell, our chief Formula 1 mechanic, possibly knows more about cars as cars than I do because he was an apprentice in a big garage in New Zealand and when a Jaguar comes in making a weird noise he knows that it's got a busted framstat. I wouldn't have a goddam clue what was wrong with it because I've never had anything to do with standard road cars. It's either a racing car, or I'd just as soon not bother."

The Alexander career as a racing engineer just grew, without a great deal of apparent patterned planning. When he completed his pressure-cooker two-year course at the aircraft engineering school he "just sort of bummed around." He wasn't particularly interested in a nine-to-five job and the excitement of motor racing offered more interest to the 21-year-old. The guys he hung around with in his hometown (Hingham, Massachusetts) were all interested in flying and they were also racing specials that they had built themselves. One of the part-time driver/flyers, John Fields, decided to get more serious at the racing game and bought a 500-cc Cooper-Norton and with Tyler looking after the little single-cylinder Formula 3 car during the 1961 season they ran 17 races with 15 wins in the national championship. The Mayer brothers were running a Formula Junior Cooper with Timmy driving and Teddy looking after the team management and quite often Fields and Mayer were running in the same race, but in different classes. Tyler didn't have anything to do at the end of the season so he took the Mayers' Cooper down to Nassau where Roger Penske drove it because Timmy was serving his stint in the army. "I wasn't really working for Teddy as a mechanic, but I ended up taking the car to several races and started working for Teddy without ever having said, 'How about a job?' or anything like that. It just happened."

Tyler worked for John Mecom's team when Roger Penske was driving the Zerex Special—a car that was to be the forerunner of all the McLaren sports cars. When the Zerex was still a single-seat Cooper Formula 1 car, Tyler had helped to rebuild it after Walt Hansgen had wrecked it in the U.S. Grand Prix at Watkins Glen. Timmy Mayer drove the car on occasions and later it was converted to a central-seat sports car and driven with great flair by Penske. The Zerex won most of the big-money sports car races in 1962, before regulations forced Penske to alter it to a more legal two-seater. This made the Zerex Special no less competitive and Tyler was working on the crew when Penske won the Guards Trophy race at Brands Hatch in 1963.

Having fulfilled his commitment to Uncle Sam, Timmy

Tyler shares victory lap with Bruce in M1B at Mosport in 1966.

Mayer drove a Formula Junior Cooper for Ken Tyrrell during 1963 and with his wife Garrell and brother Teddy lived in a rented house on an island in the River Thames. Tyler renewed his association with the Mayers and decided to join up with them again, so he resigned from Mecom's team and accompanied the Mayers to a race in Copenhagen instead of returning to America.

Bruce McLaren came to one of the Mayers' riverside lunch parties—hobbling on a cane after a frightening end-over-end crash in the German Grand Prix—to continue discussions about taking a pair of 2.5-liter Cooper-Climaxes to New Zealand and Australia for the Tasman series during January and February 1964. Wally Willmott was building Bruce's car—a special slim-line lightweight with minimum tankage—at the Cooper Car Company in Surbiton, and Tyler joined him to start building a twin car for Timmy.

"To me, Coopers were a big deal in those days because we had been running the 500, the Formula Junior and the Formula 1 car in the States, but it didn't seem to be such a big deal when I actually went into the shop."

The staff at the Cooper Car Company was something of an institution, having been with the firm since Charles Cooper first capitalized on his idea to use Fiat 500 front suspension units front and rear on a lightweight frame and install a motorcycle

187

engine to build a cheap, sturdy, competitive car for Formula 3 racing. When Tyler arrived, the racing factory hadn't changed a lot since those early days. The old hands were openly critical about American racing people who often arrived with more money than driving ability and certainly only a modicum of mechanical skills. Tyler was an exception. "I was amazed at the time, that the Cooper people were working away in a dirty dark corner of the world and I had been tossed in there by Timmy and Teddy to get on with the job and these people were very impressed that I could actually weld and do something!

"Bruce was in and out of the factory all the time the cars were being built, but I don't ever remember being formally introduced, and at the time I didn't know a great deal about him. In fact I was fairly ignorant about the whole business but I was keen on doing something I was interested in and these people seemed to be very serious about what they were doing, so I thought it would be a good bunch to tag along behind. There were so many things that I didn't know about racing cars then and this guy with the limp seemed to know a fair bit about them so I thought maybe I'd better pay a bit of attention to him and see what was going on."

From these early days working on the Tasman Coopers, Tyler stayed with Bruce as he built up the team, working first in the corner of a high-roofed, grimy shed in New Malden, then in a long narrow low-roofed factory in a run-down trading estate in Feltham, and finally in the more extensive, expensive factory at Colnbrook where the team is currently based.

"Bruce was very easy to learn from, but I find now that I didn't really learn all that much and I think I know why. After working for him for about a year and a half I found that I was doing my part of the job and he was doing his. I knew that the car had to be finished and had to be at the race and I knew how he wanted it, but we were working in parallel rather than together. Well, maybe parallel isn't quite right. Maybe it was together. We used to argue like hell over how something should be done, but we never seemed to get upset about it, and we always ended up with a reasonable solution. He knew what he wanted and after a couple of years I believed him. It's odd thinking back, because we used to argue like hell but we never said, well, screw you because I'm going to do it my way, and I guess that's why we got on so well together.

"I realize now that I should have learned more from Bruce. I got on with my own job, never reckoning he was going to write himself off, so I never bothered to get him to explain a lot of

What the public doesn't see makes what it does see impressive.

the technical or engineering things to me because *he* knew that part. That was his department. I could cope with the detail bits and pieces and make sure that the car was built, and he did the other part, saying, we should put that there, or why don't we mount that there? and I would say, well, gee, we did that last year and it's no good, and I would remember why it was no good.

"This is where I felt out of place after Bruce's death because he and I had worked so much as a team that I hadn't bothered to pay much attention to the things he did as long as the end result was right. Now I have to work with the designers and try to communicate the things that I learned on the practical side and hope that they can cope with the other side of it. I've also got to communicate what the drivers say about the feel of the car, back to the designers. It's worked out that I've fallen into doing this without even trying. All of a sudden this is what I'm doing; I'm a director of the company and I never set out to be that. I was interested in doing a job and I wanted to win. Now I reckon if you've got enough initiative to want to get on, there's no reason why you shouldn't finish up owning the place."

Tyler's career in McLaren Racing may not be the logical

climax of career for every mechanic who gets involved in motor racing but a basic technical grounding and initiative obviously help. Jim Hall's German Chaparral mechanics, Tyler points out, are among the best in the racing game and they learned a lot of their thoroughness by being trained Volkswagen mechanics. "Their Volkswagen training taught them to be thorough and not to forget things. If you were to say that racing mechanics should have any special talent, it is basically to be very, very thorough and not to forget things because you don't get another chance to fix them once the race starts."

Aircraft engineering and Volkswagen training are two avenues suggested as good backgrounds for being a racing mechanic, but as a different avenue of advancement Tyler points to Team Lotus. "Lotus has very good racing mechanics. It seems to me that when they first go there they don't have anything over anyone else but they *know* that Colin Chapman is very good—they may not like him, but they know he's good—and quite a few of the Lotus mechanics have ended up being very, very good. They respect Colin Chapman because he's had years and years of experience. They believe in him and they learn from him. Maybe part of this is that Lotus has always had very good drivers and when you're working with someone who is capable of winning a race and is giving it his 100 percent, then you give him your 100 percent. If you're working for a driver who isn't going to make it, it's easy to say, ah, why the hell bother working all night for him—he's not going to win the race anyway. Chapman has always managed to have that air of success about him or at least has had good people driving for him, and you know, I think good people go together.

"I always felt that way when I was working with Timmy and later with Bruce. I didn't know anything and Timmy didn't know anything, but we said we'd have a stab at getting to the top together. I suppose it ended up happening with Bruce because later we used to laugh and say, well, we're on our way. Let's not stop now. We'll bust our asses 'til we beat them all."

Tyler lived with Bruce and Patty McLaren when they moved from their apartment in Surbiton to a house in Walton-on-Thames, and Tyler and Bruce absorbed each other's racing lore and invented new philosophy after late dinners when they had arrived back from the workshop. "We used to say, what if there were a race tomorrow with a bunch of nobodies in the field and they paid twenty thousand dollars to win, and there was a race tomorrow with Jack Brabham, Jochen Rindt, Jimmy Clark and Jackie Stewart running—which race would you go to? We would reckon that we'd be at the race with the Brabhams and the Stewarts and the rest of them, because they were the guys to beat. You want to win, but you want to win against the best people. We used to joke about it, but we still agreed on it. I want to win, but I want to beat someone doing it. I don't just want simply to win. It's a bit like in *The Money Game*—winning is just a means of keeping score, and the better guys you beat, the better score you get."

Getting to the stage where one shares in a successful driver's career and business and thoughts is one side of the penny, but it is a hard grind getting there. A racing mechanic works endless hours—a lot of round-the-clock "all-nighters"—to get his car to the line, and he bears a lot of responsibility. The elation conquers the weariness as the race starts, but it changes to concern that all will go well with the car and he has to live with the nagging worry that something might happen, the result of something he forgot to do. Tyler Alexander says this is a worry that a racing mechanic always has to live with. A mental cross he has to bear.

"It scares the hell out of me all the time when I think of what could happen during a race. I worry about what could fall off the thing, you know—it's a lethal weapon. I guess nobody ever says anything about it, because nobody ever says anything about people getting killed in motor racing. They say, well, it'll never happen to *me*. I don't know whether it's like this with other mechanics but if the car has a shunt or something the first thing that always flashes through my mind is, Christ, what did I forget this time. I must say, as far as I know anyway, I've never forgotten anything that has caused something to happen, but it's always the first thing that flashes through our minds because there are *so many* things. You notice during a race that perhaps some of the mechanics give the impression that they don't give a damn, but you know that they *do*."

If the mechanics on a racing team worry during a race it stands to reason that a driver knows of this worry and he worries too. The top drivers in the top teams can luxuriate in the knowledge that their car has been prepared by the top mechanics, but there are drivers who, because of intimate mechanical knowledge or a nervous need to assure themselves, double-check their cars before a race. This is nerve-racking for mechanics because it shows a basic distrust to their ability, even

though it is probably no more than a habit that the driver has formed over the years with various teams. For the driver it is a part of the ritual of preparing for a race; to the mechanics this is a niggling phobia.

"I guess some of the drivers worry about their cars—the ones that know what's going on, anyway. Bruce was obviously one of the drivers who knew what was going on and what it took to prepare a car, that there were mechanical things and that somebody's hands actually did do up nuts and bolts and things. But some drivers just sit in the car and ask you which way the track goes. Maybe that doesn't happen so much now when it has gotten so competitive, and it is essential that a driver know more about what goes on.

"I've never worked with a driver like this, but there are drivers who ask various questions before they get in the car—did you remember to do this, and did you remember to do that? It's a psychological thing, I suppose, where they have a pet worry. They ask the same questions every single time they get in the car.

"Bruce was never that way. He might ask similar sorts of questions, but it was never the same thing every time. He would ask perhaps about a specific problem from the night before. 'Were you able to fix such-and-such, and if you weren't, were you able to fix it well enough so that it'll finish the race?' That sort of thing."

Between races the McLaren team mechanics check everything that is feasible to check on the cars, but their program rather depends on the amount of time they have available. If time permits, the parts that have been dismantled are sent out to be magnafluxed, or visually checked for any sign of a failure or the possible start of a tiny crack or a flaw in the material.

"In aircraft terminology we call this preventive maintenance. Even if there's nothing wrong, you pull it apart and make sure there's nothing wrong or likely to go wrong. We try to do more and better preventive maintenance than other teams."

The suspension is completely rebuilt between races. The suspension comes off the car and the uprights come completely apart. All the steel parts are magnafluxed and all the magnesium or non-ferrous metal parts are Zygloed. Generally the mechanics know which are the problem areas and these are the areas that are checked first. If there has been a transmission problem then the gearbox comes off first and is completely taken apart and checked.

"You develop priorities working on a car from experience

From the expressions you wouldn't think Bruce had just won the title.

and problems in the past, and you work from that. You have a standard list of things you try to do between races. We have a standard procedure with a checklist that we try to stay reasonably close to, say, the night before a race. If there are no problems on the car, it's a list that takes roughly four or five hours to check through. It includes taking a thorough look at the gearbox, a good look around the engine, a general check of all the brake system, the chassis itself for any physical damage, checking anything that might have happened in practice, checking the fuel system and calculating the fuel mileage from fuel checks in practice, and charging the battery for the car. These are things that most teams do as a matter of course."

Long working hours tend to cancel the more glamorous attractions of being a racing mechanic as far as the average garage mechanic is concerned, but rebuilding a car between practice and the race which could involve working all night, or all night, all the next day and the next night as well, is taken as part of the job. How do these hours affect a mechanic? Does it have an adverse effect on the job he does?

"It bothers you, yeah, when your hands get fuzzy and your

teeth feel furry and your eyes get a bit blurred, but I guess although you complain about it like hell, way in the back of your mind, as long as you've got a chance of winning the race you just keep doing it because you *know* it's got to be done. If you can do a job within reasonable working hours, fine, but if it takes three days and three nights nonstop to have it done by Friday morning at 10 o'clock because that's when it has to be done, then that's what it takes.

"The only reason you ever stop working on a racing car is because the guy drops the starting flag. Long hours affect different people different ways. It often depends on whether you're winning or losing. It's great after two or three all-nighters if you win the race or if you think you have a chance of winning the race. You may be completely buggered and collapse, but you collapse with a smile on your face!"

A close-knit relationship, a sense of trust, between the racing driver and the mechanics working on his car is important. Any bickering between them or a lack of confidence from either side gives the driver a new worry which can sometimes take the edge off his performance. One of the reasons for success with the McLaren team is the "family" relationship. Everyone knew everyone else was giving the project his utmost and at races you could almost feel a sense of high spirits. The drivers entered into this and were responsible for keeping spirits buoyant. Mechanics often have a keener sense of being able to rate a driver than perhaps outside observers do, and Tyler was of the opinion that although Denny Hulme was usually quicker than Bruce in the Formula 1 cars, Bruce was more often faster in Can-Am racing and he was easier on the cars. "Bruce was always very easy on the equipment, but perhaps that's not very fair as a comparison because Denny isn't *hard* on the equipment or the car. Bruce was easier to work with because 90 percent of the time he knew what was going on with the car and he knew how he wanted it fixed, whereas Denny knows what's wrong with the car or what feels wrong but he only has a vague idea about putting it right. That's not putting Denny down in any way, because as a race driver he could charge harder than Bruce usually—it was just that he didn't have Bruce's engineering background.

"If Bruce had set the car up the way he wanted it, Denny could climb in and drive it for a few laps and he would like it as well. Most times Denny was content to drive the car the way Bruce set it up, and quite often he was quicker than Bruce.

"Bruce was very consistent, but he obviously enjoyed driving the big powerful Can-Am cars more than he did the Formula 1

Tyler gets the signal board ready during a Can-Am race.

cars where you had to be more precise. He enjoyed something you could pitch and toss around, something that you could drive more with your right foot than with precise movements of the steering wheel."

In the early stages of the team, with the notable exception of Tyler and for a time Gary Knutson who came from Chaparral and later rejoined the Texan team, Bruce favored hiring New Zealand mechanics. This was not just a national bias, it was a hunch Bruce had that mechanics who learned their trade in New Zealand probably were more able to think for themselves, to innovate, and to improvise, than were their English equivalents. In New Zealand replacement parts were not always readily available so the broken part either had to be rebuilt or a new part made from scratch. When Bruce needed a new cylinder head for his little Ulster Austin a replacement part was out of the question so he set about welding and filing until he had completely rebuilt the old head to his own design. This was the sort of initiative he expected the mechanics on his racing team to have and he reasoned that New Zealanders were more likely to share his sort of background experience.

As the McLaren team outgrew the New Malden tractor shed and moved to the 4000-square foot factory in Feltham, the staff grew to include Bruce Harre, now a technician with Firestone; Howden Ganley, now a racing driver in his own right with sponsored drives in Formula 2 and Formula 5000; and Colin Beanland, who had accompanied Bruce to England when he won the "Driver to Europe" racing scholarship in 1958. It was generally understood that Colin Beanland had received a fee from the scholarship to work as Bruce's racing mechanic on the 1500-cc Formula 2 Cooper-Climax he drove that year, but in fact Beanland paid his own fare and only assisted Bruce where he could on the preparation of the car since he had had no training as a mechanic. At 21, then, Bruce started his racing career in Europe as a driver who also looked after his own car.

As McLaren Racing went from success to success the staff grew and Harry Pearce, an ex-motorcycle racer and racing mechanic who had looked after Bruce's Cooper when he drove for the English private entrant Tommy Atkins, joined as workshop manager. At the time of Bruce's death, the staff numbered 55 including eight on the Can-Am sports car crew in America and six at the engine shop in Detroit where Colin Beanland is now workshop manager.

Tyler Alexander has not changed a great deal since he first

Tyler and engine man George Bolthoff talk to Denny during Indy trials.

Pushing off Peter Revson's car after a pit stop in the Ontario 500.

joined up with the fledgling McLaren team as a 24-year-old in 1964. He still has a passion for cleanliness on the workshop floor and either works on the cars in a white shop coat, or in jeans and a jersey and a scuffed pair of handmade Italian Gucci shoes. The Rolex watch doesn't really match the manual work, but it fits the picture better than when he switches roles, climbing the stairs to his desk and discusses policy with the other directors or sits down to a think session with the designers. Tyler is a racing mechanic who has made good.

In conference, Bruce McLaren, Tyler Alexander, Teddy Mayer and Phil Kerr. Below, the M8A Can-Am on display at the London Racing Car Show.

10

McLAREN RACING
AS A BUSINESS

"WHEN BRUCE FIRST mentioned to me that he was leaving Coopers and going on his own, I had my doubts and told him so." Phil Kerr, then business manager for Jack Brabham, was well aware of the problems involved in getting started with a new team as he had been closely involved when Jack left the Cooper team to set up his own racing organization in 1962.

"I didn't feel that Bruce was ready for it at that stage because I thought he was too young. On reflection this was unfair judgment because it was based on the fact that when Jack went on his own he was a good deal older than Bruce—he was 32— and for this reason I thought Bruce in his mid-twenties was trying to do too much."

Phil was studying accountancy when he first met Bruce at the Muriwai hillclimb. When he was 18 he left school to join the New Zealand Forest Service as a clerk, going to the university after work. At this stage he was also secretary of the Auckland Car Club, the largest car club in the country, and on the board of control of the International Grand Prix Association. Tiring of accountancy with the state-run Forest Service, Phil left to join Arthur Harris, who had a small engineering business and handled Buckler car sales in New Zealand.

"It was beginning to get to the stage where cars and engineering were of more interest to me than pure accounting. I've never really enjoyed pure accounting because I've never had the patience to sit at a desk all day long and balance books. That's why I've always inclined towards business management studies rather than pure economics, because management offers a lot more in terms of allowing you to express ideas, and allowing you to do things other than pure accounting. But you need accounting as a basic background. It teaches you the basic principles and rules."

Bruce had mentioned to Jack that Phil was interested in some form of management job in England and since Jack was branching out into other activities and business ventures he asked Phil to come over in 1959.

Bruce was an extremely good racing driver, and his talents leaned more toward engineering and design than the business side of racing. "He didn't really need to be a businessman in those days because he was getting paid as a driver and his income was all fairly straightforward. In later years he found that he had to become a little more interested in business activities, but I don't believe that business was ever his strong forte. He was able to analyze business situations on information he had in front of him, but he never had the patience in that area as he had in others to seek out the information that was required relative to the needs of the business. But if a lot of the basic work was done he was able to assess it, and he was able to make very sensible decisions. When I joined his company later, Bruce became chairman and I was joint managing director with Teddy Mayer. What I tried to do with Bruce was to feed him information about what was happening in all the areas under my jurisdiction and then let him make decisions based on that information."

But at the beginning, the news that Bruce was thinking of leaving the Cooper team to concentrate on building his own cars came as something of a surprise to the man in whose footsteps Bruce had been following for several years.

"Jack was a little surprised," Phil recalls, "But he had known Bruce long enough to be aware of his abilities. However, I don't think Jack envisaged that Bruce in fact was going to be as dominant in some areas of racing and to produce such good cars in such a relatively short space of time. I don't think *anybody* thought Bruce would be capable of producing cars of the caliber and quality that he subsequently did."

It was Phil who had been largely responsible for Denny

202

Hulme getting his chance in the Brabham team, and in addition to his position with Jack and his companies, Phil was also looking after Denny's interests. When Denny left the Brabham Formula 1 team to drive exclusively for Bruce at the end of 1967, Phil was in a delicate position of divided loyalty and he was soon to follow Denny into the McLaren fold.

The arrangement, although appearing cumbersome at first, in fact settled down quickly with Teddy concentrating on the increased activities of the team in North America, and Phil looking after the administration of the factory on a day-to-day basis and also the Formula 1 program. They were each experts in their own fields and the division worked out well. If there was an accounting problem it came to Phil, and if it was a legal matter it was handed to the Cornell graduate.

"The general administration of the company is pretty much the same as any other commercial organization. The fact that it's a racing team presents certain complications, but generally normal business methods apply. It's important to keep the company organized using good basic commercial principles. We've endeavored to improve the efficiency of the company as a whole. We've known that internal communication between the various personnel is important and while this had tended to be overlooked, it is now vastly improved. It was also necessary to improve the efficiency of the financial control."

Like Topsy, the McLaren team just "growed," with the design, building, development, and racing of cars as the prime aim to the exclusion of almost everything else. It wasn't until the company staff had reached double figures that the suggestion of a holiday was met with anything more than an incredulous glance from Bruce who truly believed that this whole racing game was a long and joyfully involved hobby. So who needed holidays? Vacations were regarded with the same scorn as the suggestion of an 8-hour day. When the tiny team had started the hours involved were as long as it took to get a job done and all-nighters were taken for granted as part of the job. With three or four on the staff the involvement with Bruce on a personal level was compensation enough, but as the team grew and the personal relationship was diluted a little, civilization started to creep into the operation.

"Motor racing is a bit odd in that quite apart from trying to operate as a normal company, there is always an unknown element in it. You can never be sure of the really immediate future of racing, and it is becoming more expensive every year. In addition to finding that necessary finance to operate the team each year, it becomes increasingly important to control that finance."

Formula 1 racing has its own particular problems. The seasons last from March through October and in that time a group of men and equipment has to be moved from South Africa, around most of Europe, and eventually across to Canada, the United States and Mexico. The rest of the year is used up with design, building and development of new cars for the coming season and for the workshop staff this can be as hectic as it is for the race crews when the circus gets on the move during the season.

Planning for the coming season is usually started six months beforehand when the international calendar is published and arrangements are made for hotel accommodation and for garage facilities.

This is a field where experience is important. "In addition to hotels and garages you also have to plan a movements schedule which covers flights for drivers and others who may be flying to the races; you have to arrange the channel crossings for the transporter and the accompanying vehicles, and also the customs documents and insurance papers that may be required at each border." Phil is known as "Sunny Tours" when the race crews are on the move.

When the scene switches to North America, all the competing Formula 1 cars are carried on a charter flight to Canada, and are then trucked together down to Watkins Glen in New York State and finally hauled down to Mexico. The Formula 1 Constructors' Association gets together on documentation for this section of the season, but it is still comprehensive from a paperwork angle as the McLaren team ships 30 crates of spares in addition to the cars and spare engines, and the mechanics have to be familiar with the placing of all the important components. This is where the chief mechanics of racing teams have to become tour managers as well as being responsible for the preparation of the cars. When the transporter leaves the factory, the chief mechanic—Alastair Caldwell in the McLaren Formula 1 team—is responsible for the smooth-running of the trip. All possible documentation is provided for him, and he then has to see that the entourage reaches the race track.

"Alastair and the other mechanics cope well with the paperwork at the borders now purely as a result of experience in this area, and they have come to know the best approaches to the various customs offices," says Phil.

Experience is certainly the best teacher. "None of the problems are particularly difficult; the problems that arise now can easily be overcome by application. When I first started working for Jack the understanding of all the different customs requirements for the various countries was a serious obstacle to overcome, but with experience these have become straightforward. It's easy enough to phone the relevant embassy or check with the Royal Automobile Club if you are in doubt on any point.

"Quite often for Spain or France or Italy you have to apply for documentation anything up to three months ahead. If you leave it 'til the last minute, chances are you won't get what's required and your transporter and mechanics won't get through to the race. You have the responsibility of ensuring that when the transporter leaves the factory (and usually the crew is very tired after perhaps an all-nighter on final preparations) everything goes as smoothly as possible."

Any forward-thinking racing organization must consider the prospects of diversification in the future with a view to exploring other avenues connected with motor racing, and for the McLaren team the most obvious dream was a McLaren road car just as Colin Chapman's Lotus racing team now builds the road-going Elites, Elans, Sevens and Europas in addition to their

Public relations: Left, the M5-BRM Grand Prix car in New York as an art object, and right, Bruce McLaren at Marineland as a racing personality.

racing activities.

"We had felt for some time that we shouldn't just rely on racing entirely for the future, and that we should have other commercial activities, either in the nucleus stage or at least with a possibility of being developed over the next few years, so that we could become self-sufficient as an organization without depending entirely on going racing. As long as we were interested in going racing, it would have to be number one priority because (a) it is an image builder and (b) it provides the bulk of the income which would ultimately be applied to other projects. In any case winning and being competitive and expanding the name was very important to Bruce and to the team. I know Bruce got nearly as much enjoyment from seeing a McLaren car win races as he did from winning a race himself with his own car. It was a symbol of success. The fact that the name McLaren was becoming increasingly well known, particularly in North America, was due to the success of the cars as much as to Bruce's own success as a driver in Can-Am, and this was important to him."

The company is still working on long-term projects but the dream of the road car has been shelved for the moment.

In five years the McLaren organization mushroomed from the tractor shed in New Malden, through the narrow factory on the run-down trading estate in Feltham, to the relative luxury of a 7000-square foot factory on the trading estate at Colnbrook, near the little village that grew up from a coach stop on the road from London to Bath. The runways of London's Heathrow airport are deafeningly close. Immediate plans are for a move to an even larger 11,000-square foot factory which the company has purchased freehold, rather than pay the high rents for industrial property in the area. The new factory is only 100 yards along David Road from the existing premises, has three drawing offices and three management offices upstairs, with a further four offices downstairs. Out in the workshops there will be a greater area in which the three separate teams as well as the prototype building program can operate.

At the end of the 1970 season the team staff numbered 42. Teddy, Phil and Tyler are the three management personnel in terms of decision and policy-making, and they are assisted by an accountant and by Sue Winslade who acts as secretary to all three. There are three designers and two draftsmen in the drawing offices. Downstairs is the office of general manager Harry Pearce, who looks after purchasing and engineering procurement. Harry was chief mechanic on Tommy Atkins' racing team when Bruce drove for them in Formula 2 in 1959 and later on in the Tasman Series with a 2.7-liter Cooper. He has an assistant who is also in charge of quality control, checking on everything that is made in the workshops and everything that is bought out.

Don Beresford, who worked as a racing mechanic with Aston Martin and Lola before joining the McLaren team, is the works foreman and has general authority over all the workshop in addition to his special department looking after the building of the prototype McLarens behind the high wall at the end of the factory. There are three machinists, two sheet metal workers, two welders, and two general personnel in the building shop as well as a specialist fitter. Each racing team has about five mechanics, and there are floating personnel who are available to help whichever department needs assistance. Nearing the start of the racing season there can be anything up to ten new racing cars in the workshop as the crews prepare for Formula 1, Can-Am and Indianapolis. To keep the team transport rolling there is a vehicles manager who looks after servicing and the loading of the transporter as well as the other vehicles and also looks after the parts and equipment.

The giant Ford transporter holds three cars and most of the spares required for a Grand Prix, but it requires careful loading with spare engines, transmissions, suspension parts, spare body sections, wheels and the million other parts needed to keep a racing team mobile away from the base. The McLaren fleet consists of the transporter, an Econoline van that often accompanies the "mother ship" to the races, plus a Ford Transit, two Ford Thames vans, four Mini vans, and four staff cars.

The McLaren team is the only racing organization to compete in these three major fields in Europe and North America, and there have been suggestions that perhaps the Grand Prix team could be dropped in favor of the more lucrative forms of racing in the United States, but Teddy Mayer discounts this on purely economic grounds.

"Surprisingly enough the possible income from racing in Formula 1 and racing in Can-Am is fairly equal, when you take the guaranteed starting monies as well as the prize and bonus monies you earn in Formula 1 as opposed to the prize money only from the Can-Am races. However, I would say that probably two-thirds of our sponsorship is in fact allocated to us by our sponsors because we are going racing in Can-Am rather than in Formula 1.

"If we were to cut out Formula 1 we would find that the

number of designers, the size of the plant, the number of a builders, the number of mechanics—our basic overheads—would not be a great deal smaller. And the addition of the income which Formula 1 provides would more than cover that difference. Let's say all three of our racing projects cost equal amounts. In fact they do—they cost within about 10 percent of each other. If we stop doing one, our income would be cut by a third, but our costs would only be cut by about 15 percent. Our rent and rates and this sort of thing would be virtually the same. There would be some small savings—we wouldn't need the same number of mechanics, for instance—but costing it out carefully we'd save only about a sixth and we'd lose about a third of our income."

When the McLaren team first started to become successful in Can-Am racing, Bruce put a lot of the credit down to their participation in Grand Prix racing with its spur to mechanical and design development, but by the start of the 1970 season he felt the rub-off between Grand Prix and Can-Am was starting to even itself up. The M15 Indianapolis car probably owed more to the Can-Am sports car than it did to the M7 Formula 1 car.

"I think we're probably learning as much from the Can-Am cars," said Bruce. "Although it hasn't been competitive racing we've always run fairly hard in practice and we've always tried as hard as we can in terms of experiments and developments on the cars. We never set ourselves limits on design time or money that we've been prepared to spend on the Can-Am car. I think the M8 sports car is a much better car in terms of design than the old M7 Formula 1, because that was basically a copy of our Formula 2 car and that was never very good."

In terms of time Bruce McLaren achieved a tremendous amount in a short period. He left the Cooper Formula 1 team at the end of 1965 to devote all his attention to his own little racing team, and when he did so he surprised more people than Jack Brabham and Phil Kerr. It seems hard to believe that in a few years he developed his own new cars and a brand new reputation for himself as an engineer and car-builder as well as a racing driver and patron of a tiny team.

"Bruce's future was unlimited," says Phil. "Apart from the fact that we will miss him, I think the saddest thing is that while we appreciate the years that he was around, we can only wonder about the years during which I think he would have done so much more. I believe that his talents were yet to show to the full. He was just beginning to show the signs of being an innovator. He felt that he had served another apprenticeship—as a constructor a sort of extension of his earlier driver's apprenticeship—and he had jumped the first hurdle which involved engineering and designing good, sound, safe cars.

"He was learning all the time. He had this marvellous attribute of being able to retain information, assimilating all manner of engineering knowledge. He would watch what other people were doing and analyze it, rejecting what he didn't like and retaining what he did, storing it for future use.

"His imagination was working all the time. It didn't matter if you were with Bruce on an airplane, at his home or out to dinner; he would always be mulling over particular problems or cars or future projects that he might have been reminded of during the course of conversation.

"Ranked with the other leading designers of our time Bruce had some remarkable achievements to his credit at 32. At that age both Brabham and Chapman were only just beginning. They had a long start on Bruce and it wasn't until their late thirties or early forties that they came to be really widely recognized for their talents. Bruce had done so much by the time he was 32 that it is really difficult to know how much he might have achieved by the time he reached his early forties. We can only surmise. I think that Bruce would probably have surpassed the efforts of all his contemporaries and that the McLaren organization would have been a team to be even more proud of."

Early shakedown of the M15 at Indianapolis—Chris, Denny and Bruce.

11
AT THE TRACK

cLAREN DOMINATION in the Can-Am
series has been likened to the Mercedes-Benz supremacy in
Grand Prix racing in the late thirties and mid-fifties. The Mercedes reputation grew from the strict and efficient team management of Alfred Neubauer and the same clinical attention to detail is a factor in the dominance of McLaren team in the North American sports car races.

In private testing sessions and during race practice, every modification or change to the car is noted on a Vehicle Running Record along with driver comments and individual lap times. These records are filed for reference and in this way complete details of a car's behavior under certain conditions can be checked at a later date.

This Vehicle Running Record was laid out and produced by Teddy Mayer. Spaces are provided for the date, circuit, event, driver, car, weather, circuit length, total laps, total miles, fastest lap, average lap, water temperature, oil temperature, oil pressure and fuel pressure. And that is merely the heading line! Below that comes the tire section with spaces for progressive records on temperature, pressure, camber and wear. Then there are lines numbered one through fifty with a space for the lap time and room to write in alterations and their effects and driver com-

Elkhart Lake 1968: Teddy Mayer and Bruce discuss practice results.

ments.

The back of the sheet is made up of the Vehicle Specification Record which is filled out after the race with the smallest details of the setting-up of the racing car. Spaces record the date, track, event, driver, car, person making record, weather and temperature, then chassis number, engine number and gearbox number. The overall ratio comes next, then ring and pinion ratio, and the individual ratios of each of the four or five gears.

There is a section for ignition timing, spark plugs, and fuel system, then details of wheels and tires and notes on caster, toe-in, springs, anti-roll bars, ride height and wheel-weights with notes on different settings front and rear or from side to side. The conditions of brake cylinder, clutch cylinder, front and rear brakes head the second column, followed by the settings for camber, shocks, and spring length front and rear. Spaces are left to note additional specifications, difficulties that might have been encountered with equipment, and any further general comments.

"The reason we keep such detailed charts of all the testing and practice is that the whole subject of setting up a race car, and getting the last little bit of performance from it, is extremely complex," says Mayer. "The setup on the car is completely

Ontario 1970: Peter Revson tells crew what it was like out there.

interrelated. The front toe-in is related to the front camber which may be related to the caster which is related to the particular tire you have on the car and the performance is related not only to the width of the front rim, but also to the width of the rear rim which in turn is related to the pressure of the tires front and rear and to the geometry of the car. This complexity means that each change has to be carefully noted so that you are able to get back to a particular condition where you felt the car was working particularly well on a particular track."

These charts are not kept as reference for a track from year to year apart from basic information like gear ratios. The main purpose is a detailed record for use at the next race. "The reason for this is that in twelve months you will have changed tire sizes and tire construction and other things about the car so much that you really only have a small amount of information which will be useful at the track by next season. In other words we couldn't come back to, say, Spa, and use an eighth toe-in because that's what we used last year. What we could do is reason that last year we started with no toe-in and found that an eighth toe-in worked, so this year maybe more toe-in at the front will help whatever condition develops at Spa. In other

Bruce gets the M8A a little sideways during a test session.

words, you use the changes that you make at the track to guide you toward changes to make again at that track, rather than absolute identical settings."

Since these recording sheets were first used by the McLaren team they have been expanded to contain more and more different kinds of information with greater attention now being paid to tire details and to aerodynamic behavior on the car.

With a brand new McLaren on a test day the car is run for a few quiet warm-up laps to make sure there are no oil or water leaks, to bed the brakes, and to let the driver get comfortable. Perhaps the windscreen height has to be altered, some extra padding is needed in the seat, or slight adjustments are made to the position of the pedals. The driver then gradually builds up his speed with the car until he is going as fast as he can with the car set up in that particular configuration. Then the test session really starts from this baseline condition. An alteration is made, and if only a small improvement is made or the driver is not absolutely sure that the change was for the better, the car is returned to its baseline condition again for a back-to-back comparison. If a change is made and it results in an enormous improvement this then becomes the baseline condition. In this context an enormous improvement could be half a second over a ten-lap period, while a small improvement would be an average of a tenth or a fifth of a second over the same distance.

This means that the results of a test session depend to a great extent on the ability of the driver. He does not have to be good at engineering to assist in the program, but this obviously helps and in the case of Bruce it was invaluable assistance.

The basic requirement of a test driver is the ability to repeat his times for lap after lap, so that an improvement made on the car should show up as a consistent improvement on the test sheet. A fast driver is not necessarily a good driver for this sort of testing work; consistency is more important than out-and-out pace, which might not always reflect the changes that are being made.

Where Bruce was concerned he knew what was being done to the car and why, and he could analyze what difference this was making to the handling of the car while he was out on the circuit, but Denny doesn't have this gift of engineering knowledge. However, because Denny is able to reel off a series of laps at a consistent speed, the worth of any alteration to the car is always reflected in his lap times.

Tyler Alexander is fond of describing the way good preparation helps enormously in a successful racing team by saying that you can screw up a car beyond belief given twenty seconds with a seven-sixteenths wrench. It's as easy to make alterations the wrong way and ruin the setting-up if you don't approach test sessions with great care. It is also easy to be misled by behavior of the chassis or of the driver.

"At Indianapolis we found that just one turn on a spring abutment could mean two or three miles an hour—and that's a tremendous amount at Indy. If you change the rate of the springs or make just a tiny adjustment you can get the thing completely out of the ball park," says Mayer.

"We're completely dependent on what the driver says and how he feels. We can set the car up to the last tiny fraction of a degree in every direction, and each measurement can be exactly right, but if the driver's information as to whether the car feels secure, feels stable, is handling well or not, is wrong for any given reason, you can find that you're just going around in circles and no engineering in the world can tell you how to fix it.

"Indy is a perfect example of this. You can go out with a car that is set up to run at 168 mph and the driver has no problem lapping at that speed. But the next day because the driver is slightly tired or not trying quite so hard—just a very slight difference—the car will only run 165 and the driver will say it feels terrible when in fact you haven't changed a thing. This happened time and again when we first went to Indy. We made the mistake of trying to change the car for the driver to go faster, but now we park the car and wait until the driver feels right or the time of day is right."

Setting up a time schedule for race day is important so that the mechanics and the drivers know exactly when and where they will be required. In general Teddy makes out a list for the chief mechanic which tells him what time practice is, what time they have to be ready to go on the grid. A work list, which details all the items that have to be checked or altered on the cars in addition to normal preparation, is prepared the night before and given to the chief.

These time schedules are important items that can easily be overlooked. Things like traffic delays on race morning have to be taken into account when working out the movement program.

Pit equipment for Can-Am or Indianapolis racing is more extensive than in European Formula 1 races where a pit stop usually means curtains for the driver's chances anyway. In America the emphasis is on finishing a race at all costs because of the prize-money-only arrangements, but in Europe the financial arrangements are different with a fixed amount of travel expenses paid for each entry and the driver's payments based on his performance driving the previous season. The European prize money has been greatly increased under the new "Geneva" scale, extending down to 20th place. A pitstop during a 200-mile Grand Prix, then, means that it is seldom worthwhile continuing if the problem takes too long to fix, mainly because of the loss of World Championship points.

The pit setup in America includes a complete extra body—nose and tail—for each car, as well as materials to repair damage to the body, a complete set of spare wheels for each car, and quick-lift jacks ready in each pit. Air lines are rigged to power wrenches to speed wheel changes, and spare fuel is kept in cans. Oil cannot be added during a race. The team has developed a pressurized water system so that an overheating car can have water pumped in under pressure during a pit stop without unscrewing the water cap. Tools are laid out ready for use, and the signalling numbers and name boards are set out for quick selection during the race.

Teddy keeps track of his own drivers with two pairs of 60-second-sweep Heuer stopwatches, stopping one watch and starting the other as the car passes. As well as keeping every lap time for each driver, he can also record the plusses and minuses on cars ahead and behind. "If I start my watch on zero when Denny goes by," says Teddy describing a hypothetical situation, "I can wait for Jackie Stewart to go by and by glancing at the watch I can tell within a tenth or two that he is seven seconds behind Denny. Or if someone is ahead of Denny and he goes past at a minute and fifteen seconds on my watch and Denny's

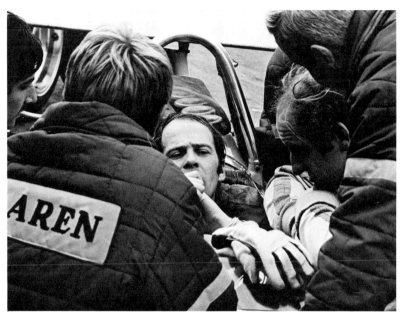

Watkins Glen 1970: the whole crew gathers around Peter Gethin's car.

lap time is one minute twenty, I know that he is five seconds ahead of Denny. On every lap I note Denny's time, his plus and his minus, and his position."

Teddy doesn't keep a lap chart and he doesn't feel that one is important in relatively short 200-mile "sprints" which most of the Can-Am and Grand Prix races are.

"In a long distance race where there could be dramatic dropouts and you may need to know whether you are seven laps behind or two in front, a lap chart would be very important, but in a short race as long as you know the laps your driver has run and the number of laps the leader has run, really it's up to the driver because he's going as hard as he can. Once in a while in a situation where it rains and you're in and out of the pits, a lap chart would be useful, but generally speaking we don't bother because you don't have enough advantage on your competitors to take it very easy, and they don't have enough advantage on you so that they can take it easy. The races aren't really long enough to play tactics. Keeping a lap chart at Indy is a mammoth task—it's one of those races where you go out and run as hard and fast as you can for the 500 miles and then find out where you are officially placed afterwards!"

McLaren dominates the Can-Am series but is just beginning its push in USAC racing. Above, Dan Gurney in M8D; below, Peter Revson in M15.

12

THE COMMERCIAL IMPORTANCE OF AMERICAN RACING

C AN-AM RACING established the McLaren team, and it made Bruce a better-known personality in America than he was in Europe. From his early races with Cooper Monacos at Laguna Seca and Riverside he became aware of the tremendous potential of American sports car racing and he wanted Cooper to become more involved, but they preferred to make their commitment in Grand Prix racing and this was one of the reasons that prompted Bruce to start up his own team.

Success in the American races brought much-needed finance to the small team, and it also helped to build a reputation that was extremely useful when Bruce and Teddy went searching for sponsors. Teddy regards Can-Am and Indianapolis racing as being much more important to the survival of the team than European Grand Prix racing.

"The reason for this is economic as much as anything. Most of our sponsorship comes from America, and generally speaking the Americans don't know very much about Formula 1. It gets less publicity in the States than Can-Am and far less coverage than Indy. Therefore if you do well in front of your sponsors in Can-Am racing or at Indy, you're doing well as far as they're concerned—they probably wouldn't be too worried if we didn't run in Formula 1 at all. In fact we divide our racing into three more or less equal parts—Can-Am, Indy and Formula 1—that all cost about the same to take part in, and all bring in about the same amount of money, so we can't afford to drop Formula 1 and only run in the States."

Initially the McLaren team ran with Firestone tires but later switched to Goodyear and has been with them ever since. Other major sponsors are Reynolds Aluminum and the Gulf Oil Corporation.

It has always been McLaren team policy to restrict the number of sponsors and the number of advertising decals on the cars, so that the major sponsors with a large investment in the team are assured of getting maximum exposure on the racing car rather than being swamped with a mass of smaller trade decals. In some cases this means that the team loses on contingency monies posted for the winner, but in the long run the team profits because its efforts at exclusivity are appreciated by the sponsoring companies.

Teddy feels that a company like Goodyear, the largest tire company in the world, goes racing because the performance image, or the association with high performance, differentiates their product from other similar products in the eyes of the public.

"To me, this is the biggest value that they get from going racing. They get a good deal of publicity from it, but the publicity is keyed to the theory that because the company is associated with successful high-performance products, it has the ability and the know-how to make production goods that are better, goods that have higher performance characteristics than other similar companies which are not associated with racing."

Long term, this involvement in racing could mean better Goodyear tires for the everyday motorist. "I think it is specious to argue that development in racing leads to development in production vehicles or in any production item. When I say racing, I don't mean sedan racing or rallying or anything of that nature because I think there is a definite tie-in there—you find things that can improve your reliability or performance, but to say that a Formula 1 tire bears relationship to the tire on a Cadillac is generally speaking pretty far-fetched. There have been instances where theories worked out in Grand Prix racing can be applied, but it's very much on a long-term basis and certainly not a direct application of racing principles.

"I have been speaking specifically of Goodyear here, but the benefit to Gulf or Reynolds is also mainly through their association with high-performance success. It's a means of getting publicity and creating an image in the public eye, rather than any great direct engineering benefit."

Bruce had the ideal sort of personality for working with sponsoring companies, and he worked hard to give good value for the financial support that the company was giving to the team. This is a relatively new area for European drivers and not many have the flair for promoting a sponsor. Stirling Moss was the first of the real professional drivers in England and he now hosts the Johnson Wax sponsorship of the Can-Am series. Jackie Stewart recently signed with Goodyear to run in the Can-Am Series with a Lola and he regards the American races as being most important for the furthering of his career.

"To give a sponsor good value for his money requires considerable effort," says Mayer. "It means that you've got to have time to do commercials and advertising shots with his public relations company for magazines, newspapers and television; you've got to make the time to do public performances, and you've got to mention him in interviews. This was another of the reasons why we decided to limit the number of sponsoring companies we could accept. You have to work to promote the image of the sponsor and in the time you have available it's impossible to project the image of more than a strictly limited number of companies. Certainly you can't promote two companies that sell the same product or even operate in similar fields."

When the team signed with Goodyear in 1967 they were told that the tire company regarded the sponsorship as an investment in a future Indianapolis program, but in fact it was 1970 before a McLaren ran at Indianapolis. When the M15 cars were being built to take the turbocharged Offenhauser Bruce talked enthusiastically about the moment when they decided to take on the "establishment" in America. "We were at Mosport listening to a radio broadcast of the 1969 race and when Denny was up in 2nd place and then dropped out, we looked at each other and said, to hell with it, let's have a go and build a car for him." As it turned out Denny wasn't able to drive in the 500 because of his accident in practice, and Chris Amon, the other scheduled driver of the all-Kiwi assault on Indy, decided that Indianapolis wasn't the place he wanted to be on May 30, so the cars started with Americans Peter Revson and Carl Williams driving.

For 1971 the McLaren team returns to Indianapolis with a completely revised program and a pair of new M16 cars. They learned a lot from their year as a "rookie" team in 1970.

"We ran too much and we ran at the wrong times," says

Teddy, outlining plans for Indianapolis the second time around. "We put a lot of emphasis on running as much as possible to find out as much as we could about the track, starting early every morning and running all day. Because of the long start-up procedure with the Offy, this meant that the mechanics had to be at the track at about 6 a.m. every morning and had to work late at night, and this pretty much wore them out. I don't think that this was necessary, and we certainly did a lot of redundant running. We were changing things on the car when in fact it was the track or the driver's mood that had changed.

"The track conditions alter a great deal between 9 in the morning when the track opens, noon and 6 p.m. when the track closes. This means that if you're running all day, you have to keep changing the car to compensate for the change in track conditions, so you're not really proving anything. The race is run between 11 a.m. and 2 p.m. so we will be doing most of our running during this period of the day and not trying to be on the track *all* the time."

The designer, Gordon Coppuck, feels there was no point in being on the track on May 1 with their three cars running nose to tail; although they made an impressive sight for a new team, all they really did was to confuse themselves. "The circuit was so dirty from the winter that the drivers couldn't get a competitive time in anyway and all we did was mess the car around trying to go as quick as we had done when we were testing in November. Next time we'll let someone else run all the dust off the track. We really got a shock when we found that we couldn't go quicker than 164 mph on those first few days in May, but we should have realized that not many of the front chargers like Foyt and Ruby were there that early—they turned up two or three days later when the track was cleaner, but by that time we had messed our car up."

Indianapolis was a track that never really appealed to Bruce. He couldn't get to grips with the necessity of having to average over 160 mph in such a confined space with all the engineering effort being aimed at making a car go through four fast left-handers. He knew there was a special science involved in that 2½-mile track, but until he went there during the November testing and later during the month of May, I'm sure he never realized just how complex that science was.

"Indy is a whole new ball game," he said in his *Autosport* column after the November tests with the new car. "First of all, you don't run much below 160 mph and most of the time you are nearer 200. In Grand Prix racing or Can-Am it's the other way around—you're not much over 160 and this is the first thing you notice.

"We hadn't been to Indy before and we didn't know much about it, but I was much more interested in finding out why and how a car is fast at Indianapolis for myself, rather than just copying all the trick things that people had developed over the years. I drove the car initially myself but then I realized that my lack of experience was going to hurt just a little. It takes quite a long time to go really fast there. Make no mistake, it's a lot more than just four left-hand corners. There's a very definite art in getting through those high-speed turns correctly. You have to run a very precise line and pattern—at least I think so—to go fast."

Denny lapped at 168 during these tests and Bruce got up to 165 and they left the Indianapolis track very pleased with their efforts. In fact Bruce went faster in November than Chris was ever able to run in May. Chris was probably somewhat unnerved by Denny's fire, and like Bruce, he was just a little unsure of what he was doing there anyway. This made it difficult for the team. With Denny driving they knew they were working with someone who had proven himself to be competitive in this special sphere of racing, and they were able to alter the car accordingly, to his suggestions. Gordon summed it up

The McLaren crew at Indianapolis after Peter Revson qualified for the 6th row inside starting spot. From left, Alan McCall, George Bolthoff, Tyler Alexander, Frank Zimmerman, Bruce, Peter and Hughie Absolom.

well. "We always had a suspicion that if Denny had been able to drive he could have run quickly enough to win the race, but we weren't sure whether the others were able to."

Tyler likened their problem to trying to sort out a Formula 1 car with a driver who couldn't tell them whether it was over-steering or understeering!

Bruce had been anxious to treat Indy as just another race, but Denny, who had been subjected to the "magic" of Indy, scoffed that it wasn't "just another race" if you had to design special shock absorbers for it! After the November tests Bruce came away saying he had never been so excited about one race before.

"We went there not knowing whether our competitors were super sophisticated or very naive. When we got there we found that there were really two classes and we were just a little surprised that there was such a depth of good equipment—we had expected to see more rubbish and less of the good quality cars," said Gordon. He and Bruce were pleased at the stir the new McLarens caused in Gasoline Alley, and they were de-lighted when the Indiana section of the Society of Automobile Engineers presented Bruce with a plaque in recognition of his contribution toward progress at Indy.

Coming home in the plane Bruce and Gordon sat together and went carefully through what they had just gathered in the way of new ideas at the Speedway, discussing ways in which these ideas could be incorporated in a McLaren for 1971. "We decided that we would have to investigate several basic shapes before coming to a decision. We wondered whether a wedge would be better, or a slim pencil shape, or a fat car. The M15 was what we called a 'fat car'. It was 45 inches wide whereas our current Formula 1 car was only 28 inches wide."

The new Indianapolis McLaren M16 is a wedge. The car that influenced it was, in fact, not an Indy car, but the Formula 1 Lotus 72 which admittedly gained its shape from the earlier 4-wheel-drive Lotus Indy cars. The McLaren has a chisel nose with the radiators mounted at the side. The 1971 car keeps the turbocharged Offenhauser and the McLaren link system in the rear suspension, but the front suspension geometry, the wheel-base and the fuel system are all altered.

The Indianapolis project grew out of the lessons learned in Can-Am racing and the M15 was very much a single-seat version of the Can-Am car, even using the same suspension uprights. The McLaren team is regarded as being super-dominant in Can-Am, but they had to serve a tough apprenticeship. The Zerex-

Olds won first time out at Mosport in 1964 and the first McLaren was a success but although the cars were fast they were dogged by trifling troubles that kept Bruce from the winner's circle time after time. In 1966 when the Can-Am Series started the Lola T70 won five of the six races and John Surtees was the champion with three wins at St. Jovite, Riverside and Las Vegas. Bruce's score was two 2nds and two 3rds, and he took 3rd in the championship behind Surtees and Donohue. His take-home pay that year was $22,560. It had also been a bad year in Formula 1 with the ineffective 4-cam Ford engine spoiling the team's chances. With the McLaren M6A and Denis Hulme the team fortunes changed in 1967. Denny won the three openers and Bruce won Laguna Seca and Riverside. He also took the title along with $62,300 and Denny was runner-up with $40,000. In 1968 it was Hulme's turn for the title and the total team pay for the series was $163,030. In 1969 the Series had grown to eleven races; the orange McLarens rumbled home to win every time and Bruce took his second Can-Am title. The 1970 Can-Am series started in the shadow of Bruce's death but Denny carried the flag to win six races, the championship and a personal total of $162,202. The team won three other Can-Ams with Dan Gurney scoring two victories and Peter Gethin one.

These winnings sound great until you add up the crippling costs of mounting such a Teutonic racing offensive, leaving nothing to chance. Mayer maintains that the costs were not covered until after mid-season in 1969 when they were winning everything in sight. Sponsorship contracts are vital to the McLaren team, and it is this lack of sponsorship that has kept the other major European teams out of the series.

Phil Kerr says that sponsors always receive value in return from the team. "It was always a good two-way trade. There were always reciprocal benefits. I don't think Bruce ever knowingly would have made an association with other people or companies where he couldn't or wouldn't keep his part of the bargain. Every effort was made to give the fullest possible value, and in terms of reward the sponsoring companies did very well. There was good publicity from the association with the winning team, and there were also technical benefits because Bruce very frequently became involved with the competition department or the research or technical divisions of the companies and there would be an interchange of information. He could seek information from these people, but would willingly provide information on what he had found applying their products or ideas to his racing cars."

225

Typical of this information interchange was the relationship with Harold Macklin in the Automotive Division of Reynolds Aluminum at Richmond, Virginia. Macklin had been working with his development team for twelve years perfecting an all-aluminum engine block which dispensed with cast iron cylinder sleeves and he was well advanced with the alloy block for the engine to power the new Chevrolet Vega when the contract was signed with McLaren Racing. The contract obviously had a publicity rub-off for all Reynolds products—from foil wrap to their ideas for building all-aluminum car bodies that could be reclaimed like aluminum beer cans—but Bruce was obviously more interested in the engine developments. Macklin and McLaren discussed building a 390 alloy version of the Can-Am Chevrolet engine and during 1969 Bruce was whispering excitedly about progress on this new power unit. In fact, it never ran in a racing car until late in the 1970 season, when Denny won the Laguna Seca race using the new Reynolds engine. Back in Richmond, Macklin was already making plans to reduce the size of the water jackets (the all-aluminum block dissipates heat better without the iron liners) and increase the capacity of the engine up to what he considered to be a safe limit of 525 cubic inches—8.6 liters.

In the five seasons since the Can-Am series started there have been 39 races, and 37 of these have been won by Chevrolet engines! Underlining the McLaren dominance in recent years—remember they won nothing in 1966—McLaren cars, including private entries, have won 31 times against six wins for Lola, and one each for Chaparral and Porsche. Denny Hulme, two-time Champion, is the top winner in the series with 17 J-Wax medals. Bruce won nine, followed by John Surtees with four, Dan Gurney with three, Mark Donohue with two, and Phil Hill, John Cannon, Peter Gethin and Tony Dean with one win each.

Ken Tyrrell, Jackie Stewart's entrant in Formula 1, maintained that he was not impressed so much by the string of McLaren victories in Can-Am racing as by the fact that the cars were always around at the finish of the race. "If you compared our record of finishes in Formula 1 with McLaren in Can-Am, it wouldn't look too bright. You can't win if you don't finish."

The secret of the McLaren success was reliability built from sound engineering. "Our basic design is good," Bruce said while the finishing touches were being put to the new Can-Am cars for 1970. "Our sports cars came from our original tube-frame cars which came from Coopers. Since then we have put in a tremendous amount of development and improvement every

Besides the silverware there's all that money! Hulme, St. Jovite, 1969.

year. If someone wants to compete with us, they can copy what we've got, but they will lack the background of research and experiment that taught us the lessons we built into our new cars. Other people can copy, but they will be doing it blindly and in doing that they can make a mistake.

"I often say to people in our drawing office and to the mechanics and engineers, 'Copy if you understand exactly why, but don't just copy blindly because the moment you do that, you're in terrible trouble.' You have to find out *why* something is done that way, do an experiment to find out why, and *then* you can copy something. In short, this is just plain good engineering. And this is why our cars are so good—they're well engineered."

Above, Elva-built M1Cs (Mk 3s) ready for shipment to American customers. Below, Peter Agg and John Bennett inspect an M4B.

13

PRODUCTION CARS & SPECIAL PROJECTS

"WHEN WE PLANNED the original Mc-Laren, it was going to be just that. A special car built by my pocket-sized team, around me, and for me. The idea was for us to win races. The prototype McLaren was almost a freehand affair and when we built it in 1964 we speculated on the possibilities of handling production ourselves, figuring on a limited line of six, but when we looked at delivery schedules and production costs on the car we were building, we shuddered and decided there were enough problems and costs involved in running one team car without buying a customer's woes when we sold a production model." Bruce was talking about the team's first year when production was a pipedream of the immediate future.

When the M1A was so successful there were several inquiries for copies but after consideration Bruce decided against going into production, even on a limited basis. That was when Frank Nichols of Elva Cars came to the factory in Feltham with a proposition to handle production of "customer" McLarens. Elva was at this stage building small-capacity sports/racing cars in its factory at Rye on the Kent coast.

The Lambretta Trojan group rescued Nichols' Elva company after it had gone into liquidation, re-forming it as Elva Cars

(1961) Ltd, and at Nichols' suggestion a deal was arranged between Peter Agg, managing director of Lambretta Trojan, and McLaren Racing, whereby the Elva company would build production McLaren sports cars for sale as McLaren-Elvas.

The agreement was signed on November 21, 1964, and work started immediately to have the first McLaren-Elva ready for the London Racing Car Show in January.

There were 24 M1A McLaren-Elvas sold. There were difficulties with the first run of production cars, firstly because the prototype was being raced in America at the time of the initial discussions and secondly because most of the McLaren team—which numbered six at the time—went to the Tasman series during January and February 1965 with the two Coopers for Bruce and Phil Hill. Another problem was that there were no manufacturing drawings. It was one thing for the racing team to build a one-off car as they went along, but quite another to set up a manufacturing process for a run of several cars.

"When you build a prototype car," said Bruce, "the most sensible method is to settle upon the suspension geometry you want first. Then the basic chassis structure is drawn to accommodate that geometry. Most of the bits and pieces—roll bars, steering column mounts, battery mounts, brake lines, switches, instruments, body fasteners, etc., are put into the chassis wherever your experience tells you they will fit and work. To lay all that out in two dimensions on the drawing board would take the best part of a year and the design would be obsolete by the time it got to the track. But these drawings have to be made in order to build a series of cars and this was the first snag we encountered. We had problems getting wheels designed and cast in time, and then came drama with the bodies. The prototype had an aluminum body built in a back alley by two old-timers in the panel-beating game in under three weeks, and this body was to be used as a mold for the production bodies which were to be in fiberglass to cut down costs."

Because Bruce was on the Tasman series at the time the molds were made he wasn't able to pass judgement and when he returned to England he found that the bodies were not quite to his liking, but by then it was too late.

"Building a racing car is not the simplest task you can undertake and building a series of them just multiplies the difficulties by the number of cars you intend making."

The M1A was designed specifically for the Oldsmobile engine, although customers for the first cars tried fitting Chevrolet and Ford engines with varying degrees of success. The M1B (or

The first Elva-built M1A, with charmer, at London Racing Car Show.

the Mk2 as it was known in America) catered to other engines and during 1965 and 1966 Trojan built 28 of these cars. The M1B and M1C (known as the Mk 3) were improvements and revisions on the spaceframe theme of the original prototype M1A, with modifications being passed on from the current cars raced by the McLaren team. Trojan built 25 M1C McLarens, for a total of 77 cars following the basic lines laid down by Bruce for the M1A.

In 1967 the new monocoque M6A sports car swept the opposition aside in the Can-Am series and for 1968 Trojan built a production version called the M6B and sold 26. In 1969 an attempt was made to homologate a GT version of the M6 Can-Am car for long-distance racing, but despite technically meeting the F1A requirements, it was not accepted as a Group 4 car and only four M6GTs were built. David Prophet raced one in England, Bruce had one as a development vehicle for a possible McLaren road car, one was shipped to a customer in America, and a fourth was built by Trojan for its own display purposes. Trojan still talks of producing a road car and Peter Agg reckons that with a "cooking" V-8 engine he could produce a road-going McLaren GT for around 6500 Pounds (about $15,600) including taxes in England.

The M4 Formula 2 monocoque designed by Robin Herd at the beginning of 1967 was put into production by Trojan later that year and sold as a chassis for Formula 2, 3 or American

An "M12GT" was recently built up using one of the M6GT body shells.

Formula B racing, but lack of time for development made the pretty little M4 one of the least successful McLaren cars.

The M12 customer car for 1969 used an M6-type chassis with a body along the lines of the 1968 M8A team cars and 14 of these were built. The M8C was further refinement of the M6/M12 line, differing from the M8A in that pontoons behind the rear bulkhead were provided to ease the installation of engines other than the aluminum Chevrolet that was a stressed member on the works M8A and M8B. Eight M8Cs were sold in 1970. For 1971 the production model will be the M8E which is a copy of the original M8 with the monocoque ending abruptly behind the cockpit. Customers can order the M8E with M8C-type pontoons to aid engine mounting if they do not wish to use the engine as a stress-bearing member.

During 1970 a prototype known as the M8E was built and tested by Denny Hulme at Goodwood. This was in fact a reversion to the narrower track and body of the M8B but with a low wing mounted to a frame over the transmission instead of the high wing of the M8B or the fins and wing of the M8D. This car was never raced because the monocoque tub was needed as a spare to replace the tub in Denny Hulme's car after it was damaged in an accident at the Road Atlanta race in September.

An important project for Trojan was the line of single-seat M10 cars for the 5-liter Formula 5000 in England, Formula A in America and the Tasman series. In 1969 and 1970 Peter Gethin won the Formula 5000 Championships in England using an M10A and an M10B. John Cannon won the Formula A title with an M10B in America in 1970, and that season in England Sir Nicholas Williamson won the British Hillclimb Championship with an M10B. Patsy Burt also won the British Sprint

Championship in 1970 with her older M3 single-seater. Trojan sold 20 M10As and 22 M10Bs.

The McLaren/Trojan alliance has resulted in a peculiarly happy marriage for both companies, since Trojan benefits by the specialist racing experience of the works team and modifications can be passed on to the production models when significant improvements have been made in the works cars. The McLaren team gets the enormous advantage of being free of 90 percent of the worries normally associated with production and they can also take advantage of the Trojan stocks of components when building up prototype cars.

Peter James Agg, 41, is a businessman to the tips of his handlebar moustache and he pushes eagerly ahead with new developments in his group of companies. On the road he drives a Bentley and an Iso Grifo and as a hobby he has a historic front-wheel-drive Derby Maserati racing car. Bruce wondered at first whether his specialized racing team would be able to work side by side with this sort of old-school-tie chappie, but he soon discovered that Agg's approach was strictly British executive and businesslike.

The Lambretta-Trojan group of companies includes the Lambretta motor scooter concession for Great Britain and they market around 10,000 of these scooters each year. Agg personally

The Ferguson torque converter and 2-speed gearbox fitted to an M1A.

owns Suzuki (Great Britain) Limited and has handed the running of the company over to Lambretta. Next to Honda, Agg's Suzuki operation is the largest distributor of motorcycles in England, selling also about 10,000 a year. Included in the group is the national distributorship for Homelite chain saws and 20,000 of these are sold annually. Agg also has the agency for the Italian Iso cars but the sleek Grifo GT costs around 8500 Pounds (about $20,400) in 7-liter form and is over-priced on the British market.

The total staff of the group numbers around 270 and this includes a property company with a complete construction crew that built the offices and factories on the Lambretta-Trojan 15-acre estate at Purley.

The racing division is housed at present in a 10,000-square foot factory but Agg talks of moving to another factory on the estate with an area of 27,000 square feet and branching out into the engine-building side of racing. In 1970 Frank Gardner's Formula 5000 Lola was extremely competitive using a Chevrolet engine built by Louis Morand in Switzerland and Agg has arranged to handle sales of this engine in England. They will build 5-liter engines for Formula A/5000 and 7-liter units for Can-Am races and the Group 7 Inter-Series which is increasing in popularity and bringing Can-Am cars into Europe.

In the Suzuki workshops ideas from the McLaren car-building construction have been borrowed in the form of an aluminum monocoque for a trials bike weighing 30 pounds less than the normal tube frame, and much stronger.

Some of the McLaren car-building staff have moved to Trojan from Colnbrook to help with the liaison between the racing team and the production cars, and Bill Meace, who ran the production at the old Elva company (the name has been dropped now in favor of the Trojan label on the cars) works closely with Harry Pearce at Colnbrook.

THE AUTOMATIC MCLAREN

Jim Hall's Chaparrals were hard cars to beat in 1964 and Bruce put a lot of credit for their pace down to the fact that Hall was using a form of automatic transmission. To try and counter this advantage, Bruce talked with Tony Rolt at Harry Ferguson Research and a special Ferguson torque converter with a 2-speed gearbox behind it was adapted to fit the M1A sports car in 1965. In the initial testing at Oulton Park Chris Amon took half a second off the lap record set the year before by Jim Clark in a Formula 1 Lotus.

This performance prompted Bruce to enter the automatic car in the Tourist Trophy at Oulton Park in May, but the problems that manifested themselves that weekend spelled the end of the Ferguson project. A seal in the torque converter shifted after Bruce had done seven laps in the first practice session and the mechanics stripped the unit to mend it. After only one lap in the second practice a connecting rod broke in the engine and with only eight laps of practice done Bruce had to settle for 2nd fastest time behind John Surtees in the Lola and the crew worked all night to install a new engine.

There was a special technique in making a grid start with the car because the transmission had a tendency to creep and the driver had to sit on the grid with his left foot hard on the brake, his right foot building up revs with the accelerator and the car trying to overcome the brakes and crawl forward!

Bruce took the lead in the TT when the Surtees Lola's steering failed after a couple of laps, but after 10 laps fluid started leaking from the torque converter again and Bruce stopped. Tyler and the other mechanics stripped the still-secret unit on the pit bench with the cars thundering past a few feet away and had the transmission repaired in time for the start of the second heat. Bruce stormed off the back of the grid and caught Jim Clark in the Lotus 30, setting a new track record of 100.4 mph in the process, before the oil pressure started to drop and he pitted before the engine destroyed itself again.

After an investigation of the problems they had suffered in the TT they discovered that the operation of the torque converter kept the engine working too low in the rev range and this was causing pre-ignition and blowing the engines.

The automatic McLaren had proved itself to be a record-breaker, but the team was not convinced that the mechanical problems associated with the transmission were worth solving, and it seemed likely that they would be better rewarded putting

The Ford GTX was driven to 5th place at Riverside in 1965 by Amon.

the same effort into further development on the sports car using a conventional transmission.

THE FORD GTX

Bruce, Richie Ginther and Roy Salvadori were the first test drivers hired by Ford for development work on the GT40 and Bruce and Phil Hill drove a GT40 in its first race at the Nurburgring 1000-Km in 1964. The car dropped out of 2nd place when a weld failed in the rear suspension. Bruce was impressed with the potential of the Ford GT and he worked well with Yorkshireman Roy Lunn who had designed the front-wheel-drive Cardinal with an advanced design crew at Dearborn before the car was handed over to Ford in Germany to become the Taunus 26M. Lunn was also responsible for the little 1.7-liter mid-engined open two-seater that was known as Mustang 1, a vehicle built to test public reaction to a possible Ford sports car. Later Lunn worked with Eric Broadley on the development of the GT40 which was closely based on the Lola GT that Broadley had built in 1963.

Toward the end of the 1964 season Lunn and McLaren discussed the chances of the McLaren team building up a special open version of the GT40 to see if it had potential in American sports car events. This was a suitable arrangement for the growing McLaren team because, as Teddy Mayer said later, Ford contracts to do *anything* at that time were extremely lucrative. From the Ford point of view the McLaren team was ideally suited to build a big sports car because of its experience in this field, and the liaison with Bruce was already well established.

The result was that the McLaren team was given a prototype GT40 (chassis number GT40/110) with a 7-liter engine and the go-ahead to start the development project. Gary Knutson was put in charge of the car, known as the GTX, converting it into an open car and radically altering the structure. The GTX emerged much lighter than the GT40 with a single-sheet aluminum monocoque in place of the GT40's 23-gauge sheet steel hull. One of Ford's main objects in handing the GTX project over to the McLaren team was to have the work done quickly and efficiently and to decide whether to pursue the aluminum monocoque or go to the new honeycomb material for the new cars they were developing.

Chris Amon raced the GTX at Mosport, Riverside and Nassau, but finished only once, placing 5th at Riverside. At the end of the season the GTX stayed in America and was altered with a new nose with the larger windscreen required by the regulations for long-distance races. It was entered in the 1966 Sebring 12-hour race and it won, driven by Ken Miles and Lloyd Ruby. After that race the car was scrapped, but Ford had benefited from the development of the GTX at Feltham—the new 7-liter Mark 4 Ford cars used the honeycomb sheet in their monocoque tubs. Bruce and Mario Andretti won the 1967 Sebring race in the first of the Ford Mk 4s and the Gurney/Foyt Mk 4 won at Le Mans the same year.

ALFA ROMEO ENGINES IN FORMULA 1

At the beginning of 1970 an arrangement was made with Autodelta (the factory-owned Alfa Romeo racing team) whereby the McLaren team would supply a Formula 1 chassis to be fitted with the 3-liter Alfa Romeo V-8 and the car would be driven by Andrea de Adamich.

The engine was basically the T33 sports car unit originally built as a 2-liter in 1967 and developed to the point where it gave around 410 horsepower in 3-liter Formula 1 trim. One of the problems with the installation of the Alfa Romeo engine in the M7 chassis was that a mounting had to be arranged for the alternator which is not integral with the engine as it is on the Ford-Cosworth V-8. This M7 received a D suffix to differentiate it from the Ford-engined M7A, M7B and M7C cars.

The horsepower did not match that of the Ford but it was felt that with the resources of the Alfa Romeo company behind Autodelta, a competitive engine could be built if the Formula 1 venture were at all successful. It was also hedging against the rash of unreliability suffered during the 1970 season with the Ford engines as Cosworth struggled to look after the 70 units in use as well as track down a problem with harmonic balancing.

Later in the season De Adamich drove a new M14D McLaren with the Alfa Romeo engine fitted and Giovanni Marelli, a young ex-Ferrari racing engineer, was hired to look after the engine. The car continued to be plagued with problems relating to engine performance and reliability and at the end of the season the alliance between the Italian factory and the McLaren team was dissolved.

WHEN THE NUMBING SHOCK of Bruce's death had been replaced by a disbelief that such a thing could have possibly happened, Teddy, Phil, Tyler and Denny pushed ahead with the team's program for 1970. They lacked their late leader's drive and enthusiasm, but they were determined to keep going "for Bruce."

Denny's burned hands were still extremely painful but he spurred recovery to drive one of the M8Ds in the first Can-Am race at Mosport on June 14th. Dan Gurney had been signed to take Bruce's place and he carried the Kiwi banner to win the first two races. Denny was 3rd at Mosport and then gave the Dutch GP at Zandvoort a miss while he waited for his hands to heal properly. The team had withdrawn its entries from the Belgian Grand Prix at a mark of respect to Bruce, and for Zandvoort Dan Gurney and Peter Gethin were driving with Denny on hand to offer expert advice.

Denny made his comeback with a win in the Watkins Glen Can-Am race after engine troubles had delayed Gurney. Problems over a sponsorship clash meant that Dan was replaced in the Can-Am team by Gethin who flew out with Denny in time for the Edmonton race. Denny made it three in a row with victories at Edmonton and Mid-Ohio. Gethin had a controversial win in the Road America race when Denny was penalized for allegedly being push-started after a spin. Peter had waited for his team leader to catch up and take the flag ahead of him, but

LOOKING AHEAD

the officials credited Denny only with the laps done before his spin and he was relegated to 15th place.

Both M8Ds were damaged in race accidents at Road Atlanta and Tony Dean won in the 3-liter Porsche 908. It was the first time any car but a McLaren had won a Can-Am race since John Surtees won with his Lola at the end of the 1967 season in Las Vegas!

Denny rounded off the 1970 season with wins at Donnybrooke, Laguna Seca and Riverside and won the championship with 132 points, nearly double the score of 2nd-man Lothar Motschenbacher with 65 points in his production McLaren M12. Peter Gethin finished 3rd on final standings after his engine blew up at Riverside and ruined his chances of overhauling Lothar's score. It was the first time in four years that Team McLaren had missed traditional 1-2 championship finish.

It had been a ragged season in Formula 1 for the McLaren M14As with Bruce's death, Denny's accident at Indianapolis and then Gurney and Gethin driving only part of the season. Denny's best result was his 2nd place in South Africa with 3rds in the British, German and Mexican Grands Prix.

For 1971 Peter Gethin again teams with Hulme in Formula 1 with new M19 Ford-engined cars, but Peter Revson will join McLaren in America, driving the second Can-Am car and the second M16 wedge in the big 500-mile races at Indianapolis, Ontario and Pocono.

McLAREN CARS
BY TYPE NUMBER
1964–1971

The original M1A-Olds, painted New Zealand's black and silver colors.

Above, the first Elva-built M1A production car. Below, Phil Hill driving Bruce's M1B team car at Kent, Washington in 1965; he was 2nd.

M1A The original McLaren-built sports/racing car was a simple space frame design powered by a light and compact Oldsmobile V-8 engine. The type was put into production as the McLaren-Elva Mark 1 and versions appeared with 4.7-liter Ford V-8 power in addition to the standard 4.5-liter Olds. A total of 24 were built and met with some success, although it soon became apparent that the Olds engine was just too small for the class.

CHASSIS: Large-diameter round and square tubular frame with light alloy sheet riveted and bonded to it, forming stressed undertray and bulkheads.
SUSPENSION: Independent by unequal-length wide-based wishbones, anti-roll bar and adjustable coil spring/shock units in front. Trailing radius arms with single top links, reversed lower wishbones, anti-roll bar and adjustable coil spring/shock units at rear.
BRAKES: Dual-circuit Girling discs all around.
BODY: Four-section polyester resin with integral brake and radiator ducting and side sections housing twin fuel tanks.
ENGINE: Traco Oldsmobile 4.5-liter V-8 standard with Hewland LG 4-speed gearbox. At least one 4.7 Ford-powered example also appeared.
DIMENSIONS: Wheelbase 91 inches, front track 51 inches, rear track 51 inches.

M1B This Group 7 sports/racing car was the 1965 development of the original M1A design. Rebuilt with a new chassis, new body and many other modifications it was put into production at Elva's Rye factory and sold in the U.S. as the McLaren-Elva Mark 2. Standard Oldsmobile or optional Ford and Chevrolet V-8s could be fitted. The works cars driven by McLaren and Amon competed in the 1966 Can-Am series, using Chevrolet V-8s with Hilborn injection. Twenty-eight were made.

CHASSIS: Large-diameter round and square tubular frame with light alloy sheet riveted and bonded to it forming undertray and bulkheads.
SUSPENSION: Independent by unequal-length wide-base wishbones with anti-dive characteristics, anti-roll bar and adjustable coil spring/shock units in front. Trailing arms with lower wishbones, single top links, anti-roll bar and adjustable coil spring/shock units at rear. McLaren-Elva cast magnesium wheels, 15 x 8½ front, 15 x 11½ rear (5.50 and 6.50-15 tires).

The Nickey Chevrolet M1B driven in the USRRC series by Charlie Hayes.

The late-1966 M1B team car had nose slots plus fins and wing in back.

Above, Bob Bondurant driving the Dana Chevrolet M1C at Riverside. Below, Bruce in the M2A-Oldsmobile tire test car at Goodwood.

BRAKES: Dual-circuit Girling discs all around, 12½-inch diameter front and 11½-inch diameter rear.

BODY: Four-section polyester resin with integral brake and radiator ducting and side sections housing twin 25-gallon rubber fuel cells.

ENGINE: Traco Oldsmobile 4.5-liter V-8 standard with single-plate Schiefer clutch and 4-speed Hewland LG gearbox. Hypoid ring and pinion with limited-slip differential standard in this transmission. Chevrolet and Ford engines and ZF transmission optional equipment.

DIMENSIONS: Wheelbase 91 inches, front track 51 inches, rear track 51 inches, overall length 146 inches, width 64 inches, height to top of windscreen 31 inches, weight less fuel 1300 pounds distributed 40 percent front/60 percent rear.

M1C

While the works team ran its first monocoque sports cars in the 1967 Can-Am series, the Trojan-built customer cars were still space-frame developments of the original design. These M1C variants, sold as Mark 3s, were generally provided with Chevrolet engines although Oldsmobile and Ford options were still listed. The model was a further improved and developed M1B with a separate spoiler wing at the tail. Twenty-five were built.

CHASSIS: Large-diameter tubular space frame with light alloy sheet bonded and riveted, forming undertray and bulkheads.

SUSPENSION: As for M1B.

BRAKES: Dual-circuit Girling discs all around, 12-inch diameter front and 11½-inch diameter rear.

BODY: As for M1B.

ENGINE: As for M1B with Chevrolet V-8 and optional 4- or 5-speed Hewland transmission; ZF still offered.

DIMENSIONS: Wheelbase 90.5 inches, front track 52 inches, rear track 52 inches, overall length 146 inches, width 66 inches, height to top of windscreen 31 inches, weight less fuel 1300 pounds distributed 40 percent front/60 percent rear.

M2A

This was an early exercise in producing a Mallite monocoque, and was the team's first single-seat design. It was the work of Robin Herd who borrowed Mallite—an aluminum/balsa sandwich material—from experience in the aircraft industry. It was light but extremely strong and this single car was used for devel-

The M2B, powered by a 3-liter version of the 4-cam Indy Ford V-8.

Above, Bruce in the M2B with the temporary Serenissima V-8 at Spa.
Below, he drives the M3 "Whoosh-Bonk" tire test car at Goodwood.

opment of the forthcoming Formula 1 car and served Firestone very well as a tire test vehicle. It used Traco Oldsmobile and Ford V-8 engines and gave rise to many rumors of McLaren having a Formula 1 car. In fact the car was never raced, but many lessons from its testing were incorporated in the M2B.

M2B
McLaren Racing's first Formula 1 car, the M2B was another Robin Herd-designed Mallite monocoque. Technically it was a spectacular success, for the chassis was probably the stiffest open-cockpit unit ever built, with a torsional rigidity approaching 10,000 lbs/ft per degree. The 1966 season was the first to be run under the 3-liter Formula 1, however, and McLaren chose a de-stroked Indy Ford V-8 for power. This unit proved extremely unreliable, suffering from fragile main bearings, and was replaced temporarily by an underpowered Serenissima V-8 in mid-season. The Ford was resurrected after some development work but was never a success and the project was shelved at the end of the year. Two chassis were built, but only one raced.

CHASSIS: Bathtub-type monocoque formed from Mallite and duralumin panelling formed over mild steel bulkheads.
SUSPENSION: Independent by upper rocker arm operating inboard coil spring/shock units with radius arm and lower wishbone in front. Upper transverse link and radius arm, lower reversed wishbone and radius arm with outboard coil spring/shock units at rear. McLaren cast magnesium wheels, 13 x 8½ front, 13 x 12 rear.
BRAKES: Girling discs all around with dual circuits and BR front calipers, AR rears.
BODY: Formed by monocoque sides apart from fiberglass nose cone and cockpit surround, and engine covers used occasionally with both engines.
ENGINE: 3-liter Ford V-8, ex-Indianapolis twincam engine later replaced temporarily by 3-liter Serenissima V-8; Borg & Beck clutch and 5-speed ZF 5DS25 transaxle.
DIMENSIONS: Wheelbase 96 inches, front track 59 inches, rear track 59 inches.

M3
The team's 1965 sports car experiences with big American V-8 engines in lightweight tubular chassis led to the design and production of this cheap and reliable space-frame single-seater in 1966. It was intended for Formula Libre, sprint and hill-

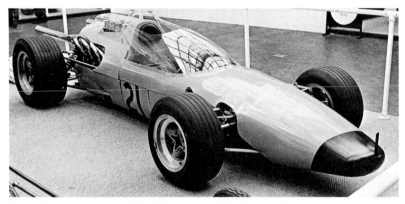

Patsy Burt's long-nosed, bubble-screen M3-Oldsmobile sprint car.

Above, Bruce at Rouen in the M4A-Cosworth Formula 2 car. Below, a production M4B-Ford Twincam built by Trojan for Formula B races.

climbs and even as a private-owner Formula 1 car, priced at 3000 Pounds as a rolling chassis. The engine bay would accept engines from 3 to 6 liters and orders were placed by such notable hillclimb drivers as Harry Zweifel and Patsy Burt. The type proved competitive and tough but only a handful were built.

CHASSIS: Large-diameter tubular spaceframe with steel bulkheads and an aluminum dash panel doubling as a bulkhead in the cockpit area. Chassis tubes carried coolant and an aluminum undertray was bonded and riveted in place to add strength.
SUSPENSION: As for M1 series but with optional 15-inch diameter rear wheels.
BRAKES: Girling 10 7/16-inch discs all around with AR calipers. Special ½-inch thick discs available for GP versions.
BODY: Polyester-resin panelling to customer preference.
ENGINE: To customer preference although engine bay was capable of accepting Oldsmobile, Ford-Cobra and Ford-Indianapolis V-8s or 3-liter Repco V-8, Maserati V-12 and 2.5 or 2.7-liter Coventry Climax 4-cylinder F1 units. Rear bulkhead designed to accept Hewland LG or ZF 5DS25 transaxles.
DIMENSIONS: Wheelbase 96 inches (required for possible Indy use), front track 51 inches, rear track 52 inches, overall length 142 inches, height to top of windscreen 29 inches, weight (with 5-liter Oldsmobile) 1100 pounds.

M4A For 1967 Robin Herd produced three major designs, for Can-Am, Formula 1 and Formula 2. The M4A was a simple bathtub type monocoque intended for Formula 2 use and it was raced by Bruce McLaren in about seven events. Some chassis also appeared in Formula 3 guise with little success, but Piers Courage raced a M4A in the 1968 Tasman series and scored the type's only major victory.

CHASSIS: Bathtub monocoque formed from aluminum panelling bonded and riveted to four mild steel bulkheads.
SUSPENSION: Single top link with radius arms and lower wishbones, outboard coil spring/shock units and anti-roll bar in front. Twin radius arms, reversed lower wishbones and single top links with outboard coil spring/shock units at rear. McLaren-Elva cast magnesium wheels, 13 x 7 front, 13 x 10 rear (5.00 and 6.25-13 tires).
BRAKES: Girling or Lockheed 10½-inch discs all around with AR calipers.

The M4B-BRM V-8 at Monaco 1967 with shortened nose and side tanks.

Above, the M5-BRM V-12 at Mosport, where it nearly won first time out.
Below, the M6A-Chevrolet Can-Am was the first orange McLaren.

BODY: Formed by monocoque sides plus fiberglass nose cone and cockpit surround.

ENGINE: Cosworth-Ford FVA 1600-cc 4-cylinder unit with five-speed Hewland FT200 transaxle.

DIMENSIONS: Wheelbase 90 inches, front track 54 inches, rear track 54 inches, overall length 121 inches, height 30 inches, weight 830 pounds.

M4B

The M4B was a production variant of the F2 design, using tuned Lotus-Ford twincam engines and Hewland HD transaxles for American Formula B racing. Another so-called M4B, the subject of this specification, was the interim 1967 Formula 1 car raced by Bruce McLaren. This was a stop-gap measure between the demise of the M2B and the appearance of the new BRM-powered M5, and had a 3-inch increase in wheelbase to accommodate a 2.1-liter BRM V-8 Tasman engine. The car was also fitted with side sponsons to provide extra tankage and was quite successful until damaged in an accident. Meanwhile the true production M4A/B line at Trojan built 25 cars in 1967-68. Formula 1 M4B specifications as for M4A apart from:

ENGINE: 2.1-liter BRM V-8 with Hewland FT200 transaxle.

DIMENSIONS: Wheelbase 93 inches, height 30 inches, weight (with ballast) about 1120 pounds to comply with F1 limit.

M5

The true 1967 McLaren Formula 1 car, the one-off M5 monocoque, was a late starter due to delays with its BRM V-12 engine. Bruce debuted the car in the Canadian GP and was a strong 2nd until he had to stop to replace a flat battery. The car was very competitive in its early races, but the V-12 was soon outstripped by the Cosworth-Ford V-8 and a new car was designed for 1968 to accept the latter unit. The M5's last race in works colors was in Hulme's hands at Kyalami, then Jo Bonnier raced the car briefly before putting it on display in his Lausanne, Switzerland, art gallery.

CHASSIS: Aluminum alloy-panelled monocoque formed over mild-steel bulkheads with long pontoons at the rear to support the V-12 engine.

SUSPENSION: Single top link with radius arm, lower wishbone, anti-roll bar and outboard coil spring/shock units in front. Twin radius arms, single top links, reversed lower wishbones, and out-

Lothar Motschenbacher in his M6B, a production version of the M6A.

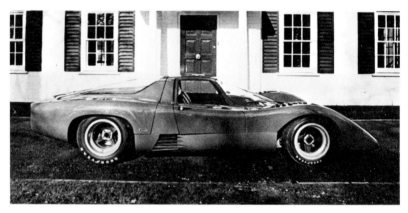

The road version of the M6GT in front of Bruce's home, above. Below, Bruce winning the 1968 Race of Champions in the new M7A.

board coil spring/shock units at rear. McLaren cast magnesium wheels, 13 x 8½ front and 15 x 12 rear.

BRAKES: Lockheed discs and calipers all around.

BODY: Formed by monocoque sides apart from fiberglass nose cone and cockpit surround.

ENGINE: 3-liter BRM V-12 with Borg & Beck clutch and Hewland DG 5-speed transaxle.

DIMENSIONS: Wheelbase 96 inches, front track 58 inches, rear track 58 inches.

M6A Bruce won the 1967 Can-Am title with this first monocoque Group 7 car, designed by a committee consisting of himself, Robin Herd, Don Beresford and Tyler Alexander. It was as simple as possible, consisting of single curvatures and square-section tubing wherever they could be used. The M6A was a pure works car and only three were built.

CHASSIS: Full monocoque formed from aluminum alloy panelling bonded and riveted to steel bulkheads and carrying two 25-gallon fuel cells in the side pontoons.

SUSPENSION: Unequal length upper and lower wishbones, anti-roll bar and coil spring/shock units in front. Upper and lower wishbones with twin radius arms anti-roll bar and coil spring/shock units at rear. McLaren cast magnesium wheels, 15 x 8½ front and 15 x 13¼ rear.

BRAKES: Girling ventilated discs front and rear, 12-inch diameter, with 16-3-LA calipers and dual hydraulic circuits.

BODY: Reinforced polyester resin panelling.

ENGINE: 5.9-liter Chevrolet V-8 with Lucas fuel injection and 5-speed Hewland LG transaxle.

DIMENSIONS: Wheelbase 93.5 inches, front track 52 inches, rear track 52 inches, overall length 155 inches, width 68 inches, height to top of windscreen 31 inches, weight less fuel 1300 pounds distributed 40 percent front/60 percent rear.

M6B The M6B was the 1968 production version of the Championship-winning M6A and differed very little from the original. It was offered by Trojan as a rolling chassis complete with transmission, mountings and exhausts, ready to accept a Chevrolet V-8 engine. It was in tremendous demand; a total of 28 were built and their specifications were virtually identical to those of the M6A.

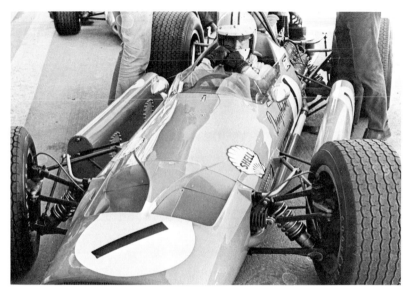

In 1968 Spanish GP the M7As had Lancia-type outrigger fuel tanks.

Above, M7A had engine cover with scoop for oil cooler at Spa. Below, small wing and makeshift sidetanks fitted to M7A at Rouen.

M6GT Following the Group 7 successes of the M6 series, a Group 4 coupe model was projected for the 1969 season. Unfortunately the type met with various problems preventing its homologation in the class and the project was shelved after just four examples had been completed. The prototype was sold to David Prophet who ran it with Chevrolet engines of various sizes and later converted it to open specification with an M6B-type body shell. Another, finished as a high-performance road car for Bruce McLaren's use, acted as the prototype of a road-car series which has yet to be produced.

M7A Robin Herd again had a guiding hand in the design of this model, the team's first Cosworth-Ford-powered Formula 1 contender. Three M7A monocoques were built for the 1968 season, to be driven by Bruce and Denny Hulme plus a spare. In the interests of accessibility, they had bathtub type monocoques which terminated behind the rear cockpit bulkhead, using the engine's crankcase as a fully-stressed rear chassis member.

CHASSIS: Monocoque with light aluminum-alloy panelling over steel bulkheads, using the engine as a stressed section aft of the cockpit, carrying rear suspension loads though a yoke over the gearbox and plates bolted beneath it.
SUSPENSION: Single top link with radius arm, bottom wishbone, anti-roll bar and outboard coil spring/shock units in front. Single top link, reversed lower wishbones, twin radius arms and coil spring/shock units at rear. McLaren cast magnesium wheels, 15 x 10 front and 15 x 15 rear.
BRAKES: Lockheed 17/3P calipers with 11.66-inch diameter discs all around.
BODY: Detachable fiberglass nose cone with separate top panel and cockpit surround. Engine cover sometimes used with various wings and spoiler arrangements.
ENGINE: Cosworth-Ford DFV V-8 with 5-speed Hewland DG300 transaxle.
DIMENSIONS: Wheelbase 94 inches, front track 58 inches, rear track 57 inches, cockpit width 28 inches, weight 1140 pounds.

M7B Starting life as M7A-3, this chassis was fitted with broad pannier fuel tanks at the beginning of 1969 as a research vehicle to test weight distribution and give room for the adoption of a four-wheel drive system. It was not very successful and was sold

Biplane wings plus nose planes on Denny's M7A at Monaco in 1969.

Above, Bruce at Brands Hatch in M7B with low, wide sidetanks and high wing. Below, the same car with low wing, driven in 1969 by Vic Elford.

to Colin Crabbe's Antique Automobiles racing team for Vic Elford to drive. He put up some excellent performances in the car before damaging it beyond repair when he was involved in Mario Andretti's accident in the German GP. Apart from the panniers its specification was little different from the standard M7As.

M7C
While the M7A-type bathtub chassis were tough and accessible they lacked some of the torsional rigidity achieved in the 1969 Formula A/5000 cars. Consequently one F1 car was built using a full "up-and-over" monocoque chassis identical to the M10A 5-liter cars and this machine, known as M7C-1, became Bruce's personal car in 1969 F1 events and was sold to John Surtees the following year. In general specification it was similar to the M7A cars.

M7D
McLaren Racing came to an agreement with Autodelta early in 1970 to build a chassis to accept one of their 3-liter Alfa Romeo T33 V-8 engines. This new chassis followed the two-year-old M7-series design but was 2 inches longer in wheelbase.

M8A
The 1968 Can-Am works cars were further developments of the successful M6A design and were again kept as simple as possible, employing single-curvature panelling and square tube sections in the monocoque, which now used the engine as a partially-stressed structural member. Three were built, dominating the championship once again, Denny taking the title.

CHASSIS: Aluminum-alloy and magnesium panelled monocoque based on steel bulkheads and using the Chevrolet engine as a partially-stressed structural member stiffening the rear bay.
SUSPENSION: Single top link with radius arm, lower wishbone, anti-roll bar and coil spring/shock units in front. Twin radius arms with single top link, reversed lower wishbone and coil spring/shock units at rear. McLaren cast magnesium wheels, 15 x 10 front and 15 x 15 rear.
BRAKES: Lockheed discs all around, 12-inch diameter with 17/3P calipers and dual aerodynamic surfaces.
ENGINE: Chevrolet V-8 with 4-speed Hewland transaxle.
DIMENSIONS: Wheelbase 94 inches, front track 57.6 inches, rear track 56 inches.

255

Above, Bruce in full-monocoque M7C at Clermont-Ferrand in 1969.
Below, separate wing replaced tray-type engine cover at Monza.

M8B Three new and further developed Group 7 works cars were built for the 1969 Can-Am series, using at least one of the original M8A monocoques. They differed from the earlier cars in body design, using wings standing high above the tail on suspension-mounted struts, and had new 7-liter engines built by George Bolthoff, an ex-Traco engineer who had replaced Gary Knutson in the team. There were minor detail differences between the M8Bs and the earlier M8As. The 1969 cars used larger wheels—15 x 11 front and 15 x 16 rear. They were unbeaten in Can-Am events and Bruce took his second Championship title.

M8C This model was the 1970 production version of the all-conquering M8-series design, but differed in some important respects. It was felt that private customers would wish to fit engines other than the Chevrolet ZL-1s used by the works, and rear-bay crossmembers were provided to support optional engines, replacing the subframes used to stress the blocks in the M8A and B models. Specifications were otherwise similar to the earlier models and demand was high, Trojan building 15 cars.

M8D Three new cars were assembled for the 1970 Can-Am Championship, and were again improvements on the basic theme. Strut-mounted wings acting on the suspension were no longer allowed so the M8D used separate airfoil sections mounted on tall fins rising from the rear fenders. These earned the car the name of "Batmobile" and with 7.5-liter engines built in Livonia, Michigan, by Bolthoff they were again successful; Hulme won another Can-Am title after Bruce was killed testing the original M8D at Goodwood. Specifications were as for the earlier M8-series cars except for the following: Front track 62.3 inches, rear track 58.5 inches, overall length 164 inches, weight 1420 pounds. Hewland LG600 4-speed transaxle fitted.

M8E The Trojan production Can-Am car for 1971, based on the prototype tested briefly by Denis Hulme at Goodwood in 1970. It has the basic shape of the M8B with a low wing instead of the side fins of the M8D. The track is narrower than the M8D, and the car has a smaller fiberglass body. The wheelbase is 95 inches with a front track of 58 inches and rear track of 55.5 inches. Wheels are 15-inch diameter with 11-inch front rims and 16-inch rear rims.

M7D driven by De Adamich had Alfa Romeo 33 V-8 in place of Ford.

Above, Denny driving his M8A to 1968 Elkhart Lake Can-Am victory. Below, the 1969 M8B was similar but had high wing, 7-liter engine.

M9 In common with Cosworth, Lotus and Matra, McLaren Racing developed a 4-wheel drive Formula 1 car during the 1969 season. The basis of the car was a simple twin-boom monocoque, with the Cosworth-Ford engine turned back-to-front and driving forward to a McLaren-designed 4wd transmission. The gearbox was just behind the driver's seat with driveshafts running along the left side of the car to tiny limited-slip differentials at front and rear. Despite extensive testing the car was only raced once, and in common with the other 4wd projects was soon abandoned.

CHASSIS: Twin-boom aluminum-skinned monocoque formed over steel bulkheads and terminating aft of the cockpit. Engine supported by a tubular subframe also providing pickups for the rear suspension.
SUSPENSION: Upper rocker arm operating inboard coil spring/shock units, and lower link with radius arm and anti-roll bar in front. Upper rocker arm operating inboard coil spring/shock units, and reversed lower wishbones, twin radius arms and anti-roll bar at rear. McLaren cast magnesium wheels, 13 x 12 front and 13 x 14 rear.
BRAKES: Girling 12-inch diameter ventilated discs front and rear, mounted inboard to reduce unsprung weight.
BODY: Formed by monocoque sides with detachable fiberglass nose cone, cockpit surround and aerodynamic surfaces.
ENGINE: Cosworth-Ford DFV 3-liter V-8 driving McLaren-designed and built 4-wheel drive transmission; torque split integral with gearbox.
DIMENSIONS: Wheelbase 95 inches, front track 59 inches, rear track 59 inches, width at cockpit 36 inches, weight 1160 pounds.

M10A McLaren was one of a comparatively few major manufacturers to produce a Formula A/5000 chassis when the class was introduced to Europe in 1969. Although it was based on Formula 1 design experience there was an interesting feedback in the M7C F1 car as described above. The M10A was extremely successful and dominated the first year of European Formula 5000. Trojan built 17 cars that first season.

CHASSIS: Full "up-and-over" monocoque with aluminum-alloy panelling bonded and riveted to fabricated steel bulkheads. Rearward-extending pontoons to support the engine.

M8C-Chevrolet was 1970 production car; this is Roger McCaig's.

M8C-Cosworth V-8 was driven in Argentina by Chris Craft/Trevor Taylor.

Above, early testing of M8D "Batmobile." Later changes, below, included vertical nose tabs and opening up of front wheel arches.

SUSPENSION: Single top link with radius arm, lower wishbone, anti-roll bar and outboard-coil spring/shock units in front. Single top link, reversed lower wishbone, twin radius arms and outboard coil spring/shock units at rear. McLaren cast magnesium wheels, 15 x 11 front and 15 x 16 rear (10.55 and 12.50-15 tires).

BRAKES: Lockheed ventilated discs all around with LA4-24 calipers.

BODY: Formed by monocoque sides with detachable fiberglass nose cone and cockpit surround and optional airfoil spoiler.

ENGINE: 5-liter (305-cubic inch) Chevrolet V-8 standard, with Hewland LG600 5-speed transaxle.

DIMENSIONS: Wheelbase 98 inches, front track 59.75 inches, rear track 60.5 inches, overall length 157.5 inches, width 77 inches, height to top of windscreen 26.5 inches, weight less fuel 1285 pounds.

M10B The 1970 development of the production Formula/5000 car differed from the original in several respects. The steering geometry was revised with low-offset front wheels, and the engine bay was altered to lower the engine mounting by 2 inches. The rear top-beam and its suspension pickups was also dropped, and a DG300 gearbox replaced the original LG600 unit, saving considerable weight. Dimensions and specifications were otherwise similar to the earlier car, and Peter Gethin won his second consecutive Guards F5000 Championship title with one of the 21 M10Bs Trojan produced.

M11 The M11 designation was not used due to possible confusion with "Mark II."

M12 This was an out-of-sequence designation applied to the 1969 production Group 7 sports/racer, which used an M8-type body on a monocoque similar to that of the M6-series cars. Standard mountings were provided for Chevrolet engines and a total of 15 cars were produced, including one with the narrower M6-type body-shell for hillclimb driver Phil Scragg. Chaparral Cars ran one M12 while its own 2G model was being developed.

CHASSIS: Monocoque with aluminum-alloy panelling bonded and riveted to fabricated steel bulkheads, with three fuel cells in

M8E is 1971 production Can-Am car; Hulme tests this 1970 prototype.

Above and below, the M9 4-wheel-drive Grand Prix car, which was not successful and was raced only once, in 1969 British GP by Derek Bell.

the sills and under the driver's knees holding 52 gallons.

SUSPENSION: Unequal-length wide-based wishbones, anti-roll bar and coil spring/shock units in front. Single top links and reversed lower wishbones with twin radius arms and coil spring/shock units at rear. McLaren cast magnesium wheels, 15 x 10 front and 15 x 15 rear (10.55 and 12.50-15 tires).

BRAKES: Girling ventilated discs, 12-inch diameter front and rear, with 16-3-LA calipers and dual hydraulic circuits.

BODY: Formed by monocoque sides with detachable fiberglass top panels.

ENGINE: Standard mountings for Chevrolet V-8 and Hewland LG 5-speed transaxle.

DIMENSIONS: Wheelbase 93.5 inches, front track 57 inches, rear track 55 inches, overall length 155 inches, width 75 inches, height to top of windscreen 30 inches, weight less fuel 1300 pounds distributed 40 percent front/60 percent rear.

M13 The M13 designation was not allocated.

M14A Three 1970 Formula 1 cars were built at the start of the season and the design team of Bruce McLaren, Gordon Coppuck and Jo Marquart had made several important innovations. Most notable of these was the adoption of inboard rear brakes in an effort to save unsprung weight.

CHASSIS: Full monocoque with aluminum and magnesium panelling bonded to fabricated steel bulkheads, terminating behind the rear cockpit bulkhead and using the engine as a fully-stressed chassis member.

SUSPENSION: Single top link with radius arm, lower wishbone, anti-roll bar and outboard coil spring/shock units in front. Single top link, reversed lower wishbone, twin radius arms and outboard coil spring/shock units at rear. McLaren cast magnesium wheels, 15 x 11 front and 15 x 16 rear.

BRAKES: Lockheed ventilated discs all around, 11.66-inch diameter front and 10.90-inch diameter rear mounted inboard.

BODY: Formed by monocoque sides with detachable fiberglass nose cone and cockpit surrounds.

ENGINE: Cosworth-Ford DFV 3-liter V-8 with Hewland DG300 5-speed transaxle.

DIMENSIONS: Wheelbase 95 inches, front track 62.4 inches, rear track 60 inches, length 156 inches, weight 1180 pounds.   **263**

M10A was a Formula A/5000 single-seater for various 5-liter engines.

M10B had minor but useful modifications. Above, Peter Gethin's Guards F5000 championship car; below, Continental F/A champion John Cannon.

M14D This was a single Formula 1 chassis built halfway through the 1970 season to accept an Alfa Romeo V-8 engine as with the M7D. It was similar to the Cosworth-Ford engine cars in all respects apart from a 2-inch increase in wheelbase (to 97 inches).

M15 The year 1970 saw McLaren's first attack on the Indianapolis 500, and the team built three new cars closely based on the simple and effective Can-Am designs. Sponsorship came from Gulf Oil, Goodyear Tires and Reynolds Aluminum, and with turbocharged Offenhauser 4-cylinder engines the three M15s proved extremely competitive in early testing. Sadly Denny was burned when his car caught fire in qualifying and Chris Amon found he could not work up to competitive speeds. Peter Revson and Carl Williams took over the two race cars, Williams finishing 9th and Revson retiring.

CHASSIS: Broad aluminum-alloy panelled monocoque formed over steel and aluminum bulkheads, with the engine acting as a semi-stressed member in the rear bay.
SUSPENSION: Single top link with radius arm, lower wishbone, anti-roll bar and outboard coil spring/shock units with adjustable ride height in front. Single top link, reversed lower wishbone, twin radius arms, anti-roll bar and outboard coil spring/shock units at rear. McLaren cast magnesium wheels with knock-off hub nuts, 15 x 10 front and 15 x 14 rear.
BRAKES: Lockheed ventilated discs, 11.97-inch diameter.
BODY: Formed by monocoque sides with detachable fiberglass upper panelling forming the nose cone and cockpit surround, engine cover and chassis-mounted aerofoil. Side fuel sponsons carrying 67 U.S. gallons.
ENGINE: 2.6-liter 4-cylinder turbocharged Offenhauser with Hewland LG500 4-speed transaxle, modified with provision for external starting.
DIMENSIONS: Wheelbase 98.69 inches, front track 57.75 inches, rear track 58.06 inches, width at cockpit 45 inches, overall length 156 inches, weight 1380 pounds distributed 30 percent front/70 percent rear.

M16 This is the wedge-shaped Indianapolis car for 1971 using the turbocharged Offenhauser engine and a Hewland LG500 4-speed transaxle. The chassis is a full aluminum monocoque with Goodyear 75-gallon fuel bags and fiberglass body panels. Wheel-

John Surtees in the Chaparral-entered M12 at 1969 Mosport Can-Am.

Bruce's last Formula 1 race, in M14A in 1970 Spanish Grand Prix.

Above, Denny in M14A with split-wing and without nose planes at Monza. Below, Carl Williams in the number-two M15 in the 1970 Indy 500 race.

base is 101 inches, with front and rear track 58 inches. Wheels are cast magnesium of 15-inch diameter front and rear with 10-inch front rims and 14-inch rear rims. Front suspension is by rocker arm and lower wishbone, and rear suspension is by reversed lower wishbone with a top link and radius rods. The M16 also uses Koni shock absorbers, Lockheed brakes, McLaren rack and pinion steering, Hewland driveshafts, Borg & Beck clutch and a Marston Excelsior radiator. Overall length 155 inches, width at cockpit 38 inches, weight 1380 pounds distributed 30 percent front/70 percent rear.

M17 The M17 designation was allocated to a 3-liter prototype sports car but the project was abandoned.

M18 The Formula A/5000 car for 1971 uses a 5-liter Chevrolet V-8 engine with a Hewland DG transaxle. It has a full aluminum monocoque chassis with a wheelbase of 100 inches, a front track of 59.5 inches and a rear track of 60 inches. It has 13-inch front wheels with 11-inch rims, and 15-inch rear wheels with 16-inch rims. Front suspension is by a lower wishbone with a top link and radius arm, while the rear suspension is by a reversed lower wishbone with a top link and radius rods.

M19 The Formula 1 car for 1971 again has the Cosworth-Ford DFV V-8 engine and Hewland DG transaxle. The car has a "coke bottle" shape not unlike the Tyrrell-Ford driven by Jackie Stewart in 1970. It has an aluminum monocoque with a wheelbase of 100 inches, a front track of 63 inches and a rear track of 62 inches. Front wheels are 13 inches in diameter with 10-inch rims and the rear wheels are 15 inches in diameter with 16-inch rims. Front suspension is by a rocker arm and lower link, and rear suspension is by top link and radius rods and a reversed lower wishbone. Koni shock absorbers, McLaren rack and pinion steering, Lockheed brakes, Borg & Beck clutch and Hewland or BRD driveshafts are used. Weight is 1230 pounds and fuel capacity 45 gallons. Ex-Brabham engineer Ralph Bellamy headed the design team.

M20 The M20 is the 1971 Can-Am team car, details of which have not yet been released.

The 1971 M16 Indy car has wedge nose and side radiators, like Lotus 72.

Above, M18 is much revised Formula A/5000 car with lower, flatter nose. Below, M19 Formula 1 car has fat body sides for better fuel placement.

Boldface indicates photograph.

Agg, Peter 7, 64, **228**, 230, 231, 233, 234

Alexander, Tyler 7, 8, 58, 60, 61, 67, 68, 81, 114, **116**, 119, 120, 121, **123**, 125, 127, 151, **153**, 158, 159, 182-199, **200**, 206, 215, **217**, **223**, 224

Alfa Romeo engine 103, **236**, 237, 238, 255, **258**, 265

Amon, Chris 66, 67, 70, 72, 73, **74**, 75, 76, 89, **92**, 93, 95, 96, **99**, **111**, 114, **123**, 153, 170, 174, **210**, 221, 223, 234, **235**, 236, 265

Andretti, Mario 93, 237, 255

Atkins, Cyril 91

Atkins, Tommy 51, 206

Austin cars 24, 25, 26, 32

Austin Seven Ulster 11, 12, 23, **24**, **25**, 26, 27, 28, 135

Austin-Healey 100 26, 27, 28, **29**, 135

Autodelta 237, 255

Bartz engines 139

Beanland, Colin 7, 26, 28, 29, 31, 34, 35, 91, **111**, 140

Belgian Grand Prix, Spa-Francorchamps 16, 45, 65, 66, 73, **86**, 87, 88, 91, 127, 131, 213, 238, **244**

Bellamy, Ralph 267

Bennett, John 64, **228**

Beresford, Don 114, 207, 251

Bolthoff, George 7, 139, 140, 144, 145, **198**, **223**, 257

Brabham, Jack 12, 25, 28, 29, 30, 31, 34, 39, 40, 41, 42, 43, **44**, 45, 48, 51, **52**, 53, 54, 55, 62, 65, 71, 73, 79, 86, 87, 97, 98, 99, 101, 106, 107, 112, 122, 132, 135, 158, **168**, 169, **170**, 173, 174, 180, 190, 191, 201, 202, 205, 208, 209

Brabham racing cars 16, **52**, 87, 101, 107, 127, 132, 173, 181, 203, 267

Brands Hatch circuit, England 36, 37, **43**, **56**, 59 63, 64, 73, 85, 88, 89, 103, 131, 154, 186, **250**, **254**

Bridgehampton circuit, New York 83, 92

British Grand Prix 41, 45, 73, 131

British Racing Drivers' Club Gold Star 102, 103

BRM racing cars 12, 36, 39, **40**, 42, 44, 48, 52, 88, 90, 158

BRM engines 77, **78**, 79, 81, 82, 88, 90, 128, **134**, **135**, 249, 251

Broadley, Eric 114, 236

Brooks, Tony 37, 42

Brown, Alan 36, 40

Burt, Patsy 15, 120, 232, 247

Caldwell, Alastair 185, 204

Canadian Grand Prix 77, 95, 134, **248**, 249

Cannon, John 92, 226, **264**

Chaparral racing cars 59, 65, 68, 69, 70, **84**, 85, **92**, 94, 107, 137, 139, 190, 226, 234, 261

Chapman, Colin 110, 121, 190, 204, 209

Chevrolet V-8 engines 12, **126**, **144**, **145**, **146**, 226

Clark, Jim 12, 51, 52, **59**, 61, 70, 79, 89, 90, 96, 107, 132, 154, 156, 190, 234, 235

Cooper, Charles 34, 45, 48, 52, 53, 62, 71, 122, 187

Cooper-Climax Formula 1 car, including Tasman 28, 29, 31, 32, **38**, 39, **40**, **41**, **42**, 44, 45, **48**, **49**, **50**, **51**, **52**, 53, 55, 58, 61, **65**, **66**, 67, 103, 135, 169, 186, 187

Cooper-Climax Formula 2 car 29, 32, 34, **35**, 36, 55, 135, **167**, 169

Cooper 1500 sports car 28, **31**

Cooper Formula 3 and Junior cars 12, 32, 150, 169, 171, 183, 186, 187

Cooper, John 36, 37, 41, 45, 52, 62, 71, 122, 150, **168**

Cooper Monaco sports car **44**, **58**, 59, 61, 62, 150, 219

Coppuck, Gordon 7, 87, 91, 109, 110, 114, 119, 121, 122, **123**, 124, 222, 223, 224, 263

Cosworth Engineering 77, 87, 97, 109, 122, 132, 141, 146, 147, 184, 237, 259

Courage, Piers 103, 247

Coventry Climax engines 40, 51, 66, 107, 129, 135, 137, 138, 247

Crabbe, Colin 255

Cunningham, Briggs 57, **58**, 60

De Adamich, Andrea 237

Dean, Tony 226, 239

Donnybrooke Can-Am race, Minnesota 239

Donohue, Mark 86, 92, 119, 225, 226

Dunedin circuit, New Zealand 28, 31

Dunlop tires 66, 154, 155

Dutch Grand Prix, Zandvoort 32, 45, 51, 77, 110, 132, 134, 238

Eagle racing cars **77**, 134, 174

Edmonton Can-Am race, Canada **92**, 238
Elford, Vic **148, 254**, 255
Elkhart Lake (Road America) Can-Am race, Wisconsin **82**, 92, **171**, 238, **258**
Elva cars 64, 229, 230, 234, 241, 247

Ferguson, Harry 234, 235
Ferguson torque converter **233**, 234, 235
Ferodo Trophy 96, 103
Ferrari racing cars 28, 37, 42, 44, 48, 61, 74, 76, 87, 89, **92**, 93, 95, 96, 127, 132, 157, 237
Firestone tires 66, 67, 73, 81, 110, 127, 129, 154, 155, 156, 161, 220, 245
Fittipaldi, Emerson 170
Ford-Cosworth DFV V-8 engines 87, 129, 132, 143, 135, **136**, 137, **138**, 141, 146, 147, 237, 249, 253, 259, 263, 265, 267
Ford GT40 61, 114, 116, 161, 174, 236
Ford GT Mk2 and Mk 4 **73**, 114, 118, 237
Ford GTX 64, 69, 70, 161, **235**, 236, 237
Ford Indy V-8 engine 107, 111, 127, **128**, 129, **130, 131**, 132, 157, 225, **244**, 245, 247
Foyt, A.J. 118, 119, 154, 222, 237
French Grand Prix 41, 44, 45, **77, 256**
From the Cockpit, by Bruce McLaren 9, 18, 26, 36, 54

Ganley, Howden **111**
Gardner, Frank 234
German Grand Prix, Nurburgring 21, **35**, 36, 37, 41, 52, 61, 77, 236, 239, 255
Gethin, Peter 16, **148**, 156, **217**, 225, 226, 238, 239, 261
Goodwood circuit, England 9, 11, 12, 13, **15** 50, 51, **63**, 64, 77, 82, 105, 113, 119, 125, 134, 160, 166, 177, 181, 232, **242, 244**, 257
Goodyear tires 14, 16, 77, 81, 154, 161, 220, 221, 265
Gulf Oil Corporation 161, 220, 265
Gurney, Dan 12, 64, 74, 77, 82, 86, **89, 93**, 96, 99, 111, 118, 119, 134, **218**, 225, 226, 237, 238, 239

Hall, Jim 68, 69, **84**, 85, 86, 92, 94, 107, 137, 190, 234
Hansgen, Walt 58, 186
Harre, Bruce **111**
Hassan, Walter 135

Herd, Robin 7, 63, 68, 70, 72, 77, 81, 86, 87, 91, 97, 107, 109, 111, 112, **113**, 114, 119, 121, 122, 123, 128, 184, 231, 243, 245, 247, 251
Hewland transmissions 64, 66, 68, 81, 91, 92, 243, 247, 249, 251, 253, 255, 257, 261, 263, 265, 269
Hilborn fuel injection 76, 241
Hill, Graham 52, 54, 90, 96, 98, 154
Hill, Phil 37, 61, 66, **69**, 73, 114, 115, 117, 154, 226, 230, 236, **240**
Hulme, Clive 166, 168, 169
Hulme, Denny 7, 8, 12, 14, 16, 30, 53, 75, 76, 78, 79, 81, **82**, 83, 84, 85, 86, 88 89, **90**, 92, **93, 94**, 95, 96, 97, 98, 100, 101, **123**, 132, **138**, 139, **148**, 156, **157, 159**, 160, 161, **164-181**, 198, 202, 203, **210**, 215, 216, **217**, 221, 223, 224, 225, 226, **227**, 232, 238, 239, 249, **252**, 253, **254**, 255, 257, **258, 260, 262**, 265, 266
Hyslop, Angus 172, 173

Ickx, Jacky 37, 97
Indianapolis 500-mile race, Indiana 14, 15, 16, 29, 99, 101, 120, **123**, 135, 154, 165, 166, 174, 178, 179, 185, 207, **210**, 216, 219, 220, 221, 222, 223, 224, 239, 265, **266**
Ireland, Innes 44
Italian Grand Prix, Monza 65, 66, 78, 79, 88, 95, 172, **174, 256, 266**

Jaguar cars 28, 30, 31, **43**, 50, 57, 87
Jensen, Ross 26, 28, 32
Jones, Parnelli 84, 85, 86

Kaser, Jim 7, 96
Kent Circuit, Washington **69, 240**
Kerr, Phil 7, 24, 25, 26, 28, 29, 43, 48, 158, 159, 173, **200**, 201, 202, 203, 204, 206, 208, 225, 238
Knutson, Gary 70, 91, 129, 138, 139, 140, 153, 236, 257

Laguna Seca circuit 57, 58, 65, 76, **83**, 84, 85, 92, **94**, 157, 219, 225, 226, 239
Lakeside circuit, Australia 53
Lambretta-Trojan group 64, 103, 229, 230, 231, 232, 233, 234, 249, 257, 259, 261
Las Vegas Can-Am race, Nevada 76, 92, **176**, 225, 239
Le Mans 24-hour race, France 57, **73**, 75, 114, 116, 117, 118, 156, 172, 174
Levin circuit, New Zealand 53
Lola racing cars **67**, 76, 82, 83, 84,

114, 138, 207, 221, 225, 226, 234, 235, 236, 239
Longford circuit, Tasmania 54, 66, 183
Lotus racing cars 12, 44, 45, 48, 51, 52, **59**, 61, 64, 70, 79, 87, 90, 96, 97, 110, 123, 132, 157, 170, 171, 205, 224, 234, 259
Lucas fuel injection 81
Lunn, Roy 7, 114, 117, 119, 236

Macklin, Harold 226
Maddocks, Owen 45
March racing cars 76, 101, 184
Marelli, Giovanni 237
Marquart, Jo 87, 91, **120**, 123, 263
Martini Trophy 67, 103
Maserati racing cars 29, 32, **33**, 58, 67
Maserati V-12 engine 128, 247
Matra cars 36, 37, 76, 91, 95, 97, 158
Mayer, Teddy 7, 18, 53, 58, 63, **54**, 81, 97, 114, **116**, 119, **123**, 127, 129, 139, 140, 146, 148-**163**, 186, 187, 188, **195, 200**, 202, 203, 206, 207, 211, **212**, 215, 216, **217**, 219, 221, 222, 225, 236, 238
Mayer, Timmy **51**, 53, 54, 58, **113**, 150, 183, 186, 187, 188, 190
Mayo, Merv 29
McLaren racing cars by type:
M1A **62, 63, 64, 67**, 68, 69, **106**, 112, **153**, 229, 230, **231, 233**, 234, **240**, 241
M1B 68, **69, 70, 74, 75, 76**, 81, 92, **108, 109**, 112, **187**, 230, 231, **240**, 241, **242**, 243
M1C **228**, 231, **242**, 243
M2A 72, **110**, 129, **139, 242**, 243
M2B **71, 72**, 107, **111, 112, 128, 131, 244**, 245, 249
M3 14, **114**, 120, 121, 233, **244**, 245, **246**
M4A 77, 82, 86, **133**, 134, 208, 231, 232, **246**, 247, 249
M4B 77, **134, 228, 246, 248**, 249
M5 77, **78, 79**, 82, 134, **135, 205, 248**, 249
M6A 8, 12, 30, **80**, 81, **82, 83, 84**, 91, 92, 113, 138, **171**, 174, 225, 231, **248**, 251, 255
M6B 92, 231, **250**, 251, 253
M6GT and "M12GT" **118** 121, 122, 231, **232, 250**, 253
M7A **85, 86**, 87, **88, 89, 90, 115**, 135, **136, 138, 173, 174, 179**, 237, **250, 252**, 253, **254**, 255
M7B **116**, 237, 253, **254**
M7C 97, 121, 237, 255, **256**, 259
M7D **236**, 237, 255, **258**
M8A **19**, 87, 91, 92, 97, 103, **104**,

117, 126, 138, 139, **142-143, 144, 145, 157, 159**, 175, **176**, 189, **200, 214**
M8B **91, 92, 94**, 97, 103, 181, **192-193, 195**, 232, 257, **258**
M8C 232, 257, **260**
M8D **10**, 12, **13**, 14, **15, 17**, 100, **148, 181, 218**, 232, 238, 239, 257, **260**
M8E 232, 257, **262**
M9 **120**, 259, **262**
M10A 97, 123, 232, 233, 255, 259, **264**
M10B 232, 233, 261, **264**
M12 232, 239, 261, **266**
M14A 99, 101, **217**, 239, 263, **266**
M14D 237, 265
M15 99, 120, 121, **123**, 140, **182, 198, 199**, 208, **210, 213, 218**, 221, **223** 224, 265, **266**
M16 221, 224, 239, 265, **268**
M18 267, **268**
M19 239, 267, **268**
M20 267
McLaren Engines, Inc. 26, 140, 163
McLaren, Amanda 87, **95**, 100, 101, 103
McLaren, Janice 21
McLaren, Leslie "Pop" 21, 23, 24, 25, 26, 27, 41, **50**
McLaren, Patty (Mrs. Bruce) 9, 32, 44, 48, 50, 51, 52, **68**, 87, **95**, 100, **101, 102**, 124, 163, 190
McLaren, Patricia, sister of Bruce 21
McLaren, Ruth 21, 41
Mecom, John 59, 151, 186, 187
Mercedes-Benz cars 8, 15, 21, 87, 119, 163, 180
Mexican Grand Prix, Mexico City 73, **79**, 96, 98, 99, 131, 132, **179**, 239
Michigan Can-Am race **93**
Mid-Ohio Can-Am race 238
Miles, Ken 74, 75, 174, 237
Monaco Grand Prix, Monte Carlo 21, 40, 45, **46-47**, 52, 67, **71**, 73, 77, 90, 97, 101, 131, 134, 135, **138**, 178, 179, **180, 248, 254**
Mosport circuit, Canada 30, **61**, 62, 63, 64, 67, 69, **75**, 83, **172**, 176, **187**, 221, 225, 236, 238 266
Moss, Stirling 12, 14, 15, 27, 39, **40**, 41, 42, 45, 51, 54, 89, **93**, 156, 221
Motschenbacher, Lothar 239, **250**
Mountain, Chuck 116, 119

Nassau circuit, Bahamas 60, 65, 103, 186, 236
Neil, Merv 28, 29
New Zealand Gold Star 32, 170

New Zealand Grand Prix 26, 28, 29, 30, 32, 41, 44, 53, 66, 169, 181
Nichols, Frank 64, 229, 230
NZIGP "Driver to Europe" scholarship 28, 29, 31, 34, 135, 169, 172

Offenhauser engines 140, 147, 165, 221, 222, 224, 265
Ohakea airfield circuit, New Zealand 25, 27, 29
Oldsmobile V-8 engine 139, 242
Ontario 500-mile race, California 199, 213, 239
Oulton Park circuit, England 61, 234, 235

Parnell, Reg 67, 170
Pearce, Harry 51, 206, 234
Penske, Roger 58, 59, 60, 65, 92, 151, 186
Phillippe, Maurice 110
Pocono International Raceway 239
Porsche cars 27, 37, 226, 239
Portuguese Grand Prix, Porto 45
Pukekohe circuit, New Zealand 53, 88

Reims circuit, France 41, 44, 45, 49, 52, 54, 112, 130, 172
Repco Engineering 73, 127, 132, 247
Revson, Peter 15, 148, 156, 182, 199, 218, 221, 223, 239, 265
Reynolds Aluminum 141, 161, 220, 226, 265
Rindt, Jochen 96, 98, 99, 100, 156, 170, 190
Riverside circuit 44, 45, 58, 64, 65, 70, 76, 80, 84, 87, 92, 111, 112, 129, 159, 175, 177, 219, 225, 235, 236, 239, 242
Road Atlanta Can-Am race, Georgia 232, 239
Rodriguez, Pedro 88
Rouen circuit, France 172, 246, 252
Ruby, Lloyd 222, 237
Rucker, Klaus von 129

Salvadori, Roy 37, 61, 71, 236
Sandown Park circuit, Australia 52
Schell, Harry 36, 37
Seagrave Trophy 102, 103
Sebring 12-hour race, Florida 42, 51, 58, 70, 135, 237
Serenissima V-8 engine 72, 73, 131, 132, 2444, 245
Sharp, Hap 70
Shuter, Frank 29, 33
Silverstone circuit, England 45, 61, 67, 89, 103
Smith, Ron 7, 15, 16, 120

South African Grand Prix, Kyalami 52, 90, 100, 101, 239, 249
Spanish Grand Prix 90, 98, 101, 115, 173, 252, 266
Spence, Mike 86
St. Jovite circuit, Canada 67, 68, 69, 74, 95, 96, 137, 192-193, 225
Stait, Eddie 63, 128
Stanton, Feo 169
Stanton, Morrie 32
Stewart, Jackie 12, 36, 39, 91, 95, 97, 98, 99, 101, 102, 150, 156, 190, 191, 216, 221, 226, 267
Surtees, John 12, 51, 54, 55, 67, 76, 82, 86, 92, 95, 99, 103, 138, 225, 226, 235, 239, 255, 260

Tanner, Reg 39
Tauranac, Ron 107
Teretonga circuit, New Zealand 32, 40, 51, 53, 88
Texas Can-Am race 195
Thompson, John 121
Traco Engineering 64, 76, 129, 130, 137, 139, 140, 241, 243, 245
Trintignant, Maurice 37, 42
Trips, Wolfgang von 37
Turner, Michael 53, 68, 112
Tyrrell, Ken 7, 36, 40, 52, 53, 71, 97, 150, 175, 187, 226, 267
United States Grand Prix 42, 45, 58, 73, 79, 89, 90, 131, 132, 135, 186

Waimate circuit, New Zealand 40
Walker, Peter 57
Walker, R.R.C., racing team 42, 45
Warwick Farm circuit, Australia 53
Watkins Glen circuit, New York 58, 73, 79, 96, 99, 131, 186, 204, 238
Weber carburetors 34, 42, 146
Wharton, Ken 28
Whitehead, Peter 57
Wigram race, New Zealand 28, 31, 53, 66
Williams, Carl 15, 221, 265, 266
Willmott, Wally 51, 60, 61, 81, 127, 130, 150, 153, 183, 184, 187
Winslade, Sue 206

Youl, John 54
Young, Eoin S. 7, 8, 9, 32, 51, 63, 65, 99, 100, 111, 150, 171

Zerex Special, Cooper-Climax and -Oldsmobile 56, 57, 59, 60, 61, 62, 63, 64, 65, 105, 106, 135, 137, 150, 151, 186, 224
ZF transmission 68, 81, 243, 245, 247
Zwiefel, Harry 121, 247